Knowledge and Investment

NEW HORIZONS IN THE ECONOMICS OF INNOVATION

General Editor: Christopher Freeman, *Emeritus Professor of Science Policy, SPRU – Science and Technology Policy Research, University of Sussex, UK*

Technical innovation is vital to the competitive performance of firms and of nations and for the sustained growth of the world economy. The economics of innovation is an area that has expanded dramatically in recent years and this major series, edited by one of the most distinguished scholars in the field, contributes to the debate and advances in research in this most important area.

The main emphasis is on the development and application of new ideas. The series provides a forum for original research in technology, innovation systems and management, industrial organization, technological collaboration, knowledge and innovation, research and development, evolutionary theory and industrial strategy. International in its approach, the series includes some of the best theoretical and empirical work from both well-established researchers and the new generation of scholars.

Titles in the series include:

Foundations of the Economics of Innovation
Theory, Measurement and Practice
Hariolf Grupp

Industrial Organisation and Innovation
An International Study of the Software Industry
Salvatore Torrisi

The Theory of Innovation
Entrepreneurs, Technology and Strategy
Jon Sundbo

The Emergence and Growth of Biotechnology
Experiences in Industrialised and Developing Countries
Rohini Acharya

Knowledge and Investment
The Sources of Innovation in Industry
Rinaldo Evangelista

Learning and Innovation in Economic Development
Linsu Kim

The Economics of Knowledge Production
Funding and the Structure of University Research
Aldo Geuna

Innovation and Research Policies
An International Comparative Analysis
Paul Diederen, Paul Stoneman, Otto Toivanen and Arjan Wolters

Knowledge and Investment

The Sources of Innovation in Industry

Rinaldo Evangelista

Researcher, Institute for Studies on Scientific Research and Documentation, National Research Council of Italy, Rome

NEW HORIZONS IN THE ECONOMICS OF INNOVATION

Edward Elgar

Cheltenham, UK • Northampton, MA, USA

Published by
Edward Elgar Publishing Limited
Glensanda House
Montpellier Parade
Cheltenham
Glos GL50 1UA
UK

Edward Elgar Publishing, Inc.
136 West Street
Suite 202
Northampton
Massachusetts 01060
USA

A catalogue record for this book is available from the British Library

Library of Congress Cataloguing in Publication Data

Evangelista, Rinaldo, 1962–
    Knowledge and investment : the sources of innovation in industry /
Rinaldo Evangelista.
        (New horizons in the economics of innovation)
    Includes index.
    1. Technological innovations—Finance. 2. Capital investments.
I. Title. II. Series.
HD45.E825   1999
658.15'2—dc21   98–33210
                                                                          CIP

ISBN 1 85898 728 8

Printed and bound in Great Britain by Bookcraft (Bath) Ltd.

Contents

List of figures   vi
List of tables   vii
Acknowledgements   ix
Preface by Chris Freeman   xi
Introduction   xiii

PART ONE   INVESTMENT IN KNOWLEDGE AND MACHINERY:
            THEORY AND PERSPECTIVES

1. Disembodied and embodied technological change: concepts
    and definitions   3
2. Disembodied and embodied perspectives on technological
    change in the economic literature   11
3. Disembodied and embodied technological change in the
    innovation literature   27
4. Embodied and disembodied perspectives on the relationship
    between technological change, firm size and market structure   47
5. Towards an integrated perspective on technological change
    and industrial structure: issues for research   68

PART TWO   EVIDENCE FROM THE ITALIAN INDUSTRY

6. An overview of innovation activities in manufacturing and
    services   83
7. Embodied and disembodied innovation strategies and the
    production structure of firms   111
8. Innovation strategies and the productive structure of firms:
    do industrial sectors matter?   132
9. Innovative patterns and technological regimes of production:
    a sectoral analysis   151
10. Embodied and disembodied patterns of technological change
    and production structure: a sectoral taxonomy   164
11. Conclusions and policy implications   181

Bibliography   186
Index   197

List of figures

5.1 Embodied and disembodied views on technological change   69
5.2 Technological change and industrial structure: the
    neo-Schumpeterian links   71
5.3 Technological change and industrial structure: embodied and
    disembodied links   77
6.1 Breakdown of innovation costs in the Italian manufacturing
    sector (1992)   94
6.2 Breakdown of innovation costs in the Italian service sector (1995) 95
6.3 Breakdown of innovation costs across European countries   96
9.1 Innovative intensity and the share of R&D and D&E expenditures 153
9.2 Disembodied innovative intensity and the share of process
    innovations   154
9.3 Disembodied and embodied sectoral innovative patterns   157
9.4 Total investment in machinery and innovative investment   158
9.5 R&D and D&E expenditures per employee and firm size   161
10.1 Scatterplot of the sectors according to the two factors 167
10.2 Disembodied and embodied innovative patterns and industrial
    structure: a taxonomy   171

List of tables

6.1 Innovating and non-innovating firms in manufacturing and services by firm size — 85

6.2 Percentages of innovating firms across firm size in Europe (manufacturing sector, 1992) — 86

6.3 Innovating and non-innovating firms in manufacturing and service industries — 88

6.4 Probability of carrying out innovative activities and R&D (logit estimates) (Italian manufacturing sector, 1990–92) — 89

6.5 Innovating manufacturing firms by type of innovation introduced — 91

6.6 Innovating service firms by type of innovation introduced — 92

6.7 Innovation expenditure by firm size (percentage values) (Italian manufacturing sector, 1992) — 97

6.8 Innovation expenditure by industry and firm size (percentage values) (Italian manufacturing sector, 1992) — 98

6.9 Breakdown of innovation costs by industry in the service sector (1995) — 100

6.10 Distribution of total sales according to the type of innovation introduced (percentage values) (Italian manufacturing sector, 1992) — 102

6.11 Sales according to the degree of novelty of the product innovations introduced (percentage values) (Italian manufacturing sector, 1992) — 103

6.12 Sources of technological information in manufacturing and services — 104

6.13 Objectives of innovation in manufacturing and services — 105

6.14 Obstacles to innovation in manufacturing and services — 105

7.1 List of production and innovative indicators used in the empirical analysis — 113

7.2 Total innovation costs and embodied and disembodied innovation expenditures (correlation and elasticity coefficients) — 115

7.3 Distribution of firms according to the type of technological activity performed across firm size classes (1981–85) — 116

7.4 Total innovation costs and embodied and disembodied innovation expenditures (correlation and elasticity coefficients) (R&D and D&E performing firms) — 117

7.5 Embodied and disembodied innovative intensity indicators and product/process innovation shares (correlation coefficients) 117
7.6 The relationship between embodied and disembodied innovation expenditures (correlation and elasticity coefficients) 119
7.7 Innovative intensity, firm size and labour productivity (correlation coefficients) 121
7.8 Determinants of labour productivity (regression estimates) 122
7.9 Innovative intensity by firm size (average values) 124
7.10 Innovation intensity and firm size by industry 126
7.11 List of variables used in the factor analysis 128
7.12 Results of the factor analysis 129
8.1 Analysis of variance at different levels of sectoral aggregation 134
8.2 Analysis of variance at different levels of sectoral aggregation and cut-off in firm size 136
8.3 Elasticity of embodied and disembodied innovation expenditures with respect to total innovation costs (LSDV estimations) 140
8.4 The relationship between embodied and disembodied innovation expenditures (LSDV estimations) 143
8.5 Firm size and capital intensity (LSDV estimations) 145
8.6 The determinants of labour productivity (LSDV estimations) 146
9.1 Innovative intensity and product/process innovation shares across sectors (correlation coefficients – 108 sectors) 152
9.2 The relationship between embodied and disembodied innovation activities across sectors (correlation coefficients – 108 sectors) 156
9.3 Innovative intensity and firm size across sectors (correlation coefficients – 108 industrial sectors) 159
9.4 Firm size, capital intensity and productivity across sectors (correlation coefficients – 108 industrial sectors) 161
10.1 List of variables used in the 'sectoral' factor analysis 165
10.2 Results of the factor analysis (108 sectors) 166
10.3 Results of the factor analysis (30 sectors) 169
10.4 Productive and technological profiles by sectoral clusters (average values) 170

Acknowledgements

This book is drawn from my Ph.D. at the Science Policy Research Unit, University of Sussex (UK). Most of the acknowledgements go thus to those who have helped me in that long venture. Accordingly I would like first of all to thank my two supervisors Keith Pavitt and Nick von Tunzelmann. On different but complementary aspects, they have encouraged me to improve focus, analytical perspective and methodology of my Ph.D. thesis first and of the book later. Comments and suggestions raised by Pari Patel, Cristiano Antonelli and Keith Smith have also been very helpful in improving the quality outcome of this book. The same is true for the very rich and detailed comments raised by an internal referee who has evaluated the outline proposal of the book.

Warm thanks go to Chris Freeman who was always very encouraging and stimulating when I first started my Ph.D. and also later when I decided to write a book based on my Ph.D. thesis. On the same line I am also indebted to Daniele Archibugi who warmly encouraged me to start my Ph.D. venture at SPRU, and to turn my thesis into a book. Many thanks go to Mario Pianta who has read several drafts and has always provided useful and sharp comments. Special thanks also go to my friend Roberto Simonetti for his great help in dealing with huge databases of more then 24 000 firms and for his support in many different matters. I also want to thank Aldo Del Santo, head of the R&D and Innovation Division of the Italian Statistical Institute (ISTAT), for making it possible to access the databases I used in this book.

I would also like to thank all my colleagues at the Istituto di Studi sulla Ricerca e Documentazione Scientifica, and in particular Giorgio Sirilli and the director Professor Paolo Bisogno, for their co-operation and patience with any work related to my Ph.D. thesis and this book. I have also benefited from a series of conferences and seminars where parts of the material contained in this book have been presented and discussed. More, in particular, I would like to mention the seminars held at SPRU and at my own Institute, the *Fourth, Fifth and Sixth International Schumpeter Society Conferences, the European Association for Evolutionary Political Economy Conference* (EAEPE) held in Copenhagen and the OECD *workshop on innovation, patents and technological indicators*.

Some of the material presented in this book is also contained in a couple of papers co-authored with some other colleagues of mine. I would like in particular to thank Daniele Archibugi, Giulio Perani, Fabio Rapiti and Giorgio Sirilli for letting me use some of the results of these joint works. Also the discussions and exchanges of ideas with Valentina Meliciani have been very useful.

Above all, however, the person I would like to thank most is Suma Athreye, whose help, encouragement and criticism have been fundamental for completing my Ph.D. and also this book.

Preface

In the last few decades there has been a resurgence of interest in the economics of technical change. This has been stimulated by the obvious importance of computers, telecommunications and the Internet in economic life and the extraordinarily rapid growth of many firms intimately involved with these new developments. Expressions such as the 'Information Society' or the 'Knowledge Economy' have entered everyday life and it is hardly possible to understand the process of structural change without taking full account of the numerous innovations in information and communications technology.

Of course, no economist of repute has ever denied the great importance of technical change from Adam Smith onwards. Even earlier, Serra in Naples had studied and demonstrated the role of skills and knowledge accumulation in advancing the prosperity of cities and of nations. However, after the classical economists relatively few scholars paid very much attention to technology, even though they acknowledged its importance. The one big exception to this generalization in the first half of this century was Joseph Schumpeter and for that reason, those economists who have more recently concentrated on technical change are often described as 'neo-Schumpeterian' or 'evolutionary' economists.

In the 1950s and 1960s, most of the work in this tradition was done by American economists, but since the 1970s this situation has changed. Whilst the leading American economists, such as Nelson and Winter, Rosenberg and Scherer have continued to make outstanding contributions to economic theory and new younger economists, such as Teece and Utterback have contributed many original ideas, there has been a resurgence of European work in this field. Italian economists such as Giovanni Dosi, Luigi Orsenigo, Daniele Archibugi, Cristiano Antonelli, Giorgio Sirilli, Roberto Simonetti and Marco Vivarelli, to name only a few, have played a leading role in this renaissance of the economics of technical change. It is in the tradition of this very creative group that Rinaldo Evangelista has contributed this brilliant book.

An admirable feature of the work of this group of Italian scholars has been the way in which they have combined empirical inquiry with original contributions to fundamental theory and this book exemplifies this feature of their work. The first five chapters discuss one of the most important problems in economic theory and in contemporary modelling of economic growth – the relative significance and interpretation of 'embodied' and of 'disembodied' technical change. The next five chapters provide a clear and very well informed account of the role of embodied and disembodied change respectively in Italian industry. A particularly valuable feature of this analysis is the further development of Pavitt's well-known sectoral taxonomy (see especially Figure 10.2). In this and in many other respects, Rinaldo Evangelista has advanced our understanding of the sources of dynamism in economic development. I commend his book most strongly to everyone with an interest in this exciting field of research.

Chris Freeman

Introduction

It is often said that technological change is a complex and multidimensional phenomenon that is difficult to generalize about or reduce to any schematic conceptual framework. Nevertheless in analysing and representing technological change – as any other complex issue – some sort of generalization is useful and necessary, both on descriptive and interpretative grounds. This holds good as long as the generalization or simplification adopted reflects important and sufficiently distinctive dimensions of the phenomenon investigated and is useful for highlighting its relation to other phenomena.

In this book I argue that the distinction between embodied and disembodied technological change is one which fulfils these requirements. Knowledge-generating activities in the form of research and development (R&D) and design on the one hand, and investment in fixed productive capital on the other, represent the two major sources of technological change in industry and are able to discriminate between major innovation patterns and technological regimes of production in the manufacturing industry. This book contributes to building an integrated perspective on technological change, stressing the importance of considering both the disembodied and embodied dimensions of innovative activities. Neither of these two perspectives on technology and innovative activities can be considered more relevant than the other. They represent two major aspects of technological change and different effects on industrial structures and performances. This book also intends to balance the 'disembodied bias' that characterizes the literature on the 'economics of technological change'. It will be shown that this bias affects both the general conceptualization of technological change, the way it is represented and measured, and the way in which innovation activities are seen as interacting with structural and production features of firms and industries.

The book is structured in two parts. Part One (Chapters 1–5) reviews the 'embodied' and 'disembodied' approaches to technology and innovation in economics and in the most recent innovation literature. Part Two (Chapters 6–10) consists of an empirical investigation of the relevance of embodied and disembodied technological change in industry and the way the different patterns of innovation are associated to the productive structure of firms and industrial sectors, as well as to their performance.

Chapter 1 provides a set of operationally useful definitions of embodied and disembodied technology, technological change and innovation activities, derived from the simple etymology of such terms. These definitions will be used as benchmarks to review the major economic approaches in Chapters 2–5 and for the construction of indicators used in the empirical analysis.

The two following chapters show that the key concepts and perspectives associated with a disembodied or embodied approach to technology and innovation have not changed significantly during the evolution of theorizing both in economics (Chapter 2) or in the more recent innovation literature (Chapter 3) and are consistent with the definitions proposed in Chapter 1. To put it in a rather extreme way, the distinction is between a conceptualization representing technology as a *stock of knowledge* (or a set of technological capabilities) as opposed to a conceptualization of technology in terms of *technical assets* (fixed capital), mainly involved in the 'production sphere'. Analogously, innovative activities have been conceptualized either as activities aimed at *producing* new technological knowledge or at *using* technologies in production through investment in fixed capital.

Chapter 4 shows that the above difference in the conceptualization of technological change also plays a role in the economic and innovation literature, which has analysed the complex relationships between technological change, firm size and market structure. In this case also, the distinction between a 'production-based' and 'embodied' perspective, implicit in most of the traditional contributions of 'industrial economics', contrasts with a prevailing 'disembodied' conceptualization of technological change, which characterizes most of the contributions in both neo-Schumpeterian and evolutionary approaches.

Chapter 5 underlines the disembodied bias characterizing the current innovation literature and urges the adoption of a more comprehensive view on technological change, one acknowledging also the role of investment as a fundamental source of innovation.

This redressing of the balance will be undertaken throughout the empirical section of the book using data generated from the Italian Innovation Surveys, carried over the last decade by the Italian Central Statistical Office (ISTAT), and covering both the manufacturing and service sectors. From such databases we will use data on *total innovation costs* sustained by Italian manufacturing and service firms for undertaking different kinds of innovative activities during the periods 1981–85, 1990–92 and 1993–95. Data on main components of such costs, namely those related to *research and development* (R&D), *design and engineering, the acquisition of know-how, trial production, innovative investment* and *marketing* along with the number of *product and process innovations* introduced will be used to identify major sectoral innovation patterns and technological regimes of production.

Three main issues are explored in the second part of the book:

1. The first question is assessing the quantitative relevance of knowledge-generating activities *vis-à-vis* innovative efforts using the technologies embodied in fixed capital. In place of the highly fragmented and impressionistic evidence so far available a clear evaluation of the two factors is made.

2. The second objective is an analysis of the relationship existing between embodied and disembodied technological activities. While the systemic and interdependent nature of the process of technological change has been much emphasized in the recent literature, there is little quantitative evidence on the effective degree of contiguity and complementarity between the different sources of innovation in industry. The specific cases where R&D, design activities and investment emerge as complements or substitutes in the innovation behaviour of firms and sectoral technological patterns will be identified.

3. The third aim of this book sheds some light on the way innovative patterns are linked with some basic characteristics of the productive structure of firms and industries. It shows that the prevalence of embodied or disembodied innovation patterns leads to different technological barriers to entry and types of economies of scale, which in turn operate as different determinants of firm size and market structure conditions.

All three empirical issues described above are investigated using both basic statistics and multivariate econometric estimates. Chapter 6 provides an overview of the basic characteristics of innovation processes in industry, looking at the diffusion, nature and economic impact of innovation activities both in the manufacturing and the service sectors. Chapter 7 uses firm-level data for an in-depth analysis of firms' innovation strategies and the way embodied and disembodied technological activities are linked with firms' size and labour productivity. Chapter 8 analyses the extent to which industrial sectors differ in the technological and productive variables contained in our data-set while Chapter 9 describes the variety of innovation patterns and regimes of production across manufacturing industries, which are then synthesized in a sectoral taxonomy contained in Chapter 10.

The concluding chapter summarizes the main findings of the book, and discusses some theoretical and policy implications which can be drawn from the empirical evidence presented.

PART ONE

Investment in Knowledge and Machinery:
Theory and Perspectives

1. Disembodied and embodied technological change: concepts and definitions

1.1 DEFINITIONS OF EMBODIED AND DISEMBODIED TECHNOLOGY, TECHNOLOGICAL CHANGE AND INNOVATION ACTIVITIES

Technology and innovation are nowadays regarded as the fundamental factors sustaining firms' competitiveness as well as aggregate economic performance and social welfare. At the same time there are few concepts which have a more undefined or casual definition basis. This in turn is due to the complex and multiform nature of the process of technological change to which are associated severe difficulties to find appropriate definitions and measurement tools.

A considerable degree of ambiguity also characterizes the labels 'embodied' and 'disembodied' attached to the terms 'technology' and 'technological change'. These concepts are not at all self-evident and are grounded on rather loose theoretical and conceptual bases. It is sufficient to say that the terminological distinction between embodied and disembodied technological change has originated only in this postwar period and within economic schools (namely neoclassical and post-Keynesian) which have attached only a limited importance to technological change. The representation and conceptualization of technology chosen by these contributions were the ones compatible with theoretical and methodological frameworks badly equipped to treat technology as an endogenous factor.

In economic theory we are, in fact, left only with a formal definition of 'disembodied technological change' built around the neoclassical 'production function' approach (see section 2.3). In the neoclassical framework, technological change has been defined as disembodied if '. . . independent of any changes in the factor inputs, the isoquant contours of the production function shift towards the origin as time passes' (Burmeister and Dobell, 1970, p. 66, quoted in Stoneman, 1983, p. 4). By default, we have embodied technological change when technological change is linked to changes of the factor inputs.[1]

Despite being formally rigorous such definitions do not give full justice to a much more rich conceptual issue regarding the essential nature of technology

3

and innovation and the way it affects the economic and social landscape. The definition of embodied and disembodied technological change, based on the production function approach, is also not able to reflect the richness of the very different approaches and theoretical categories that both in economic theory and in the most recent innovation literature can be associated to, and substantiate, such terms.

A definition of 'disembodied' and 'embodied' technological change based on the etymology of these terms seems a more appropriate way to get somewhat closer to the conceptual core of this issue.

As the term technology implies, the latter refers to a 'body of knowledge about (production) techniques'. When technology is defined in such terms, the label 'disembodied' reinforces its pure 'knowledge content'. This in turn implies that disembodied technology can be defined: (i) as knowledge expressed in some codified form (in this case technological knowledge acquires the characteristics of a public good); and (ii) or knowledge embodied in people, that is in the people who have generated it or have a full control and understanding of it.

The implicit or explicit use of an 'embodied' conceptualization of technology traditionally shared among economists, industrialists, and historians, stems on the other hand from the recognition that technology assumes its economic relevance once used as a 'production force', and more specifically when it finds its economic materialization in specific technical assets and devices used in production (embodiment process).

Tangibility and the reference to 'production' are thus the more common criteria to qualify embodied technology and differentiate it from disembodied knowledge. As mentioned by Freeman, technology '. . . is frequently used to encompass both the knowledge itself and the tangible embodiment of that knowledge in an operating system using physical production equipment' (Freeman, 1982, p. 4).

The definition of disembodied and embodied technology contained in this quotation is straightforward and in our opinion still effective in representing two fundamental forms that technology takes in the economy. However the tangible/physical qualification of embodied technology can be misleading, remaining confined only to a specific phenomenal aspect of technology. A software package is, for instance, a clear example of a technology, which though being intangible is still embodied in a well-defined operating system.

A more fundamental distinction is the one based on the extent to which technology operates in the economic system as a separate and autonomous production force, incorporated either in physical technical assets or intangible operating systems as in the case of most information technologies. The separation and autonomization we are speaking about is *vis-à-vis* the specific processes and human resources which have generated a given technology. The 'embodiment process' requires, in fact, a process of 'alienation', here meant as the possibility to split the process of generation and use of knowledge.[2] In other words what is transferred in the case of embodied technology is not pure knowledge but a production device or an operating system, which contains knowledge and is able to express its productive power.[3] Thus the specific carrier through which such knowledge is transferred (and its degree of tangibility) is of secondary importance *vis-à-vis* the process of transfer of that knowledge from the producer to the user.[4] The possibility of such a split in the process of generation and use of knowledge is, in fact, at the very basis of the historical emergence of specialized industries generating and producing technology (Rosenberg, 1963, 1976b; Athreye, 1998). The possibility of splitting the process of generation and use of technological knowledge has also been a major factor which has made possible the diffusion and economic exploitation of technology in the economy as a whole.

The distinction between embodied and disembodied technology, which is proposed in this book, thus ultimately distinguishes two distinct dimensions and forms in which technology coexists and operates in the economy. To put it in a rather extreme way, the distinction is between a technology conceived and represented as a *stock of knowledge* (or a set of capabilities) embodied in people or expressed in some codified form – that is, disembodied technology – as opposed to technology incorporated both in *tangible technical assets* and *intangible operating systems* (fixed productive capital) involved in the 'production sphere' – that is, embodied technology.

If the definitions of embodied and disembodied technology proposed above are accepted, the concept of embodied versus disembodied technological change is quite straightforward. The general process of technological change can be conceptualized as a process of *generation* of new technological knowledge as distinct from the process which leads to its *actual use* in production. The first process is clearly disembodied in nature, as long as it can be defined independently from its embodiment stage, that is from its actual use in a 'alienated' form. The process of embodied technological change refers to the actual use of technological knowledge in production activities in the form of new or improved machines, technical devices and operating systems.[5]

The term 'technological change' is usually used in a broad and macroeconomic context. However firms have been increasingly recognized as the major actors in the process of technological change. This justifies the increasing use of the terms 'innovation' and 'innovation activities' to represent the intentional and more behavioural nature of firms' strategies. In parallel with the definition of embodied and disembodied technological change, *embodied innovative activities* can then be defined as those activities undertaken by firms to introduce process technologies through investment whereas *disembodied innovative activities* consist of the generation and development of technological knowledge.

The difference with respect to disembodied and embodied technological change thus relies mainly on the firm-level connotation of innovative activities.

1.2   TECHNOLOGY EMBODIED IN INTERMEDIATE INPUTS

Economists have traditionally referred to the terms 'embodied technology' and 'embodied innovation activities' as investment in fixed capital and the process of acquisition of technologically new machinery and equipment. The vintage models (Solow, 1959; Salter, 1960), the function of technological progress proposed by Kaldor (1957) as well as the illuminating analysis of historians of technology such as Rosenberg (1963, 1976a, 1976b), all encompass a view of embodied technological change centred on the role of fixed productive capital (a more extensive discussion of the embodied perspective in the different economic schools is contained in Chapter 2).

The role played by the use of new or improved intermediate inputs as a source of technological change has also been acknowledged, although to a much lesser extent. Rosenberg himself, in his work 'Perspective on technology', points out that the substitution of inputs and the development of totally new materials represents a major source (and inducement factor) of technological advancements in modern industrial societies (Rosenberg, 1976b). The important role played by intermediate inputs in the process of technological change has also been stressed by Freeman with reference to the introduction of new synthetic materials and electronic components (Freeman, 1982). Kline and Rosenberg have made a similar point recalling the importance for user industries such as automobile, aircraft and aerospace, of upstream 'complementary' technological advancements in areas such as metallurgy, energy, glass, rubber and plastic (Kline and Rosenberg, 1986, p. 281). All this largely qualitative historical evidence has been more recently supported by empirical studies on (tangible) intersectoral technology flows, which have showed the importance of both new productive equipment and intermediate inputs as carriers of technologies between (user and producers) firms and industries (OECD, 1992a; Papaconstantinou et al., 1995).

Intermediate inputs should, therefore, also be considered as a form of embodied technology. Yet this broadening of the perspective on embodied technological change also poses significant conceptual and measurement problems.

A major conceptual problem has to do with the 'continuous' nature of economic activities consisting of the use of intermediate inputs. It can, in fact, be argued that the introduction and use in the first place of a new material and component clearly represents an innovation activity. However it is much more difficult to support such a view when the use of these inputs becomes an ordinary activity in production. In other words the repetitive use of qualitatively unchanged intermediate inputs can hardly be conceived as an innovation activity. Similarly it would be quite difficult to establish when the use of a new intermediate input would cease to be an innovative activity.[6]

On empirical grounds, there is the problem of identifying suitable proxies to measure innovative activities consisting of the use of technologically new intermediate inputs. In this respect, input–output economic and technological matrixes have been successfully used to identify the existence and direction of technological flows across industries, but are much less effective for identifying innovation processes at work (see section 3.4 for a more detailed discussion of this point).

In the light of the conceptual and practical problems mentioned above, we decided to stick to a more traditional and narrow definition of embodied technological change, one which is in line with the major streams of economic thought, which will be reviewed in Chapters 2 and 3. Such an approach is also imposed by data constraints since the database used in the empirical part of this book does not provide quantitative information on the use of intermediate inputs.

1.3 EMBODIED AND DISEMBODIED TECHNOLOGICAL INDICATORS

In empirical research, technological and innovative activities are usually measured by input and output indicators. Input indicators are those measuring the financial and human resources put into the innovation process, while innovative outputs are those measuring the output of such processes. Following the definition of disembodied and embodied technology and innovative activities given above, the traditional indicators used in the literature can be accordingly 'forced' into one of the two categories adopted here. Some technological indicators have a clear 'disembodied' connotation. This is the case of indicators built on R&D expenditures and personnel, which measure the technological and innovative efforts aiming at generating or developing technological knowledge. Patent counts can also be regarded as disembodied indicators, representing a measure of the output of such inventive innovative activities. Another typical knowledge-based indicator is built on bibliographic data, summarizing in codified form new scientific or technological knowledge. The same can be said for the data on technological flows recorded by the technological balance of payments (transfer of licences, trademarks, know-how, technical assistance), which all have a disembodied nature.

It might be argued that in many cases R&D activities are directed to generating knowledge which is eventually embodied in new intermediate products, capital goods or final products. However, by adopting the definition of disembodied technology and technological change given above, which focuses on the 'direct' knowledge-producing nature of such activities, R&D activities maintain their disembodied characteristics, as long as their direct output consists of an increase of the stock of knowledge. The indicators more commonly used to measure embodied technological activities are represented by investment in machinery, equipment and new plant, operating systems (including those intangible in nature such as software). The implicit assumption is that they all incorporate new technologies.

However, traditional input and output technological indicators have the major limitation of being unable to capture knowledge-generating activities, which take place outside formal R&D laboratories and institutions. On the other hand, the use of investment in fixed productive capital has the inconvenience that assumes that all such investment incorporates new technologies. In the last few years, innovation surveys have tried to overcome both such shortcomings capturing a wider range of technological activities, both disembodied and embodied in nature. Along with R&D, activities consisting of the design and engineering of new products and processes, the acquisition of know-how, licences and patents and trial production efforts also have been taken into account and data on innovation expenditures on such activities have begun to be collected. Innovation surveys have also included the acquisition of technologies embodied in new machinery, equipment and plants. These new data-sets allow us for the first time to explore the relevance and role of a wider range of embodied and disembodied innovation activities in industry (OECD, 1992b; OECD-EUROSTAT, 1997; Sirilli, 1997).

1.4   CONCEPTS AND DEFINITIONS USED IN THE BOOK

In the light of what has been discussed above, the following set of concepts and definitions will be used in this book, both for the literature review contained in this and the following chapter and for the later empirical chapters:

Disembodied technology: stock of technological knowledge, both embodied in people and/or expressed in a codified form;

disembodied technological change: process of advancing technological knowledge;

disembodied innovative activities: activities carried out at the firm-level to generate or develop new technological knowledge;

disembodied technological indicators: R&D expenditures and personnel, design and engineering activities, patent and licence counts, technology flows measured by the technological balance of payments and bibliometric data;

embodied technology: stock of technological productive assets consisting of machinery, equipment, plant and operating systems (both tangible and intangible);

embodied technological change: accumulation of new technical assets (machinery, equipment, plants and operating systems);

embodied innovative activities: innovative activities consisting of the use or adoption of new productive assets with enhanced technical and technological performances compared with those used before.

embodied technological and innovative indicators: investment in new machinery, equipment and plant incorporating new (or not yet used) technologies; indicators measuring the adoption and diffusion of embodied technologies.

1.5   CONCLUSIONS

In this chapter we have proposed a set of definitions for embodied and disembodied technology, technological change, and innovation activities. The rationale for such proposed definitions arises from the belief that, beyond the ambiguity surrounding such terms in the economic and innovation literature, the distinction between embodied and disembodied technological change ultimately reflects two different dimensions of technology and innovative activities. To put it in a rather extreme way, the distinction is between a conceptualization of technology conceived and represented as a stock of knowledge (or a set of capabilities) as opposed to a conceptualization of technology conceived and represented in terms of physical technical assets or intangible operating systems (software) used in the 'production sphere'. Analogously, innovative activities can be conceptualized either as activities aimed at producing new technological knowledge or as activities consisting of the use of technologies in production through investment in fixed capital. We believe that such definitions, though containing a high level of generality (and not taking into account the role of intermediate inputs), are quite effective for highlighting different perspectives in the economic and innovation literature and, on more operational grounds, allow us to build effective indicators of firms' embodied and disembodied innovative efforts to be used in empirical research.

NOTES

1. Yet, the nature of such a link has remained rather obscure in the neoclassical framework being the inputs of production defined as homogeneous factors.
2. The concept of 'embodiment' and 'alienation' used here are consistent with the ones used by Marx in relation to the process of alienation and objectification of science and technological knowledge in fixed capital (Marx [1857] 1973).
3. This does not mean that the use and adoption of embodied technologies is meant to be a passive action nor that learning by doing processes are not important. As stressed by many contributions, the use and adoption of new technologies always require an 'absorption capacity' as well as organization adjustments and changes in the skills of the labour force. Yet a significant gap does exist between the knowledge incorporated in new capital goods and the knowledge requested for their use. Moreover this gap seems to be constantly increasing in parallel with the increasing sophistication and science-based nature of most production processes and products.
4. This in turn implies that the user does not need to have a full command of the knowledge, which was necessary to generate it, nor that the user needs to fully understand the functioning of the specific technology used.
5. The labels of disembodied and embodied attached to the term 'technical change' assume a different connotation, apparently more straightforward and less ambiguous. Technical change literally refers to the changes in the techniques of production. Embodied technical change might then be identified in those changes in the production techniques which involve the use of embodied technologies, independently from the place where and time when those technologies have been developed. In this respect it is not substantially different from the concept of embodied technological change. Conversely disembodied technical and technological change do not overlap. In the case of technical change the process of generation of new knowledge is not of concern since the knowledge bases or expertise underlying such knowledge is already pre-existing. The disembodied label might only refer to those changes in the production techniques, which do not rely on changes in the production assets. As a result they refer to changes which have an organizational nature.
6. The inclusion of intermediate inputs raises an additional conceptual and empirical problem when one needs to define and measure technology as a stock variable. Considering at any given point in time all existing intermediate inputs as part of the total stock of embodied technology seems a quite extreme assumption.

2. Disembodied and embodied perspectives on technological change in the economic literature

2.1 INTRODUCTION

The purpose of this chapter is to show that the distinction between embodied and disembodied technological change, as defined in Chapter 1, is one that is able to draw a line between the major schools of thought in economics and a range of approaches in the most recent innovation literature. Such a line is not, of course, a straight one. The embodied and disembodied perspective characterizing the different approaches is often a matter of simple emphasis given to the different dimensions of technological activities. Sometimes it is only implicit in the more general conceptual framework adopted and only in a few cases is it qualified on more analytical or theoretical grounds. The definitions of embodied and disembodied technological change adopted in Chapter 1 will be used to follow such a tortuous line. Some major stages in the historical evolution of theorizing on technological change will then be identified. Accordingly the chapter proceeds in section 2.2 with the characterizations of the classical economists and Schumpeter, and carries on to analyse neoclassical economists (section 2.3) and the post-Keynesian approaches (section 2.4).

The organization of this chapter in such a chronological order is an attempt to show that a shift from an embodied to a disembodied perspective of technological change has progressively taken place and that this tendency has been reinforced by the emergence of the new contributions within the most recent neo-Schumpeterian innovation literatures and in the new emphasis given to intangible investment in the so-called 'knowledge-based economy'.

2.2 FROM THE CLASSICAL ECONOMISTS TO SCHUMPETER

2.2.1 The 'Embodied' Perspective of Classical Economists

Classical economists, particularly Smith, Ricardo and Marx, have explicitly encompassed technological change in their analysis. Technological change was seen in a rather holistic perspective, with the multidimensional nature of technological change and its complex interdependencies with the other key economic variables defining the structure and functioning of economic systems. The dynamic historical dimension in which technical change was seen as taking place was another feature of the classical approach. All these elements made the analytical treatment of technological change in these approaches difficult to reduce to any rigid and rigorous formalization or modelling.

The classical contributions also show similar characteristics with respect to some key dimensions of technology and innovative activities, and among them three interdependent aspects can be associated with, and qualify in a consistent way, the skeleton of an *embodied* conceptualization of technology and technological change, as defined in the previous section:

1. a production-centred perspective on technology and innovation;
2. an intimate link between technological advance and the process of mechanization of production;
3. the capital-deepening and labour-substituting nature of technological activities, which makes innovative activities and investment in fixed capital strongly interlinked.

The first of these refers to the centrality of the production sphere as characterizing the conceptual framework of classical economists. However the production domain is seen in a rather broad and multidimensional way, including quantitative and qualitative characteristics of the labour process, the technical physical characteristics of the tools used, and the more general organizational characteristics of production processes.

The second common feature in the approach of classical economists to technology is the presence of a clear link between technological development and the process of mechanization, that is the progressive substitution of labour by machines. Mechanization, which is the process of creation and utilization on a large scale of new machines, is identified by classical economists as the general law of industrialization and the major factor responsible for the historical increase of labour productivity. In this perspective a necessary condition for technological change to take place is precisely the presence of investment activities both at the firm-level and for the economic system as a whole. The link between technological change and investment in new machinery together with the prevalent capital-deepening and labour-saving characteristics of innovative activities is therefore the third feature common to all three classical economists mentioned above.[1]

Despite such similarities, Smith, Ricardo and Marx stress the three aspects mentioned above to a different extent and with different qualifications.

Adam Smith's work is normally recalled in relation to his original contribution on the division of labour. The process of an increasing division of labour, both at the level of the single production units and at the level of the economic system as a whole, has been seen as the key feature of the more general process of industrialization and the main source of increases of labour productivity. While the importance of the process of division of labour and its link with technological change has been recognized by other writers of Smith's time,[2] and later by Marx, a distinctive feature of the Smithian contribution is precisely the direction of causation between changes in the size of the market, the deepening of the division of labour and the introduction of new process technologies. The size of the market limits the process of division of labour, and is seen by Smith as the necessary precondition for new machines to be introduced. The automation of labour tasks is possible once they have become sufficiently simplified and specialized by the general process of increasing the division of labour.[3]

Compared to Smith's works, Ricardo's contribution appears less centred on the study of the characteristics of production activities and the labour process. His analysis of the characteristics of the labour process was undertaken within a more general effort to develop a theory of value and distribution. It is in this light that we can explain the rather tangential role given by Ricardo to techno-logical change itself and the subordination of this topic to the more general targets of his analysis. Ricardo explicitly deals with technological change only in the third edition of *On the Principles of Political Economy and Taxation* [1817] (1951) where a new chapter on machinery was added to the previous version. Even if rather marginal to the main corpus of his analysis, the vision of technological change that he has is still well within the classical tradition and is largely associated with the process of mechanization through investment. Furthermore, compared to Smith's writings, in Ricardo's works there is an explicit reference to the capital-deepening and labour-saving effects of the introduction of new technologies. These impacts of technological change on labour have been developed by Ricardo in relation to the well-known controversy with Malthus about the effects of the introduction of capital-intensive techniques on employment (Vivarelli, 1995).

The centrality of production, the importance of mechanization, and the link between technological change and the more general process of accumulation of capital, are all aspects which, along with many others, make Marx's analysis very sympathetic to those of Smith and Ricardo. The three elements are fully supported by Marx with a large number of historical references and on a more theoretical basis.

The centrality of production in the Marxian approach is at the very basis of his materialistic and dialectic vision of the evolution of the economic and social organizations. Furthermore, in Marx's works, more than in Smith's and

Ricardo's, there is an explicit analysis of the economic determinants of the general process of mechanization, the latter being seen, along with changes in the organization of the labour process, as the central feature of technological change. Such a process is seen as the result of the battle of single capitalists, and the attempt of the capitalist class as a whole, to increase 'relative surplus value', by reducing the value of the commodities, and in particular those that enter the real wages. This is obtained mainly by changing production methods (including organizational changes) and introducing labour-saving techniques.[4] For Marx, more than for Smith and Ricardo, the process of technological change is thus intrinsically linked to the investment activities of firms and to the more general process of accumulation of capital. Both the accumulation process and the continuing revolution of production techniques are, according to Marx, the specific characteristics of capitalist economies, which differentiate them from all the previous 'modes of production'.

Another aspect, which is peculiar to the Marxian perspective on technology, is the importance given to the macroeconomic conditions in which firms' innovation activities and the process of technological change take place. When the realization of profits becomes more difficult because of the emergence of periodical overproduction crises, the increased competition compels the capitalist to use technological change, along with other competitive weapons, for surviving.[5] The introduction of new (largely labour-saving) technologies becomes one of the means of inter-capitalist rivalry and a factor that spurs qualitative changes in production activities during the downturn of the business cycle.

In the analysis carried out so far we have highlighted some very common elements of the classical perspective on technological change, which qualify it as 'embodied'. This is, of course, a somewhat simplified reading of the view of classical analysis on technology. In all classical writings the endogenous nature of the process of generation of new technologies is also clearly emphasized. It is easy to show, for instance, that the emphasis put by Marx on the production-related nature of innovative activities does not contradict his extensive acknowledgement of the growing importance of science in capitalist production systems as a new 'force of production' (Marx, [1857] 1973). The two aspects are, in fact, clearly interlinked. Technological change is conceptualized as the adaptation of scientific knowledge to practical production-related problems with the progress of scientific and technological knowledge exerting its major economic and social effects by accelerating the development of the 'production forces' (Marx, [1857] (1973), [1894] (1977); Rosenberg, 1976a, 1982b; Hagedoorn, 1989). This is also true for Smith: the overall trend towards increasing levels of division of labour also applies to those economic activities consisting of the generation of new knowledge and new artefacts.[6] In this respect, although the use of new process technologies is clearly predominant, great emphasis is also given to the technological activities consisting of the generation of new ideas and innovations, as well as of the processes of 'learning by doing'.

These few examples confirm that the label 'embodied' attached to the classical perspective on technical change is somewhat reductive of their analysis. Nonetheless the reason for attaching the 'embodied' label to the classical perspective refers to the fact that investment is still seen as a necessary (or most important) vehicle to introduce such knowledge into the production system. In Marx's view the embodied conceptualization of technological change can also be associated to the emphasis given to the capital-deepening nature of techno-logical change, which leads to an ever-increasing 'technical composition of capital'. The latter can be defined as the ratio of the mass of the means of production with respect to the labour which is required to employ them. In 'value terms' this ratio is defined by Marx as 'organic composition of capital' (Marx [1894] 1983, *Capital I*, chapter 23 and *Capital III*, chapter 8).

2.2.2 Schumpeter: the Departure from an Embodied Perspective

The elements of similarity between Schumpeter and the classical economists have been widely recognized and acknowledged by Schumpeter himself (with reference to Marx) and by later literature. Such similarity is based on a clear acknowledgement of the central role that technological change plays in the dynamics of economic systems and social organizations. In Schumpeter's analysis the conceptualization of technology and innovation, as well as the macroeconomic determinants of technological change, are, however, quite different from the classical perspective.

Compared to Smith and Marx, Schumpeter is less interested in studying the characteristics of the labour process and the characteristics of technology in its production-related dimension. For the basic structure of the Schumpeterian conceptual framework innovation does not need to be restricted in its specific nature or its purpose. Especially in his early work *The Theory of Economic Development* (1934), innovative activities, and innovations, are conceived as the new 'economic facts' which make the economic system periodically depart from a situation of static equilibrium in the neoclassical sense. The emphasis is thus on any novelty introduced by entrepreneurs, almost independently of its effective and specific technological content. The role of innovation is that of allowing the innovator to gain a transitory monopolistic position, which generates a rent destined to expire as soon as the innovation is imitated and diffusion takes place. Accordingly the conceptualization and definition of innovative activities assume a broader and more general content, encompassing product, process, as well as organizational changes. At the same time innovation activities do not have any clear impact on the capital/labour relationship. The equal importance given by Schumpeter to the different forms of innovations is clear in the following taxonomy contained in *The Theory of Economic Development* where he identifies five main typologies of innovation and innovative activities:

1. The introduction of a new good – that is one with which consumers are not yet familiar – or a new quality of a good.
2. The introduction of a new method of production, that is one not yet tested by experience in the branch of manufacture concerned, which need by no means to be founded upon a new scientific discovery, and can also exist in a new way of handling a commodity commercially.
3. The opening of a new market, that is a market into which the particular branch of manufacture of the country in question has not previously entered, whether it has first to be created.
4. The conquest of a new source of supply of a raw materials or half-manufactured goods, again irrespective of whether this source already exists or whether it has first to be created.
5. The carrying out of the new organization of any industry, like the creation of a monopoly position (for example through trustification) or the breaking up of a monopoly position (Schumpeter, 1934, p. 66).

The departure of Schumpeter from the classical 'embodied' perspective on technological change emerges from the absence from this list of any reference to all those features, which were common to the classical approach. In Schumpeter's analysis the links between technology and innovation on the one hand, and characteristics of labour and production processes on the other, become much weaker and peripheral for explaining the nature, determinants and economic effects of technological change.[7] Also the strong link identified by the classical economists between investment in fixed productive capital and technological change, both at a micro-and macro-level, loses its central position in Schumpeter's analysis.[8] Similarly the nature of the relationship between technological change and economic phenomena, such as the growth in aggregate output and productivity, or the process of structural change in the economy, are rather far from the 'embodied' classical perspective based on the capital-deepening effects of technical advances.

The Schumpeterian view on the institutional setting in which innovation is generated changed from that outlined in *The Theory of Economic Development* [1912] (1934), in his later work *Capitalism, Socialism and Democracy* (1942). It has, in fact, been argued that not just one but two alternative Schumpeterian perspectives can actually be identified, later on labelled as the Mark 1 and 2 Schumpeterian models (Phillips, 1971; Freeman et al., 1982). A behavioural vision of innovative activities seen as 'heroic' entrepreneurial acts, which is at the basis of the dynamics of structural change described above, was replaced by a more stable institutional setting consisting of the prevalence and permanence of oligopolistic market structures.

The emphasis given by Schumpeter in his later work *Capitalism, Socialism and Democracy* to R&D can be seen as a decisive step towards a disembodied approach to innovative activities. The passage from the 'first' to the 'second' Schumpeter is actually based on the endogenization of a particular stage of the innovative process; that is, the stage consisting of the generation of new scientific and technological knowledge, represented by R&D activities carried out by firms through the establishment of specific laboratories.

2.3 DISEMBODIED AND EMBODIED TECHNICAL CHANGE IN THE NEOCLASSICAL APPROACH

As already mentioned in Chapter 1, the only formal definition and representation of disembodied and embodied technological change is the one developed within the neoclassical framework, and particularly with reference to the 'production function'. The latter reflects the state of technology at a given point in time, defined as the knowledge of all available techniques of production (independently of their actual use).[9] It follows from the above that using different combinations of the production factors does not represent technological change as long as one moves along the pre-existing isoquant. This implies the use of techniques already known among the economic agents.[10] In the normal textbook technological change is, in fact, represented by upward shifts of the production function, and related shifts of the isoquants.

No account is, however, given of the nature and causes of technological change, which consequently assumes a completely exogenous nature. Technological change can, however, be 'biased' according to its final effects on the relative use of the different inputs. What are termed 'non-neutral' forms of technological change, and in particular the fact that technological change can be 'biased', leading to an increased use of capital compared to labour (biased technological change in Hicks's sense) or output, cannot, however, be regarded as embodied technological change.[11] This is because the conceptualization of technological change implicit in the production function is completely independent of its final effects. It is thought of as an exogenous change in the level and nature of the knowledge (and relative techniques) available in the economic system. In this perspective technological change continues to have a purely disembodied nature. Unlike for the classical economists, innovative activities are not necessarily linked to the process of investment in fixed capital nor is there necessarily implicit in the process of technological change any process of substitution of labour by machines (mechanization in the classical perspective) or any qualitative change in the nature of the inputs and their organization.[12]

The conceptualization of technological change, which neoclassical scholars adopted in a dynamic context, continued to be exogenous and disembodied as being the only one compatible with the use of a marginalist type of production function.[13] The first explicit formulation and conceptualization of technological change of a disembodied nature can be found precisely in relation to the attempt made by neoclassical scholars to 'explain' that part of the long-term economic growth 'not explained' by the quantitative changes of the productive factors (labour and capital) (Solow, 1957; Denison, 1967, 1974). In particular Solow estimated that as much as 87 per cent of labour productivity growth (output per hour) in the US over the period 1909–49 was accounted for by the 'residual' and had nothing to do with capital formation (1957). Denison, making some growth accounting exercises for the 1950s and 1960s, showed that only 10–15 per cent of economic growth in those two decades in the US could be accounted for by capital formation in non-residential plant and equipment (Denison, 1967). The first attempt, and easiest way, to explain such a celebrated 'residual' was to attribute it to an external factor, namely technological change. The disembodied nature of technological change in such an approach is related to the fact that this new element is not a production factor in itself, and appears in the production function as a separate entity from the other productive factors. The time element is then assumed to be the explanatory factor of economic growth. As with the static production function, in this case, too, changes in the combination of the factors across time did not require qualitative changes of capital (as well as labour), and therefore did not encompass any form of embodiment of new technology in fixed productive capital.[14] Such an unrealistic assumption, and the ones on constant return to scale and factors remunerated according to their marginal productivity, lie at the heart of many criticisms addressed to the neoclassical treatment of technological change in growth accounting exercises and to their dismissal of the role played by capital accumulation. In particular later contributions have stressed the logical and practical inseparability, especially in the long run and in the presence of a deep process of structural changes, between the process of technological change and changes in the quality and quantity of the productive inputs used (Nelson, 1964,1981).

Indeed the disembodied vision of technological change portrayed in the neoclassical growth accounting literature appeared even to marginalist economists clearly insufficient to take into account one of the essential components of technological changes in a long-term perspective; that is, the qualitative changes of the productive factors and above all the qualitative changes of production equipment.

The first and clearest attempt to overcome this problem within the neoclassical stream was the proposal to employ vintage models, starting with the contributions by Solow (1959) and Salter (1960). The inclusion of qualitative changes in productive capital was obtained by decomposing the stock of capital according to different homogeneous vintages. More recent vintages have higher relative productivity because of the more recent technologies that they embody. The introduction of the stock of capital in different vintages could now take into account changes in the capital structure and the quality of fixed capital employed, stratified according to its age. In vintage models the embodied nature of technological change is not derived from its effects on the *use* of the inputs (as it is in the standard models presented previously) but from the hypothesis that new capital *embodies* new technology. This implies that investments are regarded as proper (embodied) technological activities.[15] Vintage models, by explicitly including embodied technological change in the production function, have also made the latter endogenous to the economic process. Later neoclassical contributions have pushed forward such an effort towards the endogenization of technological change though shifting towards a disembodied conceptualization of technology and innovative activities: it was the process of generation of knowledge that had to be endogenized.

2.3.1 Neoclassical Models of Growth with Endogenous Technological Change: from Arrow to the 'New Growth Theory'

In that long journey that neoclassical economists have undertaken in order first to incorporate and later to endogenize technological change in their models, the 1962 contribution by Arrow has been an important and influential work. It was the first time in the neoclassical economic tradition that the process of generation of new knowledge became endogenous to the economic process. Arrow's conceptualization of technological change seems, however, ambivalent and to some extent contradictory, as far as the distinction between embodied and disembodied technological change is concerned. In his 1962 article he expressly states that he intends to suggest 'an endogenous theory of the *changes in knowledge* which underlies inter-temporal and international *shifts in production functions*' (Arrow, 1962, p. 131 – emphasis added). This statement clearly shows Arrow's conceptualization of technology as knowledge, and technological change as the process through which new knowledge is generated. In Arrow's model the accumulation of knowledge takes the form of a process of 'learning by doing' and the latter is in turn the result of the experience and know-how accumulated in the economy. Among economic activities, investment activities (the cumulative production and use of capital goods) are identified by Arrow as the best proxy for such 'an index of experience' (p. 133).

The ambivalent conceptualization of technological change referred to, which characterizes Arrow's article, arises from the fact that, after having emphasized a knowledge-based conceptualization of technological change, he also supports an embodied conceptualization of technical change as represented in the preceding vintage models. In this respect he clearly states:

> I follow here the model of Solow and Johansen, in which technical change is completely embodied in new capital goods. At any moment of new time, the new capital goods incorporate all the knowledge then available, but once built their productive efficiency cannot be altered by subsequent learning (p. 133).[16]

In Arrow's contribution both a disembodied and embodied conceptualization therefore seems to coexist, through a double function played by investment: the latter represents an important source for the accumulation of disembodied technology (in the form of experience) and represents the only way to introduce, in an embodied form, such knowledge into the production processes.

Arrow's contribution has represented a milestone in the innovation literature and in particular for the most recent neoclassical models of economic growth. However Arrow's explicit reference to the link between investment and innovation was largely lost before the most recent contributions in the 'new growth theory', while the centrality of knowledge as a distinct factor of production has progressively taken hold among neoclassical scholars.

The relationships between investment and the innovation process are much less evident, for instance in the works of Romer, the author of two influential contributions in the new growth literature (1986, 1990). In his first model increasing returns are for the first time directly related to the stock of knowledge accumulated in the society, which enters into the production function as a new independent factor of production. The endogenous nature of technological change in Romer's models is straightforward. The stock of knowledge in the society is the outcome of firm-level investment activities. The latter in turn are the result of subjective choices between current consumption and investment in the process of generation of knowledge. Given the presence of spillovers in the production of knowledge, the stock of knowledge enters the production function as two terms: as the stock of knowledge of the single firm and as the pool of general knowledge present in the economic system. Knowledge as such becomes in these models the main source of technological externalities. The unimportant or indistinct role of investment as a form of technological activity is shown by the fact that, along with knowledge, the other factor in the production function is defined as a rather vague '. . . set of additional factors such as physical capital, labour and so forth . . . which are available in fixed supply' (Romer, 1986, p. 1014).

In Lucas's model (1988), the stock of technology is expressed in the form of human capital, that is knowledge embodied in people. Investment in technological change takes the form of investment in human resources, through education.[17] In Lucas's model 'unbounded growth' is due to the joint characteristics of non-diminishing returns in the process of accumulation of knowledge in a context characterized by the absence of any fixed factor. Externalities as well have a disembodied nature and source: they are the result of the interactions among people in the forms of exchange of information and knowledge flows.

The endogenization of technological change has been further refined by more recent contributions, by introducing into the production function innovative activities in the form of R&D. In modelling an aggregate production function, Romer (1990), Grossman and Helpman (1991, 1994) and Aghion and Howitt (1992) all distinguish between a research sector (producing knowledge) and the rest of the economy (producing ordinary goods). In some cases an additional distinction is made between a sector producing intermediate or instrumental goods and a sector producing final goods. The inclusion of a specific sector producing knowledge makes the latter the outcome of an intentional economic activity (subject to similar kinds of individual subjective choice as those envisaged in Lucas's model) as well as an input for the research sector itself. The main differences between these models relate to the effective representation of the innovative output. In the 1990 Romer model, the innovative output of the research sector assumes the form of new designs, which are used in the sector producing intermediate inputs. Changes in fixed capital related to the innovation process are also taken into account. There is, in fact, a specific emphasis on changes in the variety of capital items which are introduced by an increase in the number of new designs and intermediate products used in the final sector. It remains unclear whether these new intermediate products should be assimilated to long-lived fixed productive capital. As pointed out by Freeman and Soete, contrary to physical capital in the usual sense, these intermediate inputs do not accumulate (Freeman and Soete, 1997, p. 328). The Grossman–Helpman (1991) model does not differ significantly from Romer's one as far as the general philosophy and structure of the model is concerned. In the Aghion–Howitt (1992) model technological change, instead of increasing the varieties of intermediate product, increases the quality of intermediate and/or final products. Innovative activities are also associated with the emergence of new firms producing qualitatively enhanced products, thus recalling a Schumpeterian model of competition based on innovation.

In the new-growth literature that flourished in the last decade the somewhat heterodox view on economic growth and technological change proposed by Scott should also be mentioned (Scott, 1989). Despite Scott developing his model maintaining most of the neoclassical assumptions he also departs from the traditional neoclassical view when he looks at the sources of economic growth. Investments are, in fact, seen by Scott as the fundamental economic activities through which new technological opportunities are discovered and economically exploited. With such an approach Scott strongly criticizes both the traditional neoclassical approach to technological change and the prevalent technology-push view characterizing the more recent neo-Schumpeterian literature. As explicitly mentioned by Scott his model has been influenced by heterodox contributions and ideas such as those contained in the works of Schumpeter, Schmookler and Kaldor.

In conclusion, while some of the recent neoclassical models reviewed in this section encompass some form of embodied technological change, they are still dominated by a clear disembodied conceptualization of both innovative activities and technology. This can be argued on the basis of the following considerations: (i) technological change is exclusively, or predominantly, localized in the R&D sector; (ii) the technological output in the R&D sector takes the form of general knowledge and blueprints; and (iii) an additional qualification to such a disembodied perspective of technological change lies in the fact that even the process of generation of knowledge does not require any embodied technological asset. We have seen that only the contribution by Scott adopts a different and more 'embodied' perspective on the nature of technological change and its effect on economic growth. However it cannot easily accommodated within the new (neoclassical) growth theory.

2.4   THE EMBODIED PERSPECTIVE OF POST-KEYNESIAN ECONOMISTS

Post-Keynesian contributions are characterized by putting a strong emphasis on the role of investment for explaining long-term economic growth. In most of these contributions technological change is seen, explicitly or implicitly, linked to the overall process of capital accumulation. In the early Keynesian models technical change, however, plays a minor role. In the Harrod and Domar models, for instance, technical change is reduced to a parameter indicating the capital/output ratio, which together with the 'saving propensity' coefficient determines the rate of growth of investment and income (Harrod, 1939; Domar, 1946). Among the post-Keynesian economists, there is no doubt that Kaldor was the author who went farthest ahead in the attempt to endogenize technological change in a heterodox macroeconomic model of economic growth. In his 1957 article there is an explicit attempt to provide an alternative view (with respect to the neoclassical one) on the nature of technological change and a justification for adopting an embodied perspective. The central role of investment in the process of technological change is explicitly acknowledged in the 'function of technical progress', which ties the rate of growth of output per capita to the rate of growth of capital stock per capita (Kaldor, 1957). Kaldor's embodied perspective on technological change also emerges in his criticism of the neoclassical distinction between changes in labour productivity (and growth) due to changes in the input proportion and those due to the generation of new knowledge.[18] He explicitly states that his model departs from the neoclassical ones in the fact that:

> it eschews any distinction between changes *in the production techniques* (and in productivity) which are induced by changes in the supply of capital relative to labour and those induced by technical invention or innovation, i.e. the introduction of new knowledge. The use of more capital per worker (whether measured in terms of the values of capital at current prices, in terms of tons of weight of the equipment, mechanical power) inevitably entails the introduction of superior techniques which requires 'inventiveness' of some kind, though these need not necessarily mean the application of basically new principles or ideas. On the other hand, most, though not all, technical innovations which are capable of raising the productivity of labour require the use of more capital per man – more elaborate equipment and/or more mechanical power (Kaldor, 1957, p. 595)

The embodied vision of technological change expressed by Kaldor, and shared by other post-Keynesian economists, relies on two characteristics already present (especially the second one) among the classical economists, which are: i) the necessary link between innovation and investment; ii) the capital-deepening characteristics of both innovative activities and investment. The importance of economic activities aiming at generating and developing new knowledge is, however, not denied. On the contrary Kaldor identifies a two-way dynamic relationship between disembodied technological change and the technological absorption capacity of the economic system. The extent of the latter is, however, again measured by the level and rate of growth of investment in fixed capital. The importance of this interplay between the production and use of technological knowledge for economic growth is explicit in the following passage, which can also be read as an *ante litteram* attempt to reconcile the technology-push and demand-pull controversy, which flourished in the following decades:

> the rapidity with which a society can 'absorb' capital (i.e. it can increase its human-made equipment, relatively to labour) depends on its technical dynamism and its ability to invent and introduce new techniques of production. A society where technical change and adaptation proceed slowly, where producers are reluctant to abandon traditional methods and to adopt new techniques is necessarily one where the rate of capital accumulation is small. The converse of this proposition is also true: the rate at which a society can expand and exploit new techniques is limited by its ability to accumulate capital (Kaldor, 1957, p. 596).

The stress put by Kaldor in this passage on the importance of the generation of new knowledge makes his conceptualization of technological change somewhat closer to the disembodied perspective of the most recent neoclassical models of growth reviewed in the previous section (Romer, 1990; Grossman and Helpman, 1991; Aghion and Howitt, 1992). Marked differences, however, remain between the two approaches.

The first difference has to do with the level of the analysis. Post-Keynesian models remain aggregate and largely macro-founded, whereas all neoclassical models are still micro-founded, based on subjective utility functions and optimizing behaviours.

Secondly, as far as the conceptualization of technological change is concerned, the difference is a matter of what is really regarded as technical change and can be derived from the specific emphasis given to the different stages of the innovation process. While for Kaldor, and the other economists in his school, the stage of embodiment through investment is regarded as the crucial part of the innovation process, in the recent neoclassical 'new growth models' the emphasis is clearly shifted to the process of generation of new knowledge, and it is not very clear to what extent the embodiment stage is considered as a form of innovative activity or a way through which technology is diffused in the economy. The most important type of investment in the most recent neoclassical models of growth is that involving the accumulation of knowledge in the form of human capital, while in the Kaldorian approach the emphasis is clearly focused on investment in fixed capital.[19] These differences in perspective (that is, micro versus macro) and in conceptualization of technical change (that is, generation versus use of technology) have important implications. This is because a microeconomic and disembodied conceptualization of technology makes for a different set of determining factors and inducement mechanisms from a macroeconomic embodied conceptualization. Thus, while in the neoclassical models of economic growth, the accumulation of knowledge ultimately depends on subjective (rational) choices regarding the current or future allocation of resources, the macroeconomic post-Keynesian models of economic growth and technological change are effectively open to the influence of a wide range of macroeconomic forces. A macroeconomic approach to technological change and diffusion which re-emphasizes the role of investment is the one contained in the work of Antonelli, Petit and Tahar (1992).

2.5 CONCLUSIONS

In this chapter we have shown that, despite the terminological and conceptual fuzziness that surrounds the labels 'disembodied' and 'embodied' attached to technology and technological change, these terms can be used to identify different perspectives in the evolution of economic thought on the nature of technology and innovative activities.

The perspective of classical economists has allowed us to identify what we might define as the essential ingredients of an embodied approach to technology and innovation. Far from downplaying the role of science and knowledge the embodied perspective of classical economists can be synthesized as one that gives a central economic role to the process of adoption and use of new production technologies through investment in fixed productive capital. The labour-saving effects of technological change is also one usually stressed by classical economists and one qualifying their embodied perspective on technology.

Taking the classical perspective as a sort of benchmarking for identifying an embodied approach to technological change, it has been shown that a shift from an embodied to a disembodied perspective on technological change has progressively taken place in the evolution of economic theory with the emergence of mainstream neoclassical economics including its latest 'new-growth theory' versions. The post-Keynesian approach, and in particular the contributions by Kaldor, have on the contrary re-emphasized the key role of investment for technological change.

NOTES

1. Both Smith and Marx also recognize the presence of capital-saving technological change. Marx analyses the existence of capital-saving technologies in the third volume of *Capital* in the discussion of 'circulation' as opposed to 'production'. The capital-deepening nature of technological activities has thus to be considered as the 'prevalent form' which is assumed by technological change (Marx, [1894] 1983).
2. In particular Ure (1835) and Babbage (1883).
3. The enhancing role that the increasing division of labour has for the introduction of new technologies is evident in the following passage where Smith lists, in both logical and chronological order, the three factors responsible for the increase of labour productivity: He mentions: 'first, the increase of dexterity in every particular workman; secondly, the saving of time which is commonly lost in passing from one species of work to another; and lastly, the invention of a great number of machines that facilitate and abridge labour, and enables one man to do the work of many' (Smith, [1776] 1976, p. 17).
4. The result is the well-known Marxian law of an ever-increasing organic composition of capital, which characterizes the development of capitalist economies and which is the main factor behind the falling rate of profit (Marx [1894] 1983, *Capital I*, ch. 25). As already mentioned the existence of capital-saving technological activities were not ruled out, though they were not seen as able to offset the tendency towards an increase of the 'organic' and 'technical' composition of capital.
5. The importance of this maroeconomic inducing factor to innovation has also been stressed by Schmookler (1966) and by Mensh in his interpretation of the role of technology in the explanation of the 'long waves' (Mensh, 1975).
6. The historical and economic conditions under which the process of specialization in the production of technologically new capital goods has taken place has been stressed by Rosenberg (1976b).

7. The departure of Schumpeter from a production-centred conceptualization of technical change and its impact on the use of labour process can also be seen as a result of his full rejection of the labour theory of value.
8. On the contrary Schumpeter stresses the key role played by financial institutions in the selection of economically exploitable technologies.
9. In general terms the 'production function' can be defined as all possible (most efficient) combinations between a set of homogeneous production inputs with respect to a given output. Other requirements such as the perfect substitutability of the production factors, constant returns and convexity of the isoquants represent additional characteristics attached to the neoclassical production function.
10. This assumption has been criticized, among others, by Kaldor (1957), Rosenberg (1976a) and Nelson and Winter (1982).
11. Technological change is defined as 'neutral' (in the case of invariance of the inputs ratio), 'labour saving' (in the case of a decreased use of labour with respect to capital) and 'capital saving' (in the opposite case) (Stoneman, 1983; Coombs et al., 1987, p. 26).
12. This in turn is linked to the neoclassical 'black box approach' to production. As pointed out by Scazzieri, compared to the classical economists the upsurge of the neoclassical paradigm is characterized by a 'slow withering away of the interest in a detailed investigation of the production process, at the level both of the individual productive unit and of the economic system as a whole' (Scazzieri, 1993, p. 5).
13. Keeping the strict assumptions behind the (Cobb–Douglas) marginalist-type production function considerably limited the possibility of evaluating a long-term process of economic growth. In a dynamic context, the assumptions of constant returns to scale with respect to all the inputs and decreasing marginal productivity with respect to each input individually would have bound economic growth to the rate of growth of population.
14. Qualitative changes in the production factors are much more difficult to be treated and formally represented within the neoclassical methodological framework.
15. Along with maintaining all the restrictive assumptions implicit in the use of a production function approach, vintage models have other shortcomings. It has been noted that the technological content of investment is simply associated with the age, independently, therefore, of the actual innovative content of the fixed capital introduced at different times. Furthermore, and more important, the part of innovative activities consisting of the generation of new technological knowledge still remains exogenous to the model.
16. These were subsequently referred to as 'putty-clay' models, implying an ability to shape the technology into any desired format beforehand, but a restriction to the form it then took once it was in place. Little, if any, attention was paid to the difference in the nature of innovation implied by this metaphor.
17. Even these investment activities are a result of subjective choices of individual agents concerning the allocation of non-leisure time, under the conditions of perfect rationality and utility-maximizing behaviours of the economic agents. The alternative lies between allocating such non-leisure time to immediate consumption and to the accumulation of knowledge (human capital) through education.
18. From a different perspective this has been also criticized by Rosenberg (1976a) and Nelson and Winter (1982).
19. In a later contribution Kaldor and Mirrlees seem to enlarge Kaldor's original view on technological activities by emphasizing also the importance of disembodied forms of technological change (Kaldor and Mirrlees, 1962).

3. Disembodied and embodied technological change in the innovation literature

3.1 INTRODUCTION

The attempts made in the 1950s and 1960s by neoclassical and post-Keynesian economists to include technological change in their theoretical frameworks were characterized by different kinds of shortcomings. These were due to having introduced *ex post* technological change into conceptual frameworks not designed to encompass such a complex phenomenon and to having maintained a high level of abstraction and simplification in the way technological change was treated and represented. These efforts also paid the price, at least initially, of the extreme deficiency of data on science and technological activities. The result was an almost total lack of reliable empirical evidence on the actual role played by technological change in economic phenomena such as economic growth or productivity.

It was in response to such limitations that an ever-increasing number of scholars started to investigate more systematically, and in a much more direct way, the nature, determinants and economic effects of technological activities. Such efforts have produced over more recent decades a consistent number of contributions and important pieces of evidence forming the basis of a new body of theoretical and empirical literature labelled as 'economics of technological change', or 'economics of innovation'.

Reviewing the huge number of contributions and approaches which have flourished within this new discipline would represent a formidable effort, and would go far beyond the scope of this chapter.[1] In the following sections, in parallel with what has been done in Chapter 2, the analysis is confined to highlighting the conceptualization of technology, which is at the basis of the most significant contributions in this variegated literature, maintaining the focus on the distinction between embodied and disembodied technological change as defined in Chapter 1. The attempt is to show that also within the evolution of this new stream of literature a shift from a more balanced approach to technology to one downplaying the role of investment in productive assets has taken place.

27

In section 3.2 we start by analysing the ways in which technology has been conceptualized and measured by the empirical contributions, which have investigated the role of technology for explaining differences in the economic growth and performances across countries, sectors or firms. In the following three sections we pass on to analyse the role given to embodied and disembodied technological change by the literature on technological diffusion (section 3.3), technological flows and spillovers (section 3.4) and sectoral patterns of innovation (section 3.5). Section 3.6 looks at the analytical efforts made to explore the black box of innovation, and which have brought to the surface the complex, variegated and context specific nature of technology and the innovative process. Even when allowing for a larger number of technological sources and innovation patterns, most of these contributions have turned to a disembodied perspective on technology and innovation. Section 3.7 shows that such a turn has found its final push in the new contributions developed around the concepts of the 'knowledge-based economy' and 'intangible investments'.

3.2   DISEMBODIED AND EMBODIED PERSPECTIVES IN THE EMPIRICAL LITERATURE ON TECHNOLOGY, PRODUCTIVITY AND GROWTH

In the last two decades a new demand for data able to describe the extent, nature and economic impact of technological change at the level of firms, sectors and countries has rapidly increased. From the beginning of the 1970s, substantial efforts have been made in this direction. Data on expenditures and personnel employed for R&D activities started to be collected systematically by an increasing number of countries. Already at the beginning of the 1960s, the OECD Frascati manual gave the first international guidelines for the collection of R&D statistics. Data on patents were already registered by many national patent offices and therefore virtually available to be used. Since the end of the 1970s systematic data on R&D and patents have become the major source of information on scientific and technology activities for economists, sociologists and researchers in general, as well as for policy makers. This has in turn increased the scope for analysing on a more systematic basis the relationship between technological and economic indicators and thus the relationship between technological change and a wide range of economic phenomena (aggregate growth, productivity, trade performances and so on). The distinguishing feature of this new empirically based literature lies in the centrality given to technological change. Instead of being treated as an 'attached variable' able to enhance the explanatory power of the standard traditional economic model, or as a residual source of economic growth, innovation and technological changes were given a truly autonomous status. Technology was increasingly considered the key variable able to explain differences in the economic performances of firms, sectors and economies. In methodological terms, explanatory models based on the production function and growth-accounting exercises have been replaced by simpler, and theoretically less ambitious, econometric estimates aiming at grasping the effect of a wider range of technological factors on economic growth. This has allowed us also to overcome the pure exogenous and disembodied perspective on technological change inherent in the production function approach to economic growth.

We have seen in the previous section that the growth-accounting tradition was characterized by assuming the existence of the same long-term production function for all countries, with technology maintaining its exogenous and public nature as implicit in Solow's model. Where cross-country differences have been taken into account, the different 'residuals' found were explained as revealing catching-up processes at work, allowing for a convergence towards the technological best practice (see Denison 1967; Jorgenson and Griliches, 1967; Denison and Chung, 1976). Following Solow's model, this process of technological catching-up was also seen as disembodied, that is independent of the process of capital accumulation and factor substitution processes linked to technological change.

The role played by embodied technological change in the process of economic convergence among OECD countries taking place in the postwar period has been, on the contrary, recognized by the contributions in the empirical literature on catching-up flourishing in the 1980s (Maddison, 1979, 1982, 1991; Abramovitz, 1986, 1993). Investment, together with the initial level of per capita income, have been the variables most often used in a large series of studies on economic convergence. The latter variable has been used to measure differences among countries in their stages of economic development, and investment as a proxy for the efforts devoted to closing the technology gap. Both variables have been found to be strongly associated with economic growth across countries.[2]

In the early empirical literature on catching-up, variables reflecting innovative efforts to generate new technological knowledge and innovation such as R&D, patents and innovation counts have been given only limited space (see Fagerberg, 1987, 1988a and Verspagen, 1991 for a review). However, when such variables have been included, they have been found to have significant explanatory roles both as measures of the technological distances across countries and for explaining inter-country differences in economic growth and productivity performances. This has led Fagerberg to point out that investment, education and R&D should be seen as complementary rather than substitutive forces behind the catching-up process and economic growth (Fagerberg, 1994, p. 1171).

More recently an increasing emphasis has been given to the role that technological activities can exert not only in relation to catching-up processes but as the most effective competitive factor for firm and country performance. In this case, too, the different indicators used to measure technological activities hint at different conceptualizations about what kinds of sources of technology are supposed to be related to country economic performances and national competitive advantages.

Among the first attempts to empirically test cross-country long-run technology economic performance relationships in the Organization for Economic Cooperation and Development) (OECD) area using 'disembodied technological indicators' are the works by Pavitt and Soete (1982), who used patent statistics for the 1890–1977 period, and Soete and Patel (1985) who used R&D indicators for a more recent period. Their results support the hypothesis that long-term national economic performances are associated with scientific and technological efforts aimed at increasing the stock of knowledge and technological capabilities. In some cases the different national rates of return (elasticity) of the resources devoted to R&D activities are also quantified (Soete and Patel, 1985). Similarly, some other empirical works have related national trade performances to other 'disembodied' technological indicators such as R&D and patenting (Audretsch and Yamawaki, 1988; Greenhalgh, 1990; Amable, 1993).

More recent empirical works on the technology gap issue have adopted a broader perspective on the technological forces fuelling economic growth and competitiveness. Along with technological indicators such as R&D and patents, variables accounting for processes of adoption and diffusion of new technologies have also been taken into account. Econometric studies, which have adopted this broader perspective, include those carried out by Fagerberg (1987, 1988b, 1991), Dosi et al. (1990), Verspagen (1991) and Amable (1993). As far as the link between technology and international competitiveness is concerned, the works by Fagerberg (1988b) and Amendola et al., (1993) also deserve mention. In these empirical studies investment has been found as the variable more strongly linked to economic growth and country economic performances. In a recent work Amable and Verspagen have found significant differences across industries in the relative importance of investment, patenting activities and labour costs on trade performances (Amable and Verspagen, 1995). Pianta (1995, 1998) has shown that investment and R&D represent two distinct sources of economic growth and have a different impact on employment. Meliciani has shown the complementary role of investment and patenting for explaining economic growth and trade performance in OECD countries in the 1970s and 1980s (Meliciani, 1998).

As for the catching-up empirical literature also in these empirical studies a certain degree of ambiguity remains about whether investment should be regarded as a proper form of technological change. Investment activities are often meant to reflect only the imitation stage of innovative activities and catching-up strategies of firms and countries. The fact that any innovative process, even the most radical and original one, can indeed require substantial investment in fixed capital for mechanization, application of modern technologies and the setting up of infrastructures linked to long-term innovative projects, appears to be underestimated.

On the contrary, a clear emphasis on the propulsive role of investment in productive equipment (machinery) for economic growth can be found in the works by Wolf (1994a) and in the article by De Long and Summers (1991). Looking at the cross-country variation in the rate of economic growth during the 1960–85 period, De Long and Summers found that investment in electrical and non-electrical machinery (measured in terms of their share in gross domestic product (GDP)) was the strongest explanatory variable of inter-country differences in productivity growth. As the two authors explicitly state, the paper 'provides quantitative evidence in support of the older, traditional view that the accumulation of machinery is a prime determinant of national rates of productivity growth, and against the supposition that the private return to equipment investment mirrors its social product' (De Long and Summers, 1991, p. 446).

A completely disembodied perspective characterizes the rich empirical literature which has investigated the relationship between technological change and productivity, using firm- and sectoral-level data. The economic returns to firms' technological activities have been studied mainly through estimating the R&D elasticity with respect to the productive output. These econometric models are meant to provide an estimate of the long-term effect of R&D expenditures on firms' economic and productivity growth. By and large these exercises confirm the presence of positive effects of R&D activities, with higher elasticity coefficients found in the case of firms belonging to the higher technology sectors (see Mairesse, 1991, Griliches, 1995 and Amable and Boyer, 1992 for reviews). Other empirical works have gone even further in this direction, investigating the effects of different components of R&D activities on productivity. Mansfield (1980) found higher economic returns of 'basic' as compared to 'applied' research and Link (1981) found a larger effect of company-funded R&D on productivity compared to government-funded R&D activities. As already mentioned, the disembodied perspective of these firm-level studies on the relationship between technology and growth is straightforward. Much more rare are firm-level studies which have estimated the effect of embodied technological change on any economic performance variable (Wakelin, 1997). This seems quite surprising also considering that when rather crude proxies for process innovative activities, as in the case of process-oriented R&D

expenditures, have been used they have been found to be much more strongly related to performance variables than product-oriented R&D efforts (Audretsch and Yamawaki, 1988).[3]

3.3   DISEMBODIED AND EMBODIED PERSPECTIVES ON TECHNOLOGICAL DIFFUSION

The distinction between embodied and disembodied technological change is also able to discriminate between different ways of conceptualizing and representing the process of diffusion of technology among firms and in the economy. Theoretical models and conceptual approaches to technology diffusion, have undergone substantial changes in the last decades (Lissoni and Metcalfe, 1994). However it can be claimed that, unlike other research areas in the economics of technological change, in the diffusion literature the role and importance of embodied technological change is still explicitly recognized.[4]

Traditional diffusion models are characterized by the epidemic approach. New technologies spread across the economic systems as an epidemic. The process of imitation and adoption of a new technology can be represented by a logistic curve, which describes the contagious mechanism: after a first stage in which the rate of diffusion increases first slowly and then rapidly, the diffusion process starts to decline with the progressive saturation of the market and potential adopters of the new technology. In the early models formulated by Griliches (1957) and Mansfield (1961), innovation spreads among potential adopters according to the rate of diffusion of a specific element, that is the information concerning the characteristics of the innovation. Temporal lags in the diffusion process are due to market imperfections, and in particular to the presence of asymmetric information (on the technologies available) among the economic agents.

The disembodied perspective which might be attached to these models, is thus related to the critical role played by 'information' in the diffusion process. However in most diffusion models technology in itself, that is what is actually adopted and used in the economic systems, has a more tangible form. Diffusion refers in fact either to technologies embodied in new machinery and equipment, in the case of process technologies, or to new products, in the case that these innovations are directed towards final demand. Along with the spread of ideas, diffusion consists therefore mainly of a process of implementation of innovations embodied in intermediate products, new machinery, equipment or new products for final consumption.

An explicit acknowledgement of the fact that diffusion and adoption imply a process of investment in fixed capital has gained additional ground in later diffusion models. In the 1968 Mansfield model, the rate of diffusion is affected by the structure of capital, that is by the level of financial and physical immobilization and relevance of sunk costs. These aspects are also taken into account by Metcalfe (1981). The role of investment is also stressed when diffusion (even if rarely) is analysed in a macroeconomic perspective. In this case the expansion of the markets and demand affect the opportunity to make investments in connection with the adoption of new technologies.

An explicit reference to the embodied nature of technological activities is also present in diffusion models which have adopted a microeconomic neoclassical framework (David, 1975b; Davies, 1979). The existence of lags in the adoption process has been related to the adoption of new capital goods and is explained on the basis of the heterogeneous characteristics of the adopters. This heterogeneity is conceived of in terms of differences in the production cost structure among potential adopters, and in the fact that the characteristics of technologies and those of both producers and adopters change over time, and interact with each other, during the diffusion process. In these models the pace of the diffusion process is affected by the opportunity-cost conditions for adoption (and changes therein), which change over time by the possibility of producing the new products at lower cost as the demand for the new technologies increases and economies of scale can be exploited.

Finally, both vintage models (Salter, 1960) and post-Keynesian models of economic growth (Kaldor, 1957), reviewed in the previous section, can be thought of as implying a process of diffusion of embodied technology. In both approaches it is implicit that investment activities are associated with, and consist of, the adoption of new technologies at a firm-level as well as at a macroeconomic level. This is a point that they have in common with classical economists (Antonelli et al., 1992). In Salter's contribution, for instance, the effective alignment of the production systems to the 'best practice' depends on the rate of investment in fixed capital (Salter, 1960). In this model the actual rate of diffusion of new technologies is constrained by the embodied nature of technologies, that is by the fact that technologies consist of fixed capital and therefore affect the capital structure of firms. The presence of sunk costs related to the existing technical immobilization has an effect on the economic viability of introducing new process technologies.

The Kaldorian function of technical progress also identifies a strong connection, if not a complete overlapping, between investment and the process of adoption/diffusion of new technologies. The explicit macroeconomic framework in which the Kaldorian contribution is built opens up new perspectives on the relationship between investment and diffusion of new technologies and a different set of determinants and constraints of technological change. If diffusion at a macroeonomic level depends on the rate of investment, then the factors and forces, which govern such a variable, have an effect also on the pace of technological change. In this perspective factors such as the level of effective demand, the business cycle and all economic and institutional forces associated with investment play a relevant role in explaining technological change and the process of adoption of new technologies. This macroeconomic perspective on the relationship between technological change and investment has not been followed up until quite recently. In recent years there have been, however, some developments in this direction. The role of investment in the process of technological diffusion has been again taken into consideration in a macroeconomic framework by Antonelli et al. (1992).

3.4 EMBODIED AND DISEMBODIED TECHNOLOGICAL FLOWS AND SPILLOVERS

A clear dichotomy in the emphasis given to embodied and disembodied technological change and their effects on productivity characterizes the rich literature on technological flows and technological spillovers. In this case, too, the different indicators and methodologies used to identify technology flows (as well as their effects on productivity) hint at different conceptualizations of technology and innovation processes. In this literature differences do not refer to the localization of the upstream source of technology. The latter is always identified as the place where R&D activities are carried out (firms, sectors or even countries). The interpretative differences relate to the extent to which tangible goods are seen as the carriers of technology, and investment as the necessary channel through which innovations are used throughout the economic system. In the latter case technological flows give rise to what might be called 'embodied spillovers' as distinct from more 'disembodied or knowledge spillovers'.

3.4.1 Embodied Technology Spillovers

The use of economic input–output tables has been a common practice to measure technological flows and spillovers across industries, and implicitly reaffirms the importance of embodied technological change. Such a methodology was used for the first time by Terleckyj in 1974, followed by numerous other works up to the recent and more sophisticated work carried out in the OECD and in particular by Papaconstantinou et al. (1995, 1996) and Sakurai et al. (1996) (for a review see Mohnen, 1995). All these works have shown the critical importance of a restricted group of sectors as net producers of technology for the rest of the economic system. The works by Papaconstantinou et al. (1995, 1996) and Sakurai et al. (1996) have also shown that the technology embodied in intermediate and capital inputs account for a large share of all the technology embodied in the final output, even with considerable differences across countries.[5] It has also been shown that sectoral and country 'innovative intensity' levels change considerably when both internal R&D activities and the R&D indirectly acquired through intermediate inputs and capital goods are taken into account. In particular the inclusion of embodied R&D considerably increases the technological intensity of low- and medium-technology industries and countries specialized in such sectors.[6] The importance of technology embodied in fixed capital also seems to be confirmed by the increase in most countries over the last decade of the share of R&D embodied in capital investment, as against a relative decline of the R&D embodied in intermediate products (Papaconstantinou et al., 1995, p. 33).[7] While capital investment largely represents technological change embodied in machinery and productive equipment, intermediate products embody technological advance in raw materials and components.

The importance of embodied technological flows highlighted by these studies has encouraged other scholars to use the same methodology to investigate the technology productivity links by taking into account the impact of both direct and indirect technological sources on country economic performances. The results of these studies have confirmed a positive effect of the R&D embodied in intermediate and capital goods on productivity (Griliches and Lichtenberg, 1984; Englander et al., 1988), with more significant results obtained for the latter component (Terleckyj, 1974; Scherer, 1982a; Sveikauskas, 1986).[8]

A very comprehensive review of the literature and empirical results on technological interdependencies is contained in the book edited by Chris DeBresson (1996), one of the leading experts in this area. This author has also extensively worked on input–output technological matrixes built on the data provided by innovation survey and in particular on the Italian Statistical Institute – National Research Council (ISTAT–CNR) database. Particularly interesting is the comparison made by DeBresson et al. between the innovation matrix (measuring the intersectoral flows of innovation) and the economic input–output matrixes referring to intermediate inputs and capital flows (DeBresson et al., 1996). Quite surprising are the findings of this work, which show a rather striking dissimilarity between the innovation input–output matrix and the one on capital flows. These results contrast, in fact, with the central role traditionally given to user-producer interaction involving the capital good sector.

3.4.2 Disembodied Technology Spillovers

Although embodied technological flows can be thought of as a form of 'technological spillover', the latter term usually refers in the literature to pure 'knowledge spillovers'. As such, this symbolizes the 'leaking' of knowledge from the place where it is generated to the surrounding economic and social space. Such spillovers have thus a clear disembodied connotation inasmuch as they refer explicitly to knowledge and are (or can be thought of as) independent of any exchange or transfer of tangible goods. Since technological spillovers are seen as being associated with the outcome of R&D activities they are sometimes described as 'research spillovers' and the externalities associated with them as 'R&D externalities'.[9]

Disembodied technological spillovers and their economic impact have been studied estimating the marginal productivity (or marginal cost reduction) of 'external R&D'. Different methodologies and indicators have been used to track down such knowledge flows.

Input–output tables based on R&D and patenting have been the most widely used and those which reflect the knowledge or disembodied nature of R&D spillovers. The matrix of inter-industry technology flows proposed by Scherer in 1982 has represented a seminal work for the subsequent empirical literature in this field (Scherer, 1982a, 1982b, 1984a; Englander et al., 1988; Griliches and Lichtenberg, 1984; Hanel, 1994). The matrix was constructed by merging information on R&D expenditure and the associated patent activities with the sector of origin and destination of patents. Scherer was able in such a way to classify both R&D and patents according to industries of origin and use, hence identifying the structure of technological interdependence across sectors of production and use of innovations.

The results of the empirical literature on disembodied spillovers have confirmed the existence of substantial rates of return of external R&D. Comparative studies of the relative importance of embodied and disembodied spillovers have also been carried out with contrasting outcomes (for a review see Mohnen, 1995, p. 9). While extensive empirical evidence has shown significant returns in the case of embodied technological spillovers, Goto and Suzuki (1989) have argued, on the basis of a study of the impact of electronics technologies on other industries, that in terms of productivity increase such an impact depends on the diffusion of knowledge more than on the diffusion of new electronic equipment. The importance of the cost-reducing impact of disembodied inter-industry technological spillovers has been also found by Bernstein (1989) for Canada. Other studies have argued that the different importance of the different kinds of technological spillover depends on product or process technologies and varies from industry to industry (Levin and Reiss, 1989). However it has been correctly noted that all these empirical results are undermined by the difficulty of separating the effects of embodied and disembodied technological spillovers.

3.5 DISEMBODIED AND EMBODIED SECTORAL PATTERNS OF INNOVATION

The fact that innovation activities have both a disembodied and embodied nature has been highlighted by a series of studies, which have looked at the variety of technological patterns in industry. The major contribution in this area remains the sectoral taxonomy proposed by Pavitt, based on the study of the characteristics of about 2000 significant innovations introduced in the UK from 1945 to 1979. The taxonomy represents an attempt to describe and explain similarities and differences among firms and sectors in terms of the source, nature and impact of innovative activities (Pavitt, 1984).

The distinction of embodied versus disembodied technological change, as well as that between production and use of innovation, is explicitly emphasized in Pavitt's famous 1984 article. Along with other features (such as type of user needs and levels of appropriability), in Pavitt's taxonomy technological patterns differ in the following two aspects: (i) in the technological source used by firms to innovate, that is in the degree to which technology is generated within the sector, or it is purchased by other sectors; and (ii) in the importance of product and process innovations.

Four main sectoral patterns of innovation are identified by Pavitt:

- *Supplier-dominated* sectors, where firms rely on external technological sources. In these sectors innovative activities largely consist of purchasing new machinery and equipment and are consequently characterized by a large presence of process innovations.
- *Production-intensive* sectors, in which firms' innovative activities consist of the introduction of capital-intensive techniques aimed at exploiting economies of scale and reducing production costs.
- *Specialized-suppliers* sectors composed of firms specialized in the production of equipment and instruments which are used as process innovations by the other sectors.
- *Science-based* sectors, where firms base their innovations on R&D, and draw heavily from the more general advances occurring in the relevant scientific and technological fields.

According to this taxonomy, embodied forms of technological change, and the introduction of new process technologies through investment activities, play an important role in the *supplier-dominated* and *production-intensive* sectors. In the first sectoral category technology is acquired from other sectors and used through investment in new process innovations. An embodied pattern of technological change also characterizes the *production-intensive* firms and industries, where the acquisition of capital intensive process technologies is also accompanied by some internal innovative effort devoted to the generation, development and implementation of the process technologies used. On the contrary, in both *science-based* and *specialized-supplier* firms technological change seems to be of a more disembodied nature. However, while for the former R&D activities represent the major internal technological source, for the latter it is the accumulation of more tacit forms of knowledge associated with design and engineering activities. Investment plays a marginal role for these two latter categories of firms and industries (Pavitt, 1984).

3.6   THE EXPLORATION OF THE BLACK BOX OF (DISEMBODIED) TECHNOLOGICAL CHANGE

In recent years an ever-increasing number of scholars have begun to put the issue of understanding the micro- and firm-specific characteristics of the innovative phenomena at the top of the research agenda. This in turn arose from the dissatisfaction with the way technology and the innovation processes were conceptualized and represented by the traditional economic approaches. Schumpeter himself, the father of most of these contributions, was subject to severe criticism for an oversimplified view of the nature of innovative process. The same criticism was also addressed to the kinds of empirical study examined in the previous section that adopted a rather aggregate perspective (either at a national or at a sectoral level) using technological indicators and methodologies, which did not do justice to the actual complexity and variety of firms' innovative activities.

The methodology adopted by the new contributions has also changed in order to fulfil more analytical research objectives. A shift from a macro- to a firm-level perspective has gradually taken place. The large number of empirical studies which have explored the 'black box' of technology has led to the establishment of a set of new key concepts and 'stylized facts' about innovation processes. These have constituted the new conceptual bases and operative toolboxes used by researchers to deal with technological change.

Here we confine ourselves to highlighting only the basic concepts associated with the new perspective on innovation, focusing on those that have direct or indirect implications for our distinction between embodied and disembodied technical change.

3.6.1   The Basic ingredients of the 'New Perspective' on the Innovative Process

- A first important departure of the new perspective from the neoclassical approach, and also from the early neo-Schumpeterian literature, has to do with the conceptualization of technology. From the new attributes given to the concept and term 'technology' can, in fact, be derived most of the other aspects regarding the characteristics of innovative processes analysed below. In the new perspective technology is not just information, that is something that once generated becomes easily (and cheaply) available to everybody. A large part of technology has a tacit nature, being embodied in people, skills, competencies and organizations. From this double nature of technology stems the consequence that only to a limited extent does knowledge have the characteristics of a public good.

The part of such knowledge that is non-codifiable is largely firm- and context-specific and not transferable or marketable. These non-imitable features of innovation activities represent in turn the essential incentive for firms to undertake innovative activities. Although these concepts are not particularly new, being already contained in the early works of Schumpeter, what is new is the great emphasis given to such aspects of tacitness and partial appropriability of knowledge and technological change, up to the point where a fully consistent conceptual framework has been built around them (Nelson and Winter, 1982; Rosenberg, 1982a; Winter, 1984; Dosi, 1988).

- To the tacitness and partial appropriability of innovative activities is linked another key feature of the innovative process stressed by recent contributions: that is the *cumulative nature of the innovation process*. Cumulativeness brings into the picture the importance of the time and space dimensions of technological activities. Innovation processes occur through time and have a localized and context-specific nature, all attributes that give a path-dependent nature to technological change. This in turn is related to the 'learning nature' of innovative activities, which primarily take place in specific contexts and necessarily over time. This also changes the nature of technological knowledge, as not being confined any more to pure and codified knowledge but having a context-specific 'know-how' content (Nelson and Winter, 1982, Dosi, 1988).

- Not all technological scientific areas represent the same objective opportunity to be exploited through innovative activities. Large differences exist across technological fields and industries in the rate of return to firms' innovative efforts. These differences in the potentiality of different technologies to be exploited to generate innovation are termed *technological opportunity*. The latter can be expressed as the level of probability that a given amount of resources put into the innovation process would actually generate technological advancements (Nelson and Winter, 1982, Dosi, 1988).

- In the new perspective the existence of a large variety of technological patterns, which can be observed at firm, sectoral and even cross-country levels, has also been stressed (Saviotti and Metcalfe, 1991). These differences are partly the result of different strategic behaviours of firms and partly the result of different *technological regimes*, which define the main dimensions and boundaries of a firm's innovative activities. Technological regimes are largely technology-specific, in the sense that they depend on the paradigmatic nature of each technology, which also evolves through time (Dosi, 1988)[10]

• The emphasis on the context-specific nature of technology and on the existence of a plurality of forms of innovation activities has led to a consistent broadening of the possible locus and nature of technological change. Incremental and localized technological advances obtained as the result of day-to-day economic activities have begun to be acknowledged as a crucial source of technological progress in general and as an essential dimension of the innovative process (Rosenberg, 1976b, 1982b, Antonelli, 1995).

• The Schumpeterian perspective, especially that emerging from *Capitalism, Socialism and Democracy* (1992) and *Business cycles* (1939), based on the key importance played by scientific and technological breakthroughs, has been criticized and contrasted by one emphasizing the incremental and continuous nature of innovation activities (Rosenberg, 1976b). 'Learning' has been recognized as a central feature of the process of accumulation of technological competencies and know-how at the firm-level (Malerba, 1992). Another major criticism has been levelled against a conceptualization of the innovative process seen as a one-way sequence of distinct independent stages, starting with R&D and finishing with the use or introduction of the innovation in the production process or in the market. This model has been superseded by a more integrated model of the innovation process, characterized by the existence of different and equally important technological sources and places in which innovative activities and technological accumulation take place, and by the presence of strong linkages and complementarities between different kinds of technological source, institutions and stages of the innovation process (Kline and Rosenberg, 1986).

The new perspective on technology and innovation sketched above has undoubtedly enriched the simplified view of the innovation process contained in the traditional economic models and also in the early Schumpeterian literature. There is no doubt, however, that the new perspective has also reinforced a disembodied view of technology and innovation. The new attributes of tacitness, cumulativeness, context-specificity attached to technology and innovation activities all refer to a disembodied domain of technology. In particular technology is conceived as a composite set of resources constituted by some basic and general knowledge, plus more tacit and context-specific know-how capabilities and expertise.

The disembodied connotation carried by these new perspectives on technology and innovation can also be found in the emphasis given to the concept of *technological capabilities*, as opposed to the centrality of technological productive assets. Martin Bell and Keith Pavitt, for instance, distinguish between two stocks of resources in the economic systems, namely 'production capacity' and 'technological capabilities', and attach the label 'technological' only to the latter:

> the former (production capacity) incorporates the resources used to produce industrial goods at given levels of efficiency and given input combinations: equipment (capital-embodied technology), labour skills (operating and managerial know-how and experience), product and input specification, and the organisational methods and system used. Technological capabilities consist of the resources needed to generate and manage technical change, including skills, knowledge and experience, and institutional structures and linkages (Bell and Pavitt, 1993, p. 163).

Amendola and Gaffard come to define an even more extreme disembodied conceptualization of technology and innovative activities. According to these authors technology is defined as:

> 'an environment characterised by skills and qualifications that make it possible to devise and implement different solutions to different productive problems' while the process of innovation has been defined 'as a process of research and learning that brings about new and different skills and qualifications and thus implies the modification of the characteristics and of the structure of this resource' (Amendola and Gaffard, 1988, p. 33).

In this new stream of contributions innovation activities have thus become envisaged as progressively more and more detached from investment activities. The innovative process is increasingly seen as a searching process. The latter consists of activities aimed not only at generating new knowledge and single discoveries but as a problem-solving process, able to overcome technological bottlenecks incurred in the continuous nature of economic and technological activity. It is, however, with reference to the concept of *technological accumulation* that the emphasis on the disembodied nature of technology (as a stock) and innovative activities (as a process) of this new perspective more clearly emerges. The concept of technological accumulation no longer seems to have any physical or technical basis (in terms of technical and financial immobilization of production assets). Rather it reflects the accumulation of technological knowledge, capabilities and competencies defined in the way mentioned above.[11]

3.7   THE KNOWLEDGE-BASED ECONOMY HYPOTHESIS

A disembodied perspective of technology, innovative activities and technological accumulation has also been supported by a series of more recent
contributions which have emphasized the increasingly *knowledge-based* nature
of modern economies. Such an approach has been effectively synthesized by
a number of OECD works published in the last few years (OECD, 1992a,
1996a, 1996b; Lundvall and Johnson, 1994; Smith 1996a).

The knowledge-based economy hypothesis points out that large parts of
economic activities are nowadays linked to the generation, distribution and
use of new knowledge, which in turn are seen as the most important sources
of economic growth, productivity increases and competitiveness (OECD,
1996a, p. 7).

Put in these broad terms the knowledge-based economy hypothesis would
not necessarily support a disembodied perspective of technological change. The
knowledge content of modern economic systems has, in fact, also been referred
to as the *use* of new technologies, which includes the introduction of new
technologies embodied in intermediate inputs and tangible productive assets.
A careful reading of these contributions suggests, however, that a disembodied
perspective is clearly privileged. In describing the attributes of the knowledge-
based society the emphasis is clearly put on the process of *generation* rather
than the *use* of knowledge. Also when the use-side of knowledge is
acknowledged, it is usually stressed that what is being diffused or distributed
is disembodied knowledge either in its codified or tacit form.

Closely linked to the knowledge-based economy hypothesis, and one
reinforcing its disembodied perspective, is the one emphasizing the increasing
importance of intangible assets and investments. Taking as a reference the
definition provided by the OECD, '"Intangible investment" covers all long-term
outlays by firms aimed at increasing future performance other than by the
purchase of fixed assets' (OECD, 1992a, p. 114). Intangible investment thus
ends up embracing a set of assets and resources that go far beyond the
technology domain. The same OECD study distinguishes in this respect between
'intangible investment in technology' and 'enabling intangible investment'. The
former category includes investments in R&D, design and engineering, the
acquisition of patents and licences, scan and search activities, which are all
finalized to developing the knowledge and competence base of firms and to
introduce new products and processes. Enabling intangible investments include
those in training, information structures and organizational structures. Software
is identified as a separate fixed asset since it may be integrated in equipment
or be an essential adjunct to it and could therefore be associated to physical
investment (OECD, 1992a, p. 115).

Recent contributions, which have stressed the increasing information-based characteristics of modern economic societies, also push towards this disembodied and intangible perspective on technology and production activities. In this regard Eliasson argues that the modern firm is 'an information processor that filters people, ideas and projects to produce quality of output rather than volumes of output and that operates on knowledge capital' (Eliasson, 1989, p. 23). Also in these contributions the most important assets in the economy are knowledge and information which are reproduced and enlarged through education, training, learning and R&D activities.

The empirical evidence brought to support the knowledge-based economy hypothesis is still, however, rather casual. This is due, on the one hand, to the vagueness of the theoretical and conceptual framework used to support the knowledge-based metaphor and, on the other, to the lack of appropriate data to empirically support such a hypothesis.

The way in which the 'knowledge sector' and 'knowledge-based activities' are identified reflects such mismatching between concepts, definitions and indicators used. Within the 'knowledge sector' are usually included not only the traditionally *high-tech* industries such as computers, electronics and aerospace but also a range of very broad economic and social activities such as those linked with 'education', 'communication' and 'information'. It is even too obvious in this regard to point out that the fact that the share of GDP devoted to education increases and that also communication-related products increase their weight in final consumption is not enough to support the knowledge-based economy hypothesis and in particular does not imply that: (i) the knowledge content of the economy has actually increased; and (ii) that the knowledge generated and used in the economy is actually shared and understood by the majority of the labour force or even more by the majority of the members of the society. On the contrary there are tangible signals of an increasing polarization in the distribution of knowledge within national economies and world-wide.

Even more problematic seems the way in which *knowledge* and *non-knowledge* labour activities and jobs are identified: 'knowledge' workers are, in fact, mostly identified as those who are not engaged in the production of physical products (OECD, 1996a, p. 11). The obvious problem here is that not all workers and segments of economic and social activities dealing with intangible goods are actually involved in the process of generation and diffusion of knowledge. In particular one can think of a series of service activities, which though not being involved in the process of transformation of tangible good, are not involved in any process of generation or transformation of knowledge.

In the light of such rather loose boundaries of knowledge and non-knowledge activities, it does not come as a surprise that it is estimated that 'more than 50 per cent of GDP in the major OECD economies is now knowledge based' (OECD, 1996a, p. 9).

Following the pioneering work of Denison (1962) a new generation of growth-accounting exercises has also tried to estimate the increasing importance of human or social 'intangible' capital for economic growth. They have tried to squeeze the famous residual by 'weighting' the different labour inputs according to their (increased) levels of qualification and skills (see Denison, 1985 and Abramovitz and David, 1996, for a review). Also in this case the methodology used to measure the quality of labour (now labelled as human capital) presents many heroic assumptions and the methodology used suffers the all too well-known restrictive assumptions underlying the neoclassical production function (which in the long run become even more hard to accept).

On a parallel line, studies conducted in the US have shown that education expenditures as a share of total GDP and total gross saving have been continuously growing in this century, and these results have been used to support the knowledge-based economy hypothesis (Abramovitz and David, 1996). However the use of education expenditures and attainments for measuring 'human capital formation' still presents formidable conceptual and methodological problems. The same is true when data on education attainments are used to compare tangible and non-tangible investments and capital stocks.[12] As also mentioned in a OECD publication, which has dealt with these conceptual and methodological issues, 'Considerable conceptual and analytical work will be needed before any measure and comparison of "stocks" of the corresponding (knowledge and intangible) assets are available' (quotation in brackets added) (OECD, 1992a, p. 121).[13]

The long-term increase of the ratio between R&D expenditures, and investment in fixed gross capital or GDP seems a more robust empirical fact supporting the increasing importance of knowledge-based economy hypothesis. It should be stressed, however, that such a ratio has not experienced a dramatic increase as the knowledge-based economy hypothesis would suggest and that the bulk of investment, both in manufacturing and services, is still made up of investment in tangible assets (OECD, 1992a).

3.8   CONCLUSIONS

In this chapter we have shown that the major theoretical and empirical contributions that flourished in the last few decades in the 'economics of innovations' have moved towards a disembodied approach to technology and innovation.

Technological indicators such as R&D and patents have been by far the most used proxies for measuring firms' and countries' technological capabilities and exploring the impact of technology on the economic performance of firms, industries and countries. The innovative process has, in fact, been conceived more and more as a process of generation of new knowledge as well as scientific and technological breakthrough. The role of investment in any form, related to the use and diffusion of embodied technologies, has been analysed to a much lesser extent, with the exception of the literature on technology diffusion, inter-industry technological flows and sectoral patterns of innovation.

Most of the recent contributions, which have looked into the black box of technological change and which have recognized the importance along with R&D of other sources and forms of technological change, have also tended not to include investment in productive capital as a source of technological change. The use of technologies embodied in new machinery and equipment either have not been regarded at all as a form of innovative activity or at best a marginal role is given to them compared to other more 'disembodied' forms of techno-logical change. The contributions which over the last few years have emphasized the increasing knowledge-based characteristics of modern economies have further reinforced a disembodied perspective on technology and innovation activities. Both the conceptual framework, as well as the empirical evidence, brought to support the knowledge-based economy hypothesis has remained, however, rather impressionistic in nature.

NOTES

1. Few books attempting to draw the state of the art in this new discipline have been published over the last decade. The most comprehensive ones are those edited by Dosi et al. (1988); Dodgson and Rothwell (1994); Stoneman (1995); and Freeman and Soete (1997).
2. Despite the catching-up literature recognizing the key role played by investment for long-term economic growth, a certain degree of ambiguity remains over whether the diffusion and adoption of new technologies through investment should be regarded as a proper form of tech-nological change. In most of the cases investment activities are simply seen as a proxy for the efforts of backward countries to align their productive structures to the 'best practices'. Also the ways in which embodied technological change has been measured, that is through changes in the investment/output ratio, is not fully consistent with the capital-deepening nature of embodied technological change as envisaged by classical economists. Although the ratio of investment per employee could have acted as a better proxy for describing processes such as the increasing level of mechanization and the labour substitution effects of the introduction of new technologies, only a few authors have taken into account changes in the capital/labour ratio as a variable able to explain catching-up processes in productivity (Wolf, 1991).
3. Audretsch and Yamawaki (1988) have analysed the economic effects of product and process R&D activities on sectoral Japan–US reciprocal trade balance positions.
4. In this area of research, too, the 'new perspective' on technology and the innovation process, which will be discussed in section 3.6, has considerably changed the general perspective on diffusion, broadening its content and reinforcing a generally disembodied perspective mainly in two ways: by blurring the traditional distinction between invention, innovation and diffusion, and by focusing on the diffusion of disembodied technological knowledge rather than on embodied technology (see Metcalfe, 1994 and Lissoni and Metcalfe, 1994, for a review of the evolution of the literature on diffusion).

5. Papaconstantinou et al. (1995, p. 26) have estimated that 'acquired' or 'indirect' technology 'represents more than half of total technology intensity in Canada and Australia, has about the same weight as direct R&D intensity in Japan, Italy and the Netherlands, and it is a secondary source of technology in the remaining countries'.

6. In this work the technological content of industrial sectors of OECD countries is calculated by taking into account the R&D embodied in the intermediate and capital goods products purchased within the country and from abroad, using the Leontief inverse matrix. This makes possible the calculation of the indirect technological input of production activities and products by following the whole chain of sectoral technological transfers along the vertically integrated sectors.

7. The relative importance of technology embodied in fixed capital *vis-à-vis* that embodied in intermediate products and even direct R&D is furthermore confirmed by the fact that, as mentioned in the work by Papaconstantinou et al. (1995, 1996), the measurement of investment underestimates its importance, which is proportionate to the capital stock that is actually used in the production process (Papaconstantinou et al., 1995, p 33).

8. More ambiguous results have been obtained by Griliches and Lichtenberg (1984) and Terleckyj (1974).

9. According to Mohnen, 'R&D externalities' occur when the knowledge derived from the R&D activities of one producer has unintended consequences on the performance measures (profits, productivity, market shares and so on) of other producers (Mohnen, 1995, p. 3).

10. A technological paradigm contextual defines 'the needs that are meant to be fulfilled, the scientific principles utilised for the task, the material technology to be used' (Dosi, 1988, p. 1127). Different technological regimes are defined by different mix and degrees of those main ingredients mentioned before: (i) nature of the knowledge base (tacit/codified, general/specific); (ii) level of appropriability; and (iii) level of opportunity and cumulativeness of technological activities.

11. This emerges, for instance, in the contribution of Bell and Pavitt where technological accumulation, defined as technological learning, refers only to the process of accumulation of the second stock of resources mentioned in the main text, that is, to 'any process by which the resources for generating and managing technical change (technological capabilities) are increased or strengthened' (Bell and Pavitt, 1993, pp. 163–4). Embodied innovative activities are not meant to be part of the process of technological accumulation.

12. In particular, according to estimates carried out by Kendrick, the ratio of non-tangible stock to conventional tangible stock has passed from 0.535 to 1.150 between 1929 and 1990 (Abramovitz and David, 1996, p. 42).

13. Despite the increasing interest in intangible investment and assets, the definition and identification of such activities rest on rather shaky conceptual bases. They include a heterogeneous range of activities. The OECD publication *Technology and the Economy: the Key Relationships* (OECD, 1992a), in an attempt to identify intangible assets, has suggested that the latter should be recognized: (i) when it is separable, that is, it can be separated from all other assets without compromising the activities of the enterprise; and (ii) if its value can be determined by either its purchase cost, or by allocation of part of a global cost, or by its production cost to the enterprise. In the same work the following intangible items are included as intangible assets: R&D expenditures, know-how, industrial patterns and design, patents and licences, artistic creations and copyright, royalty payments, training and other investments in human resources, market shares, product certifications, customer lists, subscriber lists of potential customers, product brands and service brands, software and similar products (OECD, 1992a, p. 115).

4. Embodied and disembodied perspectives on the relationship between technological change, firm size and market structure

4.1 INTRODUCTION

In Chapters 2 and 3 we have shown that a shift from an embodied to a disembodied perspective on technological change has taken place in the evolution of economic theory and has been reinforced by the emergence of the most recent contributions within the 'economics of innovation'.

The purpose of this chapter is to show that a similar shift can also be found if we look at the contributions in economic and innovation literature which have looked at the complex linkages between technological change, firm size and market structure. The contributions flourished in the last few decades within the neo-Schumpeterian stream have clearly privileged a disembodied perspective on technology and innovation, departing in this way from a 'production-based' and 'embodied' perspective, which was explicitly shared among classical economists. While among classical economists, and later in the most traditional contributions in industrial economics, the emergence of large firms and concentrated market structures were seen to be associated with the use of more capital-intensive and advanced process technologies, in the neo-Schumpeterian approach the emphasis has shifted to a supposed superiority of large corporations and non-competitive markets in generating new technological knowledge and innovations.

In the next section we start analysing the embodied perspective in the relationship between technology, firms size and market structure envisaged among classical economists and implicitly acknowledged in most traditional contributions in industrial economics. In section 4.3 we examine the disembodied perspective which permeates the rich theoretical and empirical literature on innovation, firm size and market structure originated within the neo-Schumpeterian tradition. Finally, in section 4.4 we will focus on the few contributions in the innovation literature, which have analysed the relationship between innovation and firm size taking into account also the role of investment in fixed capital.

4.2   THE 'SCALE-AUGMENTING' NATURE OF EMBODIED TECHNOLOGICAL CHANGE

In Chapter 2 we have already pointed out that among classical economists the process of mechanization, the use of more and more capital-intensive techniques of production and the increasing extension of the scale of production were conceived as interdependent aspects of the process of industrial dynamics.

It was Adam Smith [1776] (1976) the first economist to stress that the division of labour and the introduction of labour displacing machines were conditioned by the extent of the market and the scale of production. An explicit reference to the close relationship between specialization, mechanization and the expansion of the scale of production can also be found in a contemporary of Smith such as Babbage (1833, pp. 212–14). In Babbage's work the advantages of specialization are obtained through the emergence of managerial and organizational functions and through the process of mechanization and automation of the labour process. In Babbage's view the capital-deepening nature of technical change was also quite central in his investigation into the causes of the emergence of modern large manufacturing factories.

Like Smith and Babbage, and other contemporary scholars such as Ure (1835), Marx also looked at technological change in its linkages with the organizational characteristics of production activities. Economic reproduction on an ever-increasing scale is, according to Marx, the characterizing feature of the capitalist 'mode of production'.

Changes of production technologies, the increase of the scale of production and concentration and centralization of capital are conceptualized by Marx as different aspects of the same historical process of industrialization (Marx, *Capital III*, [1894] 1983).[1] Technological transformations are accompanied by the formation of production systems requiring increasing levels of integration, with the growth of large combined capitals offering a base for further development of the production forces. Thus mechanization and the increase of fixed capital with respect to labour (both in technical terms and in terms of value) were seen as the major sources of technological development and an aspect strongly linked with the emergence of large firms, large combined capitals and concentrated (centralized) market structures.

Also a large part of the scientific progress in a capitalist mode of production goes, according to Marx, in the direction of an increasing industrial concentration. The progress of science and technology exerts its major economic effects by accelerating the development of the 'production forces' and fuelling the process of accumulation of capital.

The scale-augmenting nature of embodied technological change has implicitly been supported also by other contributors and scholars in the first decades of this century with a more direct reference to the size of plants and firms. This is the case of the early contributions to understanding the advantages related to the large size by Clark and Robinson which have emphasized the possibility for large firms of using more capital-intensive production techniques (Clark, 1923; Robinson, 1931).

In the neoclassical tradition as well, an explicit acknowledgement of the role played by embodied technology and technological change for the size of the business unit or the factory can be found. Marshall, for instance, explicitly states that 'capital required per head of the workers is generally greater in a large factory than in a small one' (Marshall, 1920, p. 282). On the whole, however, the upsurge of the neoclassical approach in economics has led to a progressive neglecting of the role of economies of scale as well as of their technical and technological determinants. Economies of scale are, in fact, clearly incompatible with the neoclassical assumption of decreasing returns at a micro level, which is in turn a crucial assumption for getting 'perfect' competitive equilibrium conditions. Even when economies of scale are acknowledged, the maintaining of the assumption of homogeneity of the productive factor makes it difficult to give to economies of scale a technological or a simple technical connotation.[2]

Such features, along with the exogenous role given to technology, have pushed any further attempt to investigate the role of technological change for explaining the emergence of large firms and non-competitive markets outside the mainstream of orthodox neoclassical economics.

In the postwar period, the growing importance of large corporations and oligopolistic market structures has, in fact, pushed economists to dedicate more attention to the characteristics and *modus operandi* of these organizations and markets. The price behaviours and the strategic conducts and performances of firms operating in conditions of non-perfect competition have been the object of analysis of a large body of theoretical and empirical investigations, starting with Bain's pioneering works in the early 1950s (Bain, 1956, 1959; Sylos Labini, 1956) and followed by a large number of (mainly empirical) contributions in the so-called Structure-Conduct-Performance (S-C-P) approach. In parallel, other contributions in the S-C-P literature started to re-emphasize the importance of supply-side dimensions of production structures (namely economies of scale and barriers to entry).[3] Here it is worth mentioning some of the main sources of economies of scale recalled by this literature, since they have implicitly re-emphasized the role of technological change in its production-based and embodied dimension for explaining the emergence of large corporations and concentrated market structures.[4] In this context the concept of 'indivisibilities' is emblematic.[5] Though indivisibilities might originate also from the organizational interdependencies and complementarities in production processes, such a concept has been more commonly referred to the specific characteristics of capital items and production technologies used. The most common justification for the presence of indivisibilities lies in the simple circumstance that many capital goods and plants are available only in large indivisible sizes.

The concept of 'indivisibilities', as a source of economies of scale, has been stressed not only in its strict technical sense but also in its economic nature. Economic indivisibilities refer to production inputs, which once acquired, cannot be paid according to their effective use (Baumol, 1982). The ultimate cause of such economic indivisibilities is rooted in the sunk cost nature of a large part of investment and particularly in the limited range of use of capital goods, equipment and plants.[6] Both forms of indivisibilities (technical and economic) give to investment in fixed capital and financial immobilization a key role for explaining the presence of 'static economies of scale', 'barriers to entry' and the size of production units (Baumol, 1982).

Although indivisibilities and the sunk cost nature of many technical immobilizations are usually not explicitly associated to any particular innovation pattern, it is commonly acknowledged that industries characterized by high economies of scale are also those where technological change takes the form of the introduction of capital-intensive process innovations.

Two other sources of economies of scale commonly recalled in the literature have a clear link with investment in fixed productive assets: these are the 'economies of increased dimensions' and 'economies of massed resources'. Economies of increased dimensions are usually found in process-type industries where the costs of the basic production units (storage tanks, connecting pipes and so on) increase roughly according to the area of these assets while the (productive) capacity increases according to their volume. This is known as the two-thirds or six-tenths rule (Robinson, [1931] 1958; Scherer, 1970, 1980; Pratten, 1988, 1991; Scherer and Ross, 1990). The economies of massed resources are those related to the ability to economize on spare equipment, components and materials, which have to be kept in order to meet temporary breakdowns of single items of equipment or interruption of the supply of specific intermediate components and materials (Pratten, 1988, p. 24; Scherer and Ross, 1990, p. 100). Both kinds of economies of scale characterize process-intensive industries such as chemicals, refining, production and transformation of metals and basic minerals, and more in general industries where the economization and full utilization of production assets represent a key element for the efficiency of firms (Robinson, [1931] 1958; Scherer, 1970, 1980; Pratten, 1988, 1991; Scherer and Ross, 1990). Also in these industries the exploitation of economies of scale and the establishment of large production units are likely to be associated to technological trajectories based on the use of capital-intensive process innovations.[7]

A more complex relationship between the characteristics of productive structures and patterns of innovation are those envisaged in the most recent literature on the 'economies of scope'. Economies of scope in production occur when it is less costly to combine the productions of two or more products than to produce them in separate plants or firms. The exploitation of economies of scope is sometimes presented as an alternative and more 'flexible' strategy *vis-à-vis* the exploitation of economies of scale through the production of highly standardized products. It is also often implicit that while economies of scale are associated with innovation patterns aiming at introducing cost-saving process technologies, economies of scope go in parallel with product diversification and innovation strategies oriented towards the creation of new products in response to highly volatile markets.

The existence of an actual trade-off between economies of scale and scope (and associated process/product-oriented innovation patterns) is, however, not confirmed by most of the existing empirical evidence and it is also difficult to support on theoretical grounds. It has, in fact, been noted that in most industrial practices economies of scale and scope have tended to reinforce each other, allowing for a better exploitation of firms' productive capacity (Scherer and Ross, 1990; Morroni, 1992; Harrison, 1994).[8] On more theoretical grounds, to the extent that economies of scope originate from spreading the costs of highly expensive technical immobilization over a large quantity of aggregate productive output, they are, in fact, not very different, in their economic nature, from those at the base of economies of scale (Morroni, 1992).

If this is true then technical and economic indivisibilities associated with high investment in fixed productive capital still continue to be central for explaining the presence of economies of scale and scope in production, and for justifying the presence of large firms. This also suggests that in industries where economies of scale and scope are relevant, the use of new vintages of fixed capital with enhanced performances (in terms of speed of production runs, reduction of idle times, possibility to produce a wider range of products at a lower cost) represent an important element of firms' innovation conducts.

On the whole it can be argued, therefore, that most of the theoretical and analytical literature on economies of scale and scope implicitly underline the importance of technological change in the form of the generation and use of new production techniques and consequently attach to embodied technological change an important role for explaining changes across time (and differences across industries) in the size of production units and market structures.

Such an approach is implicit also in the empirical contributions which, especially in the 1960s and 1970s, have investigated the nature and extent of economies of scale and their importance for determining the minimum efficient scale of plants and firms and the level of industrial concentration.

Many studies have looked at the long-term technological determinants of market structure. This is, in fact, the approach which is more in line with the historical perspective of classical economists reviewed in the previous section. The empirical results have however been somewhat inconclusive (see Davies and Lyons, 1988 and Scherer and Ross, 1990, for reviews). It is nonetheless surprising that in more recent times works of this type have not been carried out more extensively and that they belong nowadays to the 'archaeology' of applied industrial economics. One of the few exceptions is represented by the studies coordinated by Davies and Lyons on industrial concentration in Europe (Davies and Lyons, 1996).[9]

Also a large part of the empirical studies, which have estimated the 'minimum efficient scale' (MES) of plants and firms across industries, have maintained such a supply-side and technology-based approach to the determinants of firms' size and market structure. On the whole this empirical literature has shown that economies of scale play some role in determining the minimum efficient size of single plants and firms, and at the same time impose an upper limit on the maximum number of firms that are allowed to operate efficiently in a market of a given size (Pratten, 1971, 1988; HMSO, 1978; Lyons, 1980; Scherer and Ross 1990). Cliff Pratten, on the basis of one of the most comprehensive surveys on economies of scale in the manufacturing sector, has confirmed that the specific technologies used at the industry level play an important role for determining the different importance of economies of scale (measured through MES) across industries and for affecting market structures (that is levels of industrial concentration) (Pratten, 1971, 1988, 1991).

On the whole, however, the empirical contributions on economies of scale reviewed above, have remained largely descriptive, and not able to identify any systematic link between the presence of economies of scale and barriers to entry on the one hand and the characteristics of the production processes, technologies used, and the specific innovation patterns of firms and industries on the other.

A step in this direction has been taken by the empirical studies which have investigated the determinants of industrial concentration through cross-industry econometric estimates. Beside other variables some proxies for capturing embodied technological activities and their impact on production and market structure have also been included. Along with MES the capital intensity of production processes has been used as a proxy for capturing the importance of economies of scale and other factors indicating the presence of barriers to entry. By using an index of 'capital intensity' as a determinant of intersectoral differences in the levels of industrial concentration, these studies have resulted in the testing of some of the hypothesis set forth by the more qualitative literature on economies of sale reviewed above: the role of high overhead costs and indivisibilities in fixed capital as a source of economies of scale and barriers to entry.[10]

The results of these cross-industry econometric estimates have highlighted the following stylized facts and regularities:

1. Direct measures of the relevance of economies of scale coming from MES estimates have been found most of the time significantly correlated with the level of industrial concentration across industries, especially when differences in the actual size of the markets were taken into account.
2. The levels of capital requirement (and related financial barriers to entry) and the level of product differentiation have also been found significantly correlated with the index of industrial concentration.
3. Indicators of capital intensity as measured by the stock of productive capital per unit of labour or output, though much less used than MES, emerge as a strong explanatory determinant of market structure and firm size.[11]

These results bring empirical support to the importance of supply-side and technology-based determinants of firm size and market structure, and to the scale-augmenting role played by embodied technological change. In particular it is worth stressing the fact that even a crude indicator measuring the presence of indivisibilities, sunk costs and capital intensity (such as the stock of productive capital per unit of labour or output) has emerged in these studies as significantly correlated with industrial concentration.

These results also confirm some previous descriptive studies, which had already highlighted, on a more casual basis, a general tendency for more concentrated industries such as petroleum, steel or automobiles, to be more capital-intensive than less concentrated sectors such as textile and clothing, furniture and light engineering industries (Bain, 1956; Pratten, 1971,1991): in other words this literature confirms that the larger are the levels of technical and economical immobilization the larger is the scope for 'static' economies of scale, large-scale production units, and concentrated market structures to emerge. The implication for innovation of these stylized facts is straightforward: in the industrial sectors where such structural productive features are found innovation patterns are likely to be based on the introduction of capital-intensive process innovation (that is embodied innovative patterns).[12]

On the whole we can conclude this section by restating that both classical economists and most contributions in industrial economics have implicitly attached a great importance to technology and technological change in its embodied form for explaining the ways in which market structure evolves, and, in a more static context, for explaining differences across industries in the average firm size and industrial concentration. The most serious flaw in this literature is that they have only marginally investigated the nature and economic impact of innovation activities on production structures. In particular what is missing in this empirical literature is a systematic effort to establish a relationship between some measurable dimension of embodied innovation activities, the presence of scale economies, and associated structural aspects of production such as the average firm size of industries or the levels of industrial concentration. The reason for this has to do in turn with two interdependent factors: (i) the marginal interest that for a long time industrial economists have shown towards technological change; and (ii) the lack of appropriate data on innovation activities. Both such flaws have been overcome in recent decades by a new stream of contributions in the 'economics of technological change'. The new literature has, however, shifted towards a disembodied perspective on technological change and on its links with firm size and market structure.

4.3   THE DISEMBODIED PERSPECTIVE OF THE NEO-SCHUMPETERIAN EMPIRICAL LITERATURE

In the last two decades the relationship between innovation, firm size and industrial concentration has been explicitly addressed by a consistent number of (mainly empirical) contributions, though with a completely different approach from the one envisaged in the approaches reviewed in the previous section.

Also the origin of this literature lies in the influential works of Schumpeter. We have already mentioned that during his lifetime, he changed his views on the nature and determinants of the innovation process and the institutional setting in which it takes place. The first Schumpeterian perspective, the one which can be found in *The Theory of Economic Development* [1912] (1934), was a description of the innovation process characterizing the perfect (in a neoclassical sense) competitive environment as he saw it in the first decades of this century. Innovative activities were based on the behaviours of single entrepreneurs, often located in small firms, able to foresee commercially exploitable inventions or simply new goods or new ways of doing things. The second perspective, the one represented in *Capitalism, Socialism and Democracy* (1942), reflected the trustified-monopolistic structure of capitalism he was observing at a later stage of his life, with the predominant role of large corporations. The emergence of large corporations or units of control was related to the increasingly science-based nature of technological activities and the financial and organizational barriers to entry associated with R&D-based innovation processes. The endogenization and internalization of the scientific and technological activities within the R&D department of large firms was seen by Schumpeter as being associated with increasing levels of routinization of the innovative activities, and as a consequence, the disappearance of the heroic role of entrepreneurs (Freeman et al., 1982). Such bureaucratization of the economic and innovation activities would have eventually led to an inevitable exhaustion of the progressiveness of capitalist systems.

The publication of *Capitalism, Socialism and Democracy* inspired a large body of empirical literature focusing on the so-called neo-Schumpeterian hypotheses. The empirical issue to be investigated became whether innovative performances of large firms, or concentrated market structures, were superior to those characterizing small firms and perfectly competitive market structures.[13] The empirical studies, which have tested the neo-Schumpeterian hypotheses, have thus adopted a modified version of the relationship between market structure and economic performance *vis-à-vis* those tested in the S-C-P literature: the last two terms of the S-C-P causal chain have been substituted by indicators of innovative conducts and performance.[14]

It is with reference to the basic argumentation brought to support the neo-Schumpeterian hypotheses that we can note a clear shift of emphasis on the nature of technological change with respect to the approaches reviewed in the previous section. When explicitly mentioned the theoretical arguments focus on the advantages of large firms in funding, organizing and performing R&D activities. While in the S-C-P literature, and among classical economists, the superior efficiency of large firms and concentrated market structures were related to the use of more capital-intensive and advanced process technologies, in the neo-Schumpeterian approach the emphasis is on a supposed superiority of large corporations and non-perfect competitive markets in the process of generation of new technological knowledge and innovations.

A first, and most common, source of advantage attached to the absolute size of firms arises from economies of scale and financial barriers to entry in R&D activities. The economic justification for the presence of economies of scale in R&D and innovation activities is not substantially different from the one traditionally developed in industrial economics with respect to economies of scale in production. Pratten in his 1971 contribution on economies of scale had already pointed out that economies of scale originate also from indivisibilities and fixed costs connected to innovative activities, in particular those consisting of the generation and development of new technological knowledge and new products (Pratten, 1971). Following contributions have stressed that R&D activities, in particular, can give rise to fixed (and sunk) costs, which can lead to the same kind of indivisibilities as those originating from investment in fixed productive capital. Average R&D expenditures for unit of production decrease, in fact, as they are spread over larger volumes of production, into which the technologies developed are embodied (see Freeman, 1974; Kamien and Schwartz, 1982; Baldwin and Scott, 1987; Cohen and Levin, 1989). In this case, the presence of economies of scale are thus due to fixed costs and indivisibilities associated with investment in physical assets and infrastructure to be used for R&D activities (such as laboratories, the development and construction of prototypes and so on). Sutton regards investment in R&D and in advertising as endogenous sunk costs. The endogenous label derives from the strategic nature of these investments. 'Exogenous sunk costs' are constituted by investment in production assets which incorporate the technologies available in the economy (Sutton, 1991). According to Sutton both types of investment give rise, however, to indivisibilities, economies of scale and barriers to entry. Furthermore, as for production activities, increasing returns to R&D might also be due to the higher organizational efficiency associated with larger projects, development of specialized research institutions and larger budgets for R&D activities carried out on a systematic basis.

The intrinsically risky and uncertain nature of the innovative process has also been seen as a factor reinforcing the advantage of large firms *vis-à-vis* small firms in innovation. This is because of the obstacles that small firms usually face in funding their innovative projects in a context of highly imperfect financial markets (financial barriers to R&D), and because of the higher opportunities that large firms have in exploiting economies of scope in R&D. Economies of scope in R&D are twofold: firstly, they are related to the fact that with the size and level of diversification of R&D projects are linked enhanced possibilities of getting synergies and cross-fertilization of ideas and results; secondly, in the case of a parallel diversification in R&D and production activities, a diversified R&D portfolio allows reduction of the risk of failure and enhances the possibility of commercially exploiting the results of R&D projects in more than one market or production field (Cohen and Levin, 1989; Cohen, 1995, Cohen and Klepper, 1996). Complementarities can also emerge between economies of scope in R&D and production activities, leading to increasing returns both in production and innovation activities.

Monopolistic or oligopolistic market structures are also supposed to be more conducive to innovation compared to perfect competitive markets. This is because of the high level of risk and uncertainty characterizing innovative activities and the only partial appropriability of the economic benefits of innovation activities. The importance of *ex ante* and *ex post* monopolistic market conditions for firms to undertake risky innovative activities was already identified by Schumpeter. Incentives to innovate are present only when innovative activities are able to provide the innovator with a monopolistic power which allow firms to recover the costs of the innovative investments undertaken. On the other hand, the extra profits associated with non-competitive markets represent an important financial source for supporting risky and costly innovative activities. Conditions of non-perfect competition, such as concentrated market structures arising from different forms of barriers to entry, might therefore function as a necessary condition and stimulus to invest in R&D and innovative activities.[15]

The disembodied perspective characterizing the neo-Schumpeterian perspective on the relationship between innovation, firm size and market structure emerges even more clearly when we look at the way technological activities have been measured in empirical analyses. In particular it is straight-forward to note that only technological indicators reflecting inputs and outputs of innovative activities aimed at generating new technological knowledge have been used to compare the innovative performance of firms and industries.

The resources (financial and human) assigned to R&D have been by far the most used proxy in this research field and the one providing most of the empirical backing for the hypotheses that innovative activities increase more than proportionately with firm size and with the level of the industrial concen-tration. On methodological grounds such studies have, however, been criticized for using indicators that are biased in favour of large firms. It has been widely shown that R&D constitutes a reliable proxy of innovative activity only for large-sized firms and fails to reflect a whole series of (often non-formalized) technological activities prevalent in medium and small firms (Kleinknecht and Reijnen, 1991; Evangelista et al., 1997).

The indicators used alternatively to R&D to test the Schumpeterian hypotheses maintain a disembodied connotation as in the case of patents. In this case also the results have not been significantly different from those obtained using R&D expenditure or personnel, and anyway they have not been able to settle the dispute.

The innovative output represented by individual innovations introduced into the economic system represent a third type of indicator that has been used to test the neo-Schumpeterian hypotheses.[16] Though such an indicator captures also the innovations and technologies, which are embodied in fixed productive capital, it continues to fall short of measuring the actual diffusion of such innovations and differences in the financial commitments involved in the adoption of such innovations.

All the different indicators used in the empirical estimations of the neo-Schumpeterian hypotheses have thus implicitly assumed a disembodied perspective on innovative activities. Innovative activities consisting of the use of process technologies through investment in fixed capital have been neglected.

Moreover in particular, the empirical question of whether firm size and related market structure conditions might affect (or might be affected by) innovative activities in the form of productive investment, has for the most part not been addressed, nor have adequate indicators or alternative methodologies been developed.

4.4 NEW CONTRIBUTIONS

Over the last few years an increasing number of criticisms have been directed at both the methodological and conceptual shortcomings present in the empirical literature on the neo-Schumpeterian hypotheses.

First, it has been argued that the existence of strong sectoral specificities in the technological patterns makes testing for a relationship between firm size, market structure and innovative performance rather meaningless. This occurs when either a highly aggregated analysis or biased technological indicators are used. In any case it demonstrates the lack of significance of any kind of result obtained in such a way (Cohen and Levin, 1989; Cohen, 1995). Industrial sectors differ widely in terms of sources and nature of the innovative activities undertaken and in the levels of technological opportunity. A series of studies have, therefore, analysed the effects of firm size or the market structure on innovative intensity by taking into account single industrial sectors separately (Mansfield, 1968; Scherer, 1984b; Archibugi et al., 1995) or by adding dummy variables classifying the industry's technological characteristics (Scherer, 1967; Cohen et al., 1987; Bound et al., 1984; Scott, 1984).[17]

The consideration that the relationship between technological activities and industrial structure runs both ways, together with the acknowledgement of the dynamic nature of this relationship, represent further important steps ahead in this research field (Phillips, 1971; Nelson and Winter, 1978, 1982; Dasgupta and Stiglitz, 1980; Dosi et al., 1997). Industrial structure changes as a result of the technological activities undertaken by the firms. In this regard several authors have argued that the differences in the technological regimes, above all in terms of technological appropriability, technological opportunity and degree of diffusion of the knowledge base, can explain intersectoral differences in market structure (Levin et al., 1985; Malerba and Orsenigo, 1990, 1996).[18]

A fully dynamic framework can be found in the evolutionary models contained in the seminal contributions by Nelson and Winter (1978, 1982) and later by Dosi (1984, 1988). These authors have attempted to develop a model of dynamic competition and selection based on innovation that interacts with the process of structural change in industry. The presence of asymmetries in firm size and sectoral differences in market structures are considered neither exogenous, as in the neo-Schumpeterian empirical literature, nor associated with static technological factors as in the S-C-P perspective. In the Nelson and Winter model (1982), the structure of the industries (defined in terms of market concentration and asymmetry among firms) is seen as the result of a permanently working Schumpeterian selection process in a technological context characterized by a high uncertainty and cumulativeness of innovation activities. The latter characteristics make the existence of asymmetries and inter-firm variety (in terms of firm growth and market share) a permanent character of industries, not a temporary one as in the original (Mark 1) Schumpeterian model. Intersectoral differences in market structures are thus explained by inter-industry (and inter-technology) differences in the level of technological opportunity, appropriability, uncertainty and cumulativeness of technological activities. Unfortunately the dynamic and simultaneous nature of the linkages between technology and industrial structure features encompassed in such approaches have made such evolutionary models empirically testable almost exclusively by simulation techniques.[19]

The new empirical and theoretical contributions reviewed above have thus departed from the original neo-Shumpeterian literature in many respects. However they have maintained a clear disembodied perspective on the nature of technology and innovation and on the interaction mechanisms between the latter and the characteristics and evolution of industrial structures.

Even in the evolutionary literature, embodied technological change does not seem to play any particular role in explaining the interrelationships between firms' innovative behaviours, firms' economic growth and the evolution of market structures. If we take the most representative of such models, that is the one proposed by Nelson and Winter (1978, 1982), embodied technological change and production-related technological determinants of industrial structure do not play any specific role in explaining the evolutionary patterns of industrial structures.

This is confirmed by the following passage extracted from an article by Nelson and Winter:

> We focus here on a number of key variables that influence the evolution of market structure. The logic of the model would appear to imply that the more rapid the pace at which technological opportunities extend over time, the more uncertain is the outcome of the research project aimed at seizing new opportunities, the harder it is to imitate successful innovation, and the less the tendency of firms to restrain their output growth as they grow larger, the greater is the tendency of significant concentration to develop out of a situation that originally started out with many equal-sized firms (Nelson and Winter, 1978, p. 531).

Nelson and Winter themselves seem to admit in the following passage the absence in their model of any production-related technological determinant of industrial structure and the exclusive applicability of their model to sectors where such determinants are not relevant:

> The model would be improved if it were generalised to reflect more of the systematic influence on industry structure – for example, technological economies of scale, product differentiation, and entry conditions (Nelson and Winter, 1978, p. 543).

Dosi also seems to stress a clearly disembodied perspective on the technological determinants of industrial structure features and their evolution. In one
of his most influential articles he states that:

> the features of the evolution of each industry are, so to speak, 'ordered' by the
> patterns of learning, and by the ways the latter influence the competitive process; the
> understanding of the variety of observable industrial structures, performances, and
> their changes implies, I suggest, a sort of 'micro foundation' in the underlying modes
> by which economic agents accumulate knowledge and competencies on how to solve
> technological and organisational problems (Dosi, 1988, p. 1163).

In another part of the same article he seems to adopt a broader perspective,
including, along with the traditional evolutionary ingredients, production-
related determinants of industrial structure features: '. . . the sectoral distributions
of characteristics such as firms' size are affected by the specific characteristics
of the technological paradigms on which the production of that sector is based,
in terms of appropriability, technological opportunities, scope for automation,
and economies of scale' (Dosi, 1988, p. 1152).

4.5   CONTRIBUTIONS EMPHASIZING BOTH DISEMBODIED AND EMBODIED INNOVATION PATTERNS

In this section we finally identify the few contributions in the innovation
literature which have analysed the relationship between innovation, firm size
and market structure taking into account also the role played by embodied technological change. These contributions are very important since they represent
an attempt to close the gap between the disembodied perspective of the neo-
Schumpeterian literature and the embodied one supported by classical
economists and implicitly shared by most of the contributions in industrial
economics reviewed in section 4.2.

4.5.1   Firm Size and the Adoption of Embodied Technology

We have shown in Chapter 3 that in the diffusion models proposed by Mansfield
(1968), David (1975b) and Davies (1979), process technologies are assumed
to be both embodied in fixed capital and labour saving. Although these contributions do not belong to the stream of literature dwelling on the Schumpeterian
hypotheses, they have also clear implications for the relationship between
innovation and firm size. Absolute levels of capital requirement and its durability
are aspects that have been explicitly taken into account by Mansfield for
explaining firms' innovative decisions (1963, 1968). The importance of firm

size and market structure as factors affecting the rate of adoption of new technologies is also stressed in some of the other diffusion models reviewed in Chapter 3. In particular, in the models proposed by David (1969) and Davies (1979), the introduction of process innovations involves the presence of scale economies in production. In both these models the probability for a firm to adopt an innovation at any given time is a linear function of the logarithmic value of its size. Also Mansfield (1963) and Stoneman and Ireland (1983) have found significant empirical evidence, which shows the presence of a size effect on the rate and speed of adoption of embodied technology.

4.5.2 Firm Size and Innovation in Pavitt's Taxonomy

A clear relationship between embodied innovation patterns, firm size and market structure is also identified by Pavitt in his sectoral taxonomy, and in particular with reference to the 'production-intensive' trajectory. Pavitt explicitly mentions that the latter is the one that was previously described by Adam Smith as being 'associated with production intensive firms, namely, the increasing division of labour and simplification of production tasks, resulting from an increasing size of the market, and enabling substitution of machines for labour and as a consequence lowering of production costs increasing large-scale fabrication and assembly production' (Pavitt, 1984, p. 358). This innovative pattern is contrasted with those characterizing 'science-based' and 'specialized suppliers' firms and industries, which rely on the internal generation of technological knowledge and specific know-how and capabilities.

The variety of technological trajectories identified by Pavitt is important also because it places some limits on the extent to which the evolutionary metaphor can explain intersectoral differences in firm size and market structure. Referring to the evolutionary models he states that 'formal models of the dynamics of Schumpeterian competition, like those developed by Nelson and Winter, would more accurately reflect a varied reality in technological trajectories, if they were to explore a range of assumptions about new entrants and static and dynamic economies of scale; about pressures for market diversification, and about complementarity relations between producers and users of capital goods' (Pavitt, 1984, p. 369).

4.5.3 Patterns of Innovation and Industrial Structure in the Product Cycle Models

A model of dynamic interaction between technological change and industrial structure where both embodied and disembodied innovative patterns play a distinct role can be found in the 'product cycle' model, and more specifically in the influential works by Utterback and Abernathy (1975) and Abernathy and

Utterback (1978) as well as in the following contributions by Gort and Klepper (1982), Klepper and Graddy (1990) and Klepper (1993).

The initial contributions by Abernathy and Utterback can be thought of as technological versions of the original 'product cycle' model presented by Vernon in 1966. Compared to the original product cycle approach, in the Abernathy and Utterback model there is a clear emphasis on the technological connotation of such structural changes of industries. Such changes are the result of the changing nature of technological characteristics of production processes associated with shifts in the innovative patterns: product versus process and quality-enhancing versus cost-minimizing innovations (Abernathy and Utterback, 1975, 1978).[20] According to these authors the evolution of industries is characterized by a first stage when production technologies and product designs are not fully defined. In the early stages of the evolution of an industry most of the technological efforts of the firms are thus dedicated to matching the existing technological opportunities with the high levels of market uncertainty characterizing the emergence of new products or industries. With the growth of the industries a shift in the innovative patterns also occurs: innovation activities, from being based on product design, begin to be oriented towards the introduction of more capital-intensive techniques. The evolutionary process behind such a shift in the nature and role of innovation is described by the two authors as follows:

> As production process develops over time toward levels of improved output productivity, it does so with a characteristic evolutionary pattern: it becomes more capital intensive, direct labour productivity improves through greater division of labour and specialization, the flow of materials within the process takes on more of a straight line flow quality (that is flows are rationalised), the product design becomes more standardised, and the process scale become larger (Utterback and Abernathy, 1975, p. 641).

These changes in the technological and organizational nature of production process are a result of a progressive change of the basis of competition, which shifts from product to process innovations. This in turn accelerates the process of structural change in the industry, characterized by a progressive increase of firm size, level of industrial concentration and static barriers to entry. The dynamic interplay between structural conditions of production, models of competition and firm innovative behaviours is again synthesized by these authors as follows:

> As the product life cycle evolves product variety tends to be reduced and products become standardised. Then as a progression the basis of competition begins to shift to product price, margins are reduced, the industry often becomes an oligopoly, and efficiency and economies of scale are emphasised in production. As price competition

increases production processes become more capital intensive and may be relocated to achieve lower costs of factor inputs (Utterback and Abernathy, 1975, p. 644).

More recently there have been other contributions which have developed and improved on the original insights provided by the Utterback and Abernathy model. These contributions have strengthened the conceptual and theoretical foundations behind the simplified regularities identified by early product cycle models and provided additional empirical historical evidence.

Although these studies have highlighted much more complex dynamic interactions between technology and structural features of industries, they have by and large confirmed the key mechanisms contained in the original product cycle model. In particular changes in market structures are still related to the underlying technological transformation of industries and innovative patterns, which are based on: (i) a progressive shift from product to process innovation; (ii) the progressive introduction of more and more capital-intensive innovations; and (iii) the emergence of technologically-based economies of scale and barriers to entry (Gort and Klepper, 1982; Klepper and Graddy, 1990; Utterback and Suàrez, 1993; Klepper and Simons, 1994).

4.6 CONCLUDING REMARKS

In this chapter we have shown that the relationships between technology, innovation and industrial structure have been traditionally analysed focusing on two kinds of question and underlying causal relationships, each assuming a different perspective on technology and innovative activities.

4.6.1 From Technology to Industrial Structure

Contributions in industrial economics have been traditionally focused on the technological determinants of industrial structure. Firm size and levels of industrial concentration have been explained by the presence of technical indivisibilities, scale economies and barriers to entry. In this context technology and innovation have been seen as interacting with firm size and market structure conditions mainly in their 'embodied' dimension. Empirical research in industrial economics largely reflects such an approach. Most of the empirical studies in this area have looked at the technical determinants of firm size and industrial concentration analysing the extent and sources of economies of scale and barriers to entry as well as specific characteristics of production technologies. Indicators based on fixed capital expenditures (per employee or per unit of output) in cross-industry econometric analyses have been found positively associated with firm size and industrial concentration.

4.6.2   From Industrial Structure to Innovative Activities

A different perspective has characterized the contributions arising out of the so-called neo-Schumpeterian debate. In this literature the ways in which firm size and market structure conditions affect innovative behaviours and performances have represented the main object of investigation. With such inversion of the direction of causality, the conceptualization of technological change has moved towards a disembodied and production unrelated perspective. The technological indicators most often used have been those reflecting innovative efforts devoted to the generation and development of technological knowledge and innovations, such as R&D expenditures, patents and innovation counts. The econometric exercises, which have tested the neo-Schumpeterian hypotheses, have provided so far quite mixed and contrasting results.

4.6.3   Towards a More Complex View of Innovation Activities and their Interactions with Structural Features of Industries

Over the last two decades the evolution of the innovation literature has progressively gone in the direction of obtaining a more comprehensive picture of innovative activities and their relationship with structural features of firms and industries. In particular it has been suggested that the relationship between technology and industrial structure takes place in a dynamic context and runs both ways in the presence of wide sectoral differences in the levels of technological opportunity and appropriability conditions.

These more recent contributions seem thus to converge towards a more holistic and dynamic perspective on the relationship between technology and industrial structure, as the one envisaged in the analysis of classical economists. However still quite different mechanisms of 'dynamic interaction' between technology and industrial structure are envisaged in the two approaches. Classical economists adopt a clear production-based perspective on technological change, putting a sharp emphasis on the long-term effects that embodied technological change has on the organization of production and market structures (and vice versa). On the contrary, evolutionary approaches have identified different kinds of mechanisms, of a more Schumpeterian flavour, which govern the dynamics of technology and industrial structure. The presence of structural asymmetries and differences across firms (in terms of firm size) and industries (level of industrial concentration) are based on a more 'behavioural' and 'disembodied' vision of innovative activities.

We have also pointed out, however, that, in some of the new contributions in the innovation literature, both embodied and disembodied forms of technological change have been acknowledged as playing a part in the definition of sectoral innovative patterns (as in the case of Pavitt's taxonomy) and in explaining changes in the innovative patterns and structural characteristics of industries (as in the product cycle contributions).

NOTES

1. Marx uses the term 'concentration of capital' to indicate the process through which means of production get more and more concentrated in the hands of the capitalist class *vis-à-vis* the labour force. Centralization has to do with the division of property of capital within the capitalist class and indicates the process through which the amount of capital gets concentrated in the hands of fewer and fewer capitalists and therefore can be assimilated to what, in the current literature is termed as (industrial/financial) concentration (Marx, *Capital III* [1894], 1983 and *The Poverty of Philosophy* [1847], 1973).
2. In such a framework the presence of economies of scale can be attributed only to organizational improvements such as changes in the organization and specialization of labour allowed by an increased scale of production, but which leave unchanged the state of technology and the inputs ratio (Gold, 1981).
3. The S-C-P approach has been widely criticized especially by the recent 'new industrial organization' literature. However very few subsequent contributions have dismissed a role for technical economies of scale and barriers to entry. In most of the later contributions some estimate or proxy accounting for the scale factor such as the minimum efficient scale of firms, the number of firms, or the level of fixed costs, have continued to be taken into account (Clarke and Davies, 1982; Shaked and Sutton, 1987). The exceptions are represented by: (i) 'pure stochastic models' of market concentration such as those based on Gibrat's 'law of proportionate effect' (Gibrat, 1931); and (ii) evolutionary models entirely based on a mixture of stochastic elements and purely Schumpeterian models of dynamic competition (Nelson and Winter, 1982) where no explicit role for static and production-based economies of scale is found (see section 4.4).
4. The theoretical argumentation and the empirical evidence supporting the existence of economies of scale in production applies to a large extent also to barriers to entry. The necessary condition for such a link is that economies of scale are related to the presence of sunk costs. On this point there seems to be a good deal of agreement on the fact that the presence of economies of scale is most of the time associated with the presence of sunk costs (see Davies and Lyons 1988, and Scherer and Ross, 1990 for reviews).
5. The existence of some form of indivisibilities is a necessary prerequisite for the presence of economies of scale since, if single productive items and production processes were perfectly divisible, there would not be any technical room for economies of scale.
6. Although the labour inputs can to some extent be regarded as fund elements, depending on particular institutional norms that regulate the labour market and work conditions, high levels of technical and economic indivisibility are seen as a primary characteristics of production facilities (Morroni, 1992).
7. Economies of scale do not have only a productive connotation. Under the label 'indivisibilities' are, for instance, often found a variety of fixed cost items, which are not related to the acquisition and use of fixed productive capital. In this respect Pratten identifies the following costs, which are at least partially independent of scale: (i) the initial development and design costs for a new product; (ii) first copy costs of books, newspapers and so on; (iii) obtaining tenders and studying sources of supply for a component; (iv) office records for a batch of a product; (v) preparation of advertisements (Pratten, 1988, p. 21; see also Pratten, 1991). The role of the sunk cost nature of investment in R&D and marketing has also been stressed by Sutton (1991).
8. Particularly important cases arise when production capacity cannot be fully utilized on the basis of single-product productions because of demand constraints (market saturation and

instability of demand). As mentioned by Scherer and Ross (1990), 'assigning multiple products to a single plant with economies of scope can offset at least some of the product specific economy sacrifices attributable to low volume production' (p. 102).

9. Michael Waterson, in the book edited by Casson and Creedy, *Industrial Concentration and Economic Inequality* (1993), raises the interesting question of 'why industrial economics/industrial organisation theory has moved away from consideration of concentration and its determinants'. He points out that this is due to 'the methodological position of the New Industrial organisation, the interrelated influence of game theory and the development of contestability theory. This has in turn had an influence on the type of empirical work which is commonly pursued in recent studies' (Waterson, 1993, p. 111–112).

10. See Curry and George (1983) for a review of the results of these empirical studies.

11. See Rosenbluth (1957); Nelson (1963); Comanor and Wilson (1967); Pashigian (1968), (1969); Ornstein et al. (1973); Banerji, (1978).

12. Surprisingly enough, the relationship between firm size and an indicator of capital intensity has been empirically investigated to a much lesser extent. It is also surprising that there have not been, at least to my knowledge, econometric exercises analysing the relationships between firm size, industrial concentration and the capital intensity of production. This kind of link was explicitly addressed by most of the theoretical contributions examined in the previous sections.

13. In this respect most of the debate on Schumpeterian hypotheses contains a clear misleading reading of the historical perspective contained in the Schumpeterian analysis (at least of the work, which has mostly inspired the debate, that is *Capitalism, Socialism and Democracy*, 1942). In Schumpeter's writings there is no trace of the claim about the existence of a linear correlation between firm size, or levels of industrial concentration, and innovation performances. Schumpeter's emphasis was rather on the increasing importance in the most advanced economies of large firms or units of control in promoting technical change (see Schumpeter, 1942, ch. 5–8).

14. In both cases the relationship between 'structure' and 'performance' has been conceived in a static perspective. For a review see Kamien and Schwartz, 1982; Baldwin and Scott, 1987; Cohen, 1995.

15. As in the traditional literature on economies of scale in production, and also in the innovation literature, several counteracting forces, which might reduce the innovativeness of large firms and concentrated market structures, have been identified. Among the latter are the negative effects that excessive levels of bureaucratization characterizing large R&D laboratories can have on the researchers' incentives and on the overall efficiency of the research processes. It has also been argued that the lack of competition might weaken the incentive to innovate where it is viable to maintain large margins of profit by simply exploiting market power positions related to more static barriers to entry.

16. The most important data-bank in this connection is the one created by SPRU (Science Policy Research Unit) at the University of Sussex, which includes a sample of significant innovations introduced in Great Britain between 1945 and 1983 (Pavitt et al., 1987). Empirical studies have also been carried out on another data-bank (set up by the US Small Business Administration) concerned with the innovations commercialized and publicized in the technical literature (Acs and Audretsch, 1990).

17. Using data provided by the Federal Trade Commission's Line of Business Program, Scherer (1984b) found a positive relationship between R&D intensity and firm size in only around 20 per cent of the business lines considered, while in a much older work the effect of diversification was found to be highly significant at an aggregate level and disappeared when single industries were taken into account separately (Scherer, 1965). More recently Cohen et al. (1987) found that, once fixed industry effects were included, the size of the firms did not have any effect on R&D intensity despite finding a threshold effect in R&D.

18. The role of such factors had already been found by Scherer (1967) for the relationship between R&D intensity and level of industrial concentration and confirmed by Scott (1984) and Levin et al. (1985). In all these cases the inclusion of dummy variables for different types of industrial technology or classes of product (as proxies for different technological regimes) considerably weakened the explanatory power of industrial concentration.

19. Once again the basic reference model is the one proposed by Nelson and Winter. The results of their simulation show a general long-term trend of industrial concentration to growth as result of innovative (R&D-based) competition with parameters reflecting levels of technological uncertainty, appropriability and opportunity affecting the final level of industrial concentration (Nelson and Winter, 1978, 1982). The authors contend that the evolution of industries that such simulations emulate are consistent with direct empirical observation of the real world.
20. Their model is based on a study of a conspicuous number of innovations in five different industries.

5. Towards an integrated perspective on technological change and industrial structure: issues for research

5.1 ALTERNATIVE PERSPECTIVES ON TECHNO-LOGICAL CHANGE AND THE DISEMBODIED BIAS

In Chapter 1 we argued that, despite the terminological and conceptual fuzziness, which surrounds the labels 'disembodied' and 'embodied' attached to technology and innovation activities, these terms can be used to differentiate two key dimensions of technology and innovative activities. The distinction we have drawn is one between a conceptualization of technology conceived of as a stock of knowledge (or a set of capabilities) as opposed to one in terms of production assets (fixed productive capital). Analogously, innovative activities can be conceptualized either as activities aimed at producing new technological knowledge or as activities consisting of the use of technologies in production through investment in fixed capital (see Figure 5.1). In the previous chapters we have shown that such distinction allows us to draw a line between the major schools of thought in economics and different approaches in the most recent innovation literature.

In general terms, neither of the two different perspectives on technology and innovative activities and their effects on industrial structure can be defined as better or worse. They grasp different aspects (or stages) of such a multidimensional phenomenon as technological change as well as different kinds of effects and determinants of technology and innovation on industrial structure features. Nevertheless these perspectives, if taken separately, remain to some extent partial, not communicating with each other, and therefore unable to grasp the overall dimension of technological activities and their diversified effects on economic reality. This requires us in turn to move towards an integrated perspective on technological change – one encompassing both embodied and disembodied innovation activities.

5.1.1 The 'Disembodied Bias' in the Innovation Literature

The economic analysis of technological change and innovation in recent years seems on the contrary characterized by a shift in the conceptualization of tech-

Innovative Activities

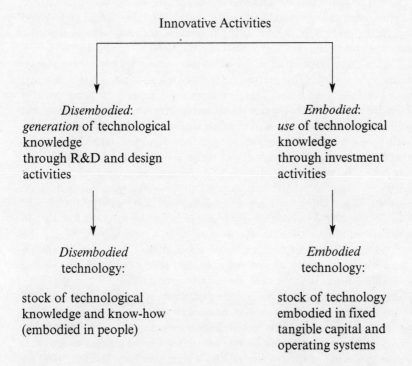

Disembodied:
generation of technological
knowledge
through R&D and design
activities

Embodied:
use of technological
knowledge
through investment
activities

Disembodied
technology:

stock of technological
knowledge and know-how
(embodied in people)

Embodied
technology:

stock of technology
embodied in fixed
tangible capital and
operating systems

Figure 5.1   Embodied and disembodied views on technological change

nological change from an embodied to a disembodied perspective. Such a
process has received a pronounced push with the emergence of the so-called
'economics of technological change' as a new and independent area of
theoretical and empirical research. In this new stream of literature, investments
in fixed productive capital seem to have progressively lost their centrality in
the analysis of technological change, while increasing attention has been given
to innovative activities aimed at producing new technological knowledge. This
has happened as part of a more general perspective emphasizing the increasing
knowledge-based features characterizing modern 'post-industrial' societies.

    The shrinking interest of scholars in embodied technological change was first
reflected in the Schumpeterian emphasis on the increasing importance of
science-based technological advancements and the endogenization of the process
of generation of new knowledge, and has been later reinforced by the neo-
Schumpeterian empirical research. The more recent shift from a macroeconomic
approach to technological change to one emphasizing the firm-specific
dimensions of innovation activities has not changed such a perspective.

There is no doubt that looking into the 'black box' of technological change has represented an important breakthrough in this discipline. It has highlighted the complex and varied nature of the innovative process, which cannot be reduced to a linear and one-way model centred on R&D. It is also true, however, that even in this new perspective the quantitative importance of the innovative activities represented by embodied technological change has remained somewhat in the shadow. This has happened despite it being widely acknowledged that it is the actual use of technology which affects micro- and macroeconomic performances. When the existence of differences in the nature of technological change has been recognized, these have been related to different ways of generating and accumulating knowledge, technological capabilities and know-how. The most common terms and concepts associated with the term 'technology' are 'knowledge' or 'capability', while innovative activities are described as activities of 'learning', 'searching' and 'solving problems'. Investment related to innovative activities and technological diffusion, both in the forms of direct purchasing of equipment and machinery, and the development of internal resources for the application of new technologies on an industrial scale, are not considered as being a central part of the innovative efforts of the firms, with the exception of few contributions.[1]

We have also seen that such a disembodied perspective is clearly reflected in the indicators developed and used to measure technological performances and estimate their economic effects. Technological indicators such as R&D, patents, licences and innovation counts, measuring exclusively the innovative activities aimed at producing new technological knowledge, have been developed and are largely used, whereas equally developed indicators of the innovative efforts consisting of the use and diffusion of these new technologies through investment in new process technologies have not been developed, and are not generally used in empirical analysis to explain innovative or economic behaviours and performances. The recent trend in many countries to design and carry out innovation surveys following the guidelines set by the OECD's 'Oslo Manual' represents a very promising step ahead in this respect. Among the different types of innovation activities, which are covered by the survey, the Oslo Manual also includes those related to 'the acquisition of machinery and equipment with a technological content connected to either product or process innovations introduced by the firm' (OECD, 1992b, p. 32; see also OECD-EUROSTAT, 1997).[2] However the actual use of these data to measure relevance and the economic impact of embodied technological activities has been so far very limited.

5.1.2   The Disembodied Bias in the Analysis of the Relationship between Innovation, Firms' Size and Market Structure

The empirical debate on the relationship between firm size, market structure and innovation has also favoured a disembodied view of technology. Figure 5.2

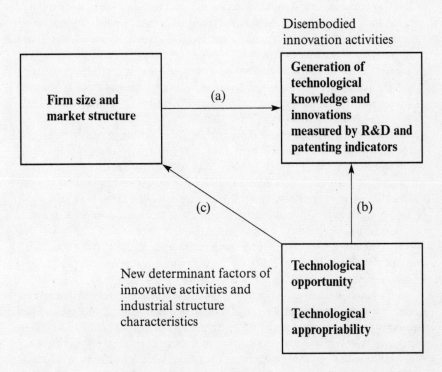

Figure 5.2   Technological change and industrial structure: the neo-Schumpeterian links

synthesizes the main relationships analysed by the innovation literature reviewed in Chapter 4. Most of the empirical works, which have characterized the neo-Schumpeterian debate, have been testing the effect of market structure and firm size on the innovative performance (link (a)). Innovative performance has been defined and conceptualized in a fully disembodied perspective, and measured through R&D, patent activities and innovation counts. We noted in Chapter 4 that the more recent contributions have enriched and integrated such a picture by stressing the role of (sector- and firm-specific) characteristics of technological regimes, mainly differences in technological opportunity, appropriability conditions and knowledge base. These differences have been seen as most fundamental in influencing the nature and levels of innovative activities (link (b)) and the characteristics of the industrial structure (link (c)). However, as pointed out in Chapter 4, these new contributions also continue to maintain a generally disembodied perspective on the nature of technology and innovative activities and their links with industrial structure features. Even when the interplay between firm size, market structure and innovation has been reinterpreted in a truly dynamic Schumpeterian perspective (that is evolutionary contributions), the dominance of a disembodied approach to technology and innovative activities is confirmed. The disequilibrating role of technological change in creating asymmetries among firms, and in shaping the dynamics of market structures, is seen again in terms of R&D strategies and the building up of firm-specific technological capabilities (Nelson and Winter, 1982; Dosi 1982,1984; Malerba and Orsenigo, 1990).

In both neo-Schumpeterian and evolutionary contributions, organizational and productive factors connected to the diffusion of innovations embodied in investments in fixed capital do not have any specific role in determining technological opportunities and appropriability conditions and in influencing the dynamics of industrial structure. Differences between firms and sectors in terms of the nature of production processes, relevance of economies of scale, or static barriers to entry, related to the capital intensity of firms, specific process technologies used and firms' investment patterns, are also not considered as characteristics directly related to the domain of technological change and firms' innovative activities, and as a result they are not taken into account.[3]

In the 'economics of technological change' the production-related dimensions of technology have been progressively considered to be the object of the analysis of another economic discipline, namely industrial economics, where firm (or plant) size and market structure conditions are related (alongside other factors) to sector-specific characteristics in the production sphere, that is technological characteristics underlying firms' production and cost functions which in turn determine the presence and level of indivisibilities in production, economies of scale, barriers to entry (see Chapter 4, section 1).[4] As we have seen in this literature also, the role of technological change is neglected. Although the fact that technology affects the basic industrial structural characteristics in its embodied-productive nature is implicit in most of these analyses, actual attempts to investigate the relationships and regularities, which should be found between such technologically determined conditions of industrial structure and the level and nature of embodied technological activities at firm and industry level, have been rarely carried out.

5.1.3   The Rediscovery of Investment as a Form of Technological Change

In recent years there have been a certain number of contributions, which have rediscovered the importance of embodied technological activities and technological diffusion. Investment seems to have regained a place, for instance, in the new contributions in the 'new growth theory' (Romer, 1990) and in more heterodox approaches such as those proposed by Scott (1989) and Antonelli et al. (1992). In empirical research, as well, investment has been found to play an important role, along with other technological inputs, in the explanation of cross-country differences in growth rates (Dosi et al., 1990; De Long and Summers, 1991; Maddison, 1991; Wolf, 1991, 1994a, 1994b; Amendola et al., 1993; Pianta, 1995; Meliciani, 1998). These studies follow earlier contributions, which had already looked at differences between industrial sectors in terms of the technological sources used by firms. Among the latter the efforts in the improvement of process technologies through R&D and also through investment have been identified as important, in different degrees for different sectors (Pavitt, 1984) and in different stages in the evolution of industries (Utterback and Abernathy, 1975; Abernathy and Utterback, 1978; Gort and Klepper, 1982; Klepper and Graddy, 1990; Klepper and Simons, 1994). The importance of taking into account the diffusion of embodied technologies across firms, sectors and countries has been also pointed out in recent empirical works by the OECD (Papacostantinu et al., 1995).

Yet quantitative and reliable evidence on the actual relative importance of investment as an independent source of technological change, as compared to innovative efforts aiming at producing new technological knowledge, is still lacking. Also the specific impact of embodied technological activities on firms and industry economic performance and their productive structure has been under-investigated. The second part of this book is precisely intended to start filling these gaps.

5.2 EMPIRICAL TARGET OF THE BOOK AND METHODOLOGY

The ultimate target of this book is to show the importance of adopting an integrated perspective on technological change, one acknowledging the role of both disembodied and embodied technological change. In addition this contribution is intended to try to balance the aforementioned 'disembodied bias' that seems to characterize specifically the innovation literature in two broad respects recalled above: (i) in the general conceptualization of technological change and the way it is represented and measured; and (ii) in the way innovation activities are seen as interacting and associated with structural and production features of firms and industries.

The empirical section of this book thus aims at shedding light on the three following issues:

1. the quantitative importance of both disembodied and embodied innovation activities at an aggregate level and across industrial sectors and firm-size classes in both manufacturing and services;

2. the relationships between embodied and disembodied technological change in firms' strategies and sectoral patterns of innovation;
3. the relationships between embodied and disembodied technological change and the other production-related features of industries and firms, namely firm size, the capital intensity of production processes and the presence of economies of scale.

The empirical analysis will use data generated by three different innovation surveys carried out in Italy by the Italian statistical office (ISTAT) in collaboration with the National Research Council of Italy (ISTAT–CNR innovation surveys) and namely:

*   the first ISTAT–CNR innovation survey, which has collected data on innovation activities carried out in the manufacturing sector in the period 1981–85;
*   the second ISTAT–CNR innovation survey (which was part of the Community Innovation Survey (CIS) co-ordinated by EUROSTAT) which has covered innovation activities in the manufacturing sector during the period 1990–92.
*   the most recent ISTAT–CNR innovation survey in the service sector covering the period 1993–95.

As already mentioned innovation surveys provide a very rich range of information regarding firm-level quantitative and qualitative aspects of innovative activities. More particularly firms are asked to indicate the type of innovation introduced (product or process), the type of innovative activities performed, the expenditures sustained for performing such activities, the economic output or impact of the innovations introduced and other more qualitative information regarding the sources of information used, the objectives pursued with innovation and the hampering factors of technological activities. Particularly relevant for the issues we are dealing with in this book are the data on firms' innovation costs. Such costs refer to the expenditures incurred by firms for carrying out activities aiming, on the one hand, at generating, developing and acquiring new technologies in a disembodied form (R&D, design and engineering activities, the acquisition of patents and licences) and, on the other, those consisting in the acquisition and use of technologies embodied in fixed productive capital (innovative investment). The relative importance of product and process innovation in firms' innovation strategies represents another important piece of information provided by innovation surveys, and one able to capture firms' innovation efforts consisting of the use of new production technologies *vis-à-vis* innovation strategies focused on the generation and development of new technologies embodied in new products.

The empirical targets listed above, and the data and methodologies used, are discussed in greater detail below.

a. The quantitative importance of embodied and disembodied technological change

The first empirical target consists of filling the already-mentioned gap present in the literature on the quantitative importance of firms' innovative efforts in the use of new technologies through investment embodied in fixed capital by comparison with more disembodied technological activities.

Data on innovation costs and product/process innovation provided by the ISTAT–CNR surveys will be used to answer the following questions:

1. How much do firms spend on producing technological knowledge compared to what they spend on using it?
2. How and to what extent do firms and sectors differ in the mix (product/process) and amount of innovative activities carried out? What are the major sources of such variance?

Disembodied technological activities will be proxied by firms' expenditure on R&D, design and engineering activities while embodied technological activities will be measured by innovative expenditures on technologically new equipment and machines. In a complementary way, the different propensity towards product and process innovation will be used as a proxy for firms' innovative efforts in producing and using technologies, embodied respectively in new production processes and products.[5]

b. The relationship between embodied and disembodied technological change

The presence of close linkages and feedbacks among the different stages of the innovation process has been much emphasized by several contributions in the recent innovation literature. The linear and R&D-centred representation of the innovation process has been substituted by one envisaging a much more complex and interactive nature of innovative activities as represented by the Kline and Rosenberg 'chain model' (Kline and Rosenberg, 1986). There is, however, little systematic and quantitative evidence on the effective degree of contiguity and complementarity among the different components of the innovative process at firm as well as sectoral level, while we have seen that the relationship between embodied and disembodied innovative activities is not explicitly addressed on a more conceptual basis either.[6] A key aspect investigated in the following chapters will be thus the relationships between the main components of innovative activities, and the way the latter define different innovative patterns along with different propensities towards product versus process innovations. Moreover what we will be looking for is the presence of complementary or substitutive relationships between the different sources of technological change and, in particular, between R&D, design and innovative investment, across firms, industries and more aggregated sectoral groupings.

c. *Innovation and the productive structure of firms and industries: key links and main sectoral patterns*

The third objective of our empirical analysis consists of identifying main patterns of innovation in manufacturing and the way these are linked with the productive structure of firms and industries. The size of firms (business units), the capital intensity of production processes and level of labour productivity will be used as proxies for identifying the presence of scale factors, barriers to entry and increasing returns both in production and innovation activities.

As already mentioned, the relationship between innovation, firm size and market structure has been the object of a large amount of empirical research in the last two decades. We have seen that most of the empirical literature in this field has been hampered by two factors: (i) the exclusive focus on disembodied innovation activities and performances and the omission of investment in fixed capital as source of technological change; and (ii) the difficulty of effectively taking into account industry specificities both in firms' innovative patterns and in the role played by production-related technological determinants of firm size and market structure.

The ISTAT–CNR databases show a comparative advantage in both respects. They look in detail at the variety of innovative patterns in industry and at the ways in which these could be associated with firm size and market structure conditions. By using these data we will be able to jointly take into account the relationships between innovation and industrial structure envisaged in the neo-Schumpeterian literature, explicitly referring to disembodied innovative activities (link (a) in Figure 5.3) and those implicitly considered by the classical and the S-C-P perspective specifically addressing the role of the capital-deepening nature of investment associated with scale factors (link (b)).

The questions, which we will try to answer, can thus be summarized as follows:

1. Is there any systematic relationship between firm size and: (i) the type of innovation activity undertaken (R&D, design and investment); (ii) the type of innovative output generated (product/process), (iii) the overall financial commitment to innovation (total innovation expenditure)?
2. In which industries do these relationships emerge more clearly?

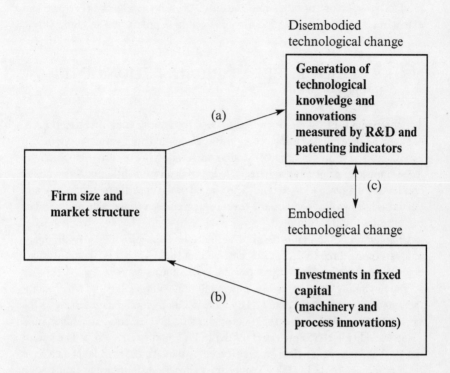

Figure 5.3   Technological change and industrial structure: embodied and disembodied links

3. What is the relative importance of scale factors in R&D and production for explaining differences in firm size across industries?
4. How do R&D, investment and firm size affect labour productivity?

The kind of empirical analysis proposed in this book does not pretend to be exhaustive with respect to all other possible ways in which the relationship between technology, firm size and market structure can be conceptualized and empirically investigated.[7] In particular the data provided by the ISTAT–CNR innovation surveys do not allow us to analyse such a relationship in a dynamic and evolutionary perspective.[8] In other words, we will not be able to empirically test those contributions and models which have identified mechanisms of a more Schumpeterian (evolutionary) flavour governing the interaction between firms' innovation behaviours and the evolution of industrial structures.

The empirical analysis contained in Part Two will focus on those dimensions of technological activities reflecting more permanent determinants of the productive structure of industries and firms, as reflected by the presence and extent of economies of scale and barriers to entry in production and innovation.

5.3   OUTLINE OF THE EMPIRICAL SECTION OF THE BOOK

The three main sets of empirical issues described above (that is subsections a, b, c) will be investigated using descriptive statistics and multivariate econometric estimates. The following chapters, rather than following the order in which the three empirical issues have been listed, address them from different perspectives and levels of aggregation of data. The choice of the specific methodology and database used will depend on the level of aggregation of the data and number of variables jointly examined.

Chapter 6 is essentially descriptive in nature and provides a preliminary analysis of the three ISTAT–CNR data-sets and an overview of the basic characteristics of the innovation process in manufacturing and services.

The remaining chapters use an 'integrated' innovation industrial database for the manufacturing sector obtained by merging innovation data referring to the period 1981–85 with data on sales, employment, investment in machinery and value added (for 1985) provided by the ISTAT industrial survey. The use of the 1981–85 innovation data-set was forced by the fact that firm-level data have been made available by ISTAT only for that period. Furthermore only with respect to the 1981–85 innovation data-set was it possible to make a firm-level merging between innovation and economic data.

Chapter 7 uses 'firm-level data' from our innovation industrial database for an in-depth analysis of firms' innovation strategies, looking more in particular at: (i) the importance of the different components of technological activities in firms' total innovative efforts; (ii) the existence of complementary/substitutive relationships between embodied and disembodied innovative activities and product and process innovation; and (iii) the relationship between innovation, firms' size and labour productivity. In Chapter 8 we establish whether industrial sectors significantly differ in all the technological and productive dimensions covered by our data-set. In Chapter 9 we look into the variety of innovation patterns and productive structure across industries in manufacturing using sectoral average data for 108 industrial sectors. In Chapter 10 a taxonomy, which identifies main sectoral patterns in innovation and technological regimes of production activities, is proposed. Chapter 11 summarizes the main findings of the empirical work contained in Chapters 6–10, and discusses some theoretical and policy implications which can be drawn from the empirical evidence presented.

NOTES

1. We have seen that the exceptions are represented by some contributions in the literature on 'technological diffusion', on 'intersectoral technological flows' and on 'sectoral patterns of innovations'.

2. Even so a certain degree of ambiguity still remains about the extent to which such activities should be regarded as innovation. Firstly, the OECD Oslo Manual fully adopts the Rosenberg–Kline chain innovation model in which embodied technological change does not appear (Kline and Rosenberg, 1986); secondly, the use of new technologies through investment in technologically new machinery and equipment seems to be relegated to the diffusion stage (p. 22). The fact that any innovative process, even the most radical and original one, can require substantial investment in fixed capital for mechanization, application of modern technologies and setting up R&D infrastructures, appears to be underestimated.

3. As pointed out in the previous chapters, Pavitt's taxonomy has represented an important breakthrough in this context (Pavitt, 1984). The identification of different technological trajectories and sectoral patterns of technological change is based on differences in the sources and nature of the innovative activities as well as on structural and more 'production-based' characteristics of firms and industrial sectors.

4. The marginal role given to technology and innovation by the traditional literature in industrial economics is clear when one looks at the theoretical and empirical contributions which have dealt with the characteristics and determinants of the economies of scale and barriers to entry (Chapter 4). Economies of scale have been largely conceived of in a static perspective and changes in the proportion of the productive factors and in the technologies used have usually not been taken into account (Gold, 1981). In the previous chapter we have pointed out that to find an analysis of the relationship between technological change and economies of scale in production in a dynamic perspective we have to go back to the works of Smith (1791), Marx [1894] (1983), Marshall, (1920), Clark (1923), and Robinson [1931] (1958). More recent theoretical investigations of these issues are contained in Morroni (1992) and Scazzieri (1993).

5. The second Italian innovation survey was part of the European Community Innovation Survey (CIS). It has, therefore, adopted a harmonized questionnaire prepared by EUROSTAT. In the CIS questionnaire two additional innovation items have been included in the list of innovation activities included in the first Italian survey: (i) the acquisition of know-how, patents and licences; and (ii) tooling-up and trial production activities. The acquisition of know-how, patents and licences will still be regarded as disembodied technological activity consisting of firms' innovative efforts aiming at acquiring (through external sources) disembodied technological knowledge. Tooling-up and trial production activities are not easily interpretable as embodied or disembodied; however, as it will be shown in Chapter 6, these activities absorb a rather marginal share of total innovation costs.

6. Recent contributions have shown, mainly through cross-country analyses, the presence of a certain degree of complementarity between intangible investment (R&D, training, education) and investment in physical capital. Most of these analyses remain, however, very aggregate in nature and rely upon very crude proxies for intangible and tangible investment (see OECD, 1992a for a review).

7. In the light of the literature reviewed in Chapter 4 two different sets of relationships and approaches can be conceptualized and empirically tested. The first has to do with the interplay between firms' innovation performances and their impact on the evolution of market structures (emerging from selection processes based on firms' innovative behaviours). A second approach adopts a more 'static' view highlighting the ways in which sector-specific innovation patterns are intertwined with the characteristics of products, production processes, markets and demand patterns governing the different industries. The static nature of the data-set used in our empirical analysis is better suited to the second approach.

8. This is due to the fact that the two innovation surveys in the manufacturing sector cannot be used to build a panel data-set.

PART TWO

Evidence from the Italian Industry

6. An overview of innovation activities in manufacturing and services

6.1 INTRODUCTION

The purpose of this chapter is to provide an overview of the basic characteristics of the innovation process in manufacturing and services, as they emerge from a preliminary analysis of the data provided by the ISTAT–CNR innovation surveys. In Chapter 5 we pointed out that, compared to more traditional technological indicators, innovation surveys are able to capture a wider range of quantitative and qualitative aspects of innovation processes. In this chapter the potentialities of the ISTAT-CNR databases will be shown investigating:

1. the actual diffusion of the innovative phenomenon within manufacturing and services;
2. the very nature of the innovation activities undertaken by manufacturing and service firms, in particular distinguishing between: (i) those related to generation and development of technological knowledge and new products; and (ii) those consisting of the use of technologies embodied in new equipment, machinery and production processes;
3. the economic impact of innovation activities on sales, that is the actual percentage of total production, which is affected by innovation through the introduction of new products and processes;
4. a set of more qualitative aspects characterizing firms' innovation strategies.

The chapter is organized as follows: section 6.2 analyses the level of diffusion of innovation activities in Italian manufacturing and services looking at the percentage of innovating firms across main industries and firm size classes. Section 6.3 looks at the relative importance of process and product innovation while section 6.4 quantifies the importance of the different sources of technology looking at the role played by embodied and disembodied technological activities in manufacturing and services. Section 6.5 explores the economic impact of innovation looking at the percentage of sales linked to the introduction of new or improved products and production processes. Section 6.6 looks at the importance of different information sources used by firms for their innovation activities, different objectives pursued with the technological innovation and different factors hampering innovation. The concluding section summarizes the results presented in this chapter.

6.2   THE SPREAD OF INNOVATION IN MANUFACTURING AND SERVICES

Innovation is nowadays regarded as one of the most fundamental factors sustaining firms' competitive strategies and performances. Yet there is little evidence on the actual spread of the innovative phenomenon within the industrial structure. This can be estimated using data provided by innovation surveys and, in particular, looking at the percentage of the firms which have introduced, in a given period of time, a technological innovation: either a product or a process innovation or both. This is the definition of 'innovating firm' used in this and the following chapters.

Table 6.1 shows the total number of firms which have been involved in the second ISTAT–CNR innovation survey in manufacturing and in the most recent one in services, along with the percentage of innovating firms in the two different periods covered by the surveys (1990–92 and 1993–95 respectively). Data are reported for manufacturing and services as a whole and at the level of the main firm size classes within these two sectors.[1]

Table 6.1 shows that both in manufacturing and services, roughly one-third of the firms have introduced at least one technological innovation in the periods 1990–92 and 1993–95. A similar percentage of innovating firms was also found by the first innovation survey in the manufacturing sector and referring to the period 1981–85.[2] In both manufacturing and service sectors the innovative phenomenon involves, however, a much larger portion of the industrial structure: 61.5 per cent of employees of the Italian manufacturing industry in 1992 and 63.7 per cent of employees in services in 1995 were, in fact, concentrated in innovating firms.

Table 6.1 also shows that both in manufacturing and services innovation is a much more widespread phenomenon among large firms than small firms. Only one-fourth of the firms with less than 50 employees in manufacturing have innovated during the period 1990–92 while 84.3 per cent of manufacturing firms with over 1000 employees have innovated in the same period. The same pattern is found in services and a very similar picture was found using data referring to the Italian manufacturing sector in the period 1981–85 (Archibugi et al., 1991). On the whole Table 6.1 shows that a rather strong similarity is found between manufacturing and services in the patterns of diffusion of innovative activities in the industrial structure and in the way it correlates with firm size.

Table 6.1 *Innovating and non-innovating firms in manufacturing and services by firm size*

Classes of employees	Manufacturing firms (1990–92)			Service firms (1993–95)		
	Total firms	% of innovating firms on total firms	% of employees of innovating firms on total firms	Total firms	% of innovating firms on total firms	% of employees of innovating firms on total firms
20–49	15109	25.9	27.5	13934	25.9	26.4
50–99	4142	40.8	41.6	2844	38.6	38.5
100–199	2012	48.0	48.7	1269	43.4	42.8
200–499	1041	58.5	59.8	822	50.9	51.7
500–999	292	74.0	74.5	238	65.1	66.2
1000 and over	191	84.3	91.5	195	79.0	88.8
Total	22787	33.1	61.5	19302	31.0	63.7

Table 6.2 Percentages of innovating firms across firm size in Europe (manufacturing sector, 1992)

Classes of employees	Denmark	Spain	France	Italy	Luxemburg	The Netherlands	Norway	Germany (*)	Ireland (*)	Belgium (*)	Total Europe
20–30	33.8	29.1	28.9	22.4	17.9	40.4	21.9	65.9	63.4	41.8	28.2
31–50	53.9	33.6	33.7	31.9	31.0	53.2	48.8	82.3	76.7	62.4	36.3
51–100	64.5	44.6	43.8	41.0	38.1	69.9	54.8	85.9	80.5	54.3	49.1
101–300	72.8	62.0	48.1	49.9	44.8	78.8	65.8	86.9	79.0	80.6	60.9
301–1000	77.2	81.7	71.7	68.2	75.0	84.3	86.5	94.6	95.0	90.6	80.5
1001 and over	91.3	86.8	84.7	85.2	100.0	94.9	92.9	94.7	88.9	95.5	90.1
Total	65.0	42.2	43.6	33.3	24.8	65.7	40.6	83.2	73.2	67.2	43.4

Note: (*) Countries with low response rates: values likely to be overestimated. See also footnote 9.

Source: Evangelista et al. (1998). Elaboration on CIS database.

A strong positive relationship between firm size and the presence of innovation activities is also found across main European countries, as emerges in Table 6.2, which use data provided by the CIS. The percentage of European manufacturing firms, which have introduced innovations in the period 1990–92, is higher than the one found in Italy, rising up to 53 per cent of the total. This figure, however, is likely to be somewhat overestimated. This is due to the very low response rate obtained in many European countries, which are likely to be associated to samples biased in favour of innovating firms (Evangelista et al., 1998).[3]

The actual spread of the innovative phenomenon changes considerably across industrial manufacturing sectors and services' activities as indicated by Table 6.3. Manufacturing sectors showing the highest percentages of innovating firms (with more than 50 per cent of innovating firms in 1990–92) are aerospace, office machinery, radio, TV and precision instruments. Manufacturing industries showing the lowest percentage of innovating firms are textile, clothing and footwear, wood products, minerals and non-metal products, where more than two-thirds of the firms have not introduced any innovation during 1990–92.

In the service sector the industries showing the highest percentages of innovating firms are (as expected) R&D services, insurance, banking and other financial services with around or above 60 per cent. Conversely, in retail trade, hotels and restaurants, cleaning and security, innovative firms are a minority, between one-tenth and one-fifth of the total.

On the whole, the evidence presented so far confirms that industrial sectors and firm size prove to be important factors for determining the presence of innovation activities within firms and, in particular, that only a minority of small firms are involved in any innovative activity. This kind of evidence, however, does not allow us to test whether large firms are more likely to be innovative independently from the industry in which they operate. Recent contributions have argued that precisely because of the presence of marked sectoral specificities in the levels of technological opportunity and appropriability, the relationship between firm size and innovation studied at the level of the entire manufacturing industry can provide spurious indications regarding the actual importance of the size factor as a determinant of innovation (see Cohen, 1995).

To check whether any sectoral and size 'composition effects' exist we have estimated two logit equations in which the mere presence–absence of the innovative phenomenon (equation 1) and R&D activities (equation 2) in the Italian manufacturing industry in 1990–92 are considered as the independent variables (see Table 6.4). In both equations we used firm size as regressors (measured by the logarithm of the number of employees) and the industrial sector firms belonged to (expressed by 24 sectoral dummies variables). Another two variables were included as controlling factors, namely the geographical location of the firm (identified by five regional dummies) and the fact the firm belongs to an industrial group.[4]

Table 6.3 Innovating and non-innovating firms in manufacturing and service industries

Manufacturing sectors (1990–92)	Total firms (*)	% of innovating firms on total firms
Aerospace	31	67.7
Office machinery	48	64.6
Radio, TV, telecommunications	249	59.8
Precision instruments	435	50.3
Mechanical machinery	2713	48.9
Chemicals	759	48.4
Motor vehicles	445	44.7
Synthetic fibres	31	41.9
Rubber and plastic	866	41.8
Oil	89	39.3
Electrical machinery	989	38.7
Printing and publishing	496	38.3
Paper	732	38.3
Metals	643	37.9
Metal products	2874	33.4
Other transport	272	32.7
Food, drink, tobacco	1501	31.2
Mineral and non-mineral	1486	29.7
Wood	622	28.8
Other manufacturing	1679	26.0
Textile, clothing, footwear	5435	19.5
Total manufacturing	22445	33.3

Service sectors (1993–95)	Total firms (*)	% of innovating firms on total firms
R&D	67	97.0
Insurance	157	63.1
Banking	917	61.8
Other financial	163	61.3
Computing and software	972	54.3
Advertising	137	51.1
Engineering	263	50.2
Technical consultancy	105	41.9
Other business	454	37.4
Wholesale trade	4469	35.0
Shipping/sea transportation	117	33.3
Legal, accounting	540	30.7
Land transportation	1510	29.8
Travel/transport	1201	29.0
Trade/repair of motor vehicles	1319	28.0
Waste disposal	255	27.8
Security	395	25.6
Retail trade	2522	20.1
Hotels and restaurants	2186	19.6
Post and telecommunications	55	10.9
Cleaning	1220	10.5
Total services	19024	31.3

Note: *The differences in the totals between Tables 6.1 and 6.3 are due to the exclusion of sectors with a low number of firms.

Table 6.4   Probability of carrying out innovative activities and R&D (logit estimates) (Italian manufacturing sector, 1990–92)

Dependent variables	Equation 1 presence of innovative activities		Equation 2 presence of R&D activities	
Number of observations	22787		22787	
Concordant	70.0%		77.5%	
Discordant	29.7%		22.1%	
−2 Log L	2774		3725	
Score	2641		3837	
Intercept	−3.972		−6.114	
Belonging to an industrial group	0.166		0.327	
Not belonging to an industrial group	reference		reference	
Log of employees	0.578		0.742	
North-west	0.771		1.361	
North-east	0.454		1.496	
Centre	0.208		1.127	
South	0.067^*		0.612	
Islands	reference		reference	
Office machinery	1.486	(1)	1.927	(1)
Aerospace	1.276	(2)	1.544	(3)
Radio, TV, telecommunications	1.212	(3)	1.578	(2)
Precision instruments	0.962	(4)	1.415	(4)
Mechanical machinery	0.875	(5)	1.219	(5)
Pharmaceuticals	0.71	(6)	1.097	(6)
Rubber and plastic	0.648	(7)	0.637	(10)
Chemicals (excluding pharmaceuticals)	0.584	(8)	0.894	(7)
Motor vehicles	0.579	(9)	0.800	(8)
Printing	0.558	(10)	−0.700	(18)
Paper	0.467	(11)	$−0.221^*$	(21)
Electrical machinery	0.435	(12)	0.776	(9)
Metal products	0.411	(13)	0.262	(13)
Oil	0.324^{**}	(14)	0.572	(12)
Metals	0.296	(15)	0.021^{**}	(16)
Wood	0.203^*	(16)	$−0.130^{**}$	(22)
Other transport	0.17^{**}	(17)	0.254	(14)
Food, drink, tobacco	0.16^*	(18)	$−0.129^{**}$	(23)
Mineral and non-mineral products	0.116^{**}	(19)	0.086^{**}	(15)

continued

Table 6.4   continued

Dependent variables	Equation 1 presence of innovative activities		Equation 2 presence of R&D activities	
Clothing	−0.913	(20)	−1.287	(19)
Leather and footwear	−0.319	(21)	−0.225	(11)
Synthetic fibres	−0.06[**]	(22)	0.599[*]	(20)
Textile	−0.015[**]	(23)	−0.279	(17)
Other manufacturing	reference		reference	

Note: Ranking in brackets.
No[*] = significant at least at 95% level.
[*] = significant only at 90% level.
[**] = not significant at 90% level.

Source: Evangelista et al. 1997.

The coefficients of the different variables represent an estimate of the probability of a firm with given characteristics (size, sector, geographical area, membership of a group) to be innovative or perform R&D. In the case of the dummies' variables the coefficient can be interpreted as a gross index of the relative importance of the characteristic of the firm taken into account by the dummies.

The estimated coefficients indicate that the probability of firms being both innovative and performing R&D increases monotonically with firm size and increases considerably for industrial sectors, which are usually labelled as those characterized by high technological opportunities, namely aerospace, radio, TV and telecommunications, precision instruments, mechanical machinery and pharmaceuticals. These results confirm, therefore, that the industry in which firms are located and firm size are both important factors for explaining the presence of innovation activities.[5] Table 6.4 also shows that the probability of a firm being innovative and able to perform R&D increases if the firm is a member of an industrial group. It is much higher among firms in the north-west and lower in other areas, with a minimum level in the south and Islands. The positive effect of firm size on the probability to introduce innovation should not come as a surprise if one considers large firms are multiples of small production units. However this is less obvious in the case of performing R&D. This is because R&D activities are much more permanent and systematic activities in their very nature.

6.3   PRODUCT AND PROCESS INNOVATION IN MANUFACTURING AND SERVICES

The product/process innovation mix is deemed to be an important dimension of firms' innovation strategies and an area covered by innovation surveys. While product innovations are usually associated with the creation of new markets or with the quality enhancement of existing products, process innovations are introduced for reducing costs, rationalizing or increasing the flexibility and performance of production processes.

Table 6.5   Innovating manufacturing firms by type of innovation introduced

Manufacturing sectors	% of firms introducing product innovation	% of firms introducing process innovation	% of firms introducing product and process innovation
Aerospace	95.2	85.8	81.0
Office machinery	100.0	71.0	71.0
Radio, TV, telecommunications	93.3	75.8	69.1
Precision instruments	91.8	72.1	63.9
Mechanical machinery	92.8	69.8	62.6
Chemicals	91.6	75.5	67.1
Motor vehicles	86.4	82.9	69.3
Rubber and plastic	87.3	87.0	74.3
Oil	74.3	80.0	54.3
Electrical machinery	87.7	78.1	65.8
Printing and publishing	57.5	95.0	52.5
Paper	70.0	90.0	60.0
Metals	69.3	95.9	65.2
Metal products	76.7	87.4	64.1
Other transport	89.1	77.3	66.4
Food, drink, tobacco	70.3	93.6	63.9
Mineral, non-mineral products	71.4	87.3	58.7
Wood	67.6	91.1	58.7
Other manufacturing	84.4	83.8	68.2
Textile, clothing, footwear	71.9	86.0	57.9
Total manufacturing	79.7	83.0	62.7

Table 6.6   Innovating service firms by type of innovation introduced

Service sectors	% of firms introducing service innovation	% of firms introducing process innovation	% of firms introducing process and service innovation	% of firms declaring the distinction not applicable (in any case)
R&D	79.4	94.1	73.5	30.8
Advertising	75.0	75.0	50.0	28.6
Security	71.8	55.3	27.1	14.9
Cleaning	69.4	44.9	14.3	54.7
Shipping/sea transportation	69.0	55.2	24.1	23.1
Banking	68.3	83.7	52.0	22.0
Engineering	67.9	67.9	35.8	19.7
Computing and software	65.4	77.3	42.7	21.0
Land transportation	60.9	62.4	23.3	14.7
Legal, accounting	53.6	78.6	32.1	27.1
Hotels and restaurants	51.9	60.0	11.9	33.9
Retail trade	48.7	62.6	11.3	28.0
Wholesale trade	46.7	76.0	22.7	26.4
Trade/repair of motor vehicles	46.2	68.1	14.3	25.5
Technical consultancy	45.7	85.7	31.4	0.0
Waste disposal	44.3	80.3	24.6	5.6
Insurance	41.8	91.0	32.8	25.3
Travel/transport services	37.1	71.1	8.2	35.6
Other business services	34 9	76.7	11.6	20.6
Other financial services	34.5	100.0	34.5	32.0
Total	53.4	72.6	25.9	25.6

Table 6.5 shows the breakdown of innovating firms in manufacturing as a whole and across main industrial sectors according to the type of innovation introduced during 1990–92. For the manufacturing sector as a whole, the most diffused typology is process innovation, which has been introduced by 83 per cent of innovating firms with no substantial differences across industries: only in the machinery sector is the percentage of firms introducing process innovation below the 70 per cent threshold. Product innovations have been introduced by a slightly smaller percentage of manufacturing firms (79.7 per cent). They are introduced by almost the totality of innovating firms in the

chemical and pharmaceutical industry in the machinery sector and aerospace. The most striking result of Table 6.5 is, however, the joint presence of both process and product innovation in firms innovation strategies in the manufacturing sector.

In services the applicability of the distinction between product and process innovation is more problematic. As indicated by many contributions this is due to the co-terminality between production and consumption, which characterize most service activities (Miles, 1993, 1996).

There is, however, little quantitative and systematic evidence on the actual difficulty faced by service firms in separating product and process innovation. In order to shed some light on this issue, in the Italian innovation survey service firms have been asked to specify the type of innovation introduced (distinguishing between product and process/delivery innovation) and to indicate whether they had introduced innovations for which the distinction between product and process was not applicable. Table 6.6 shows that only one-fourth (25.6 per cent) of innovating firms in the service sector have not been able (in any case) to distinguish between product and process-delivery innovations.[6] For the remaining innovating firms (that is those able to apply the product/process distinction) the introduction of new or improved ways of producing and delivering services represent by far the most common typology of innovation, with 72.6 per cent of the firms indicating they have introduced process innovation. Process innovations are introduced by almost the totality of firms in service sectors as diverse as R&D (94.1 per cent), insurance (91 per cent), banking (83.7 per cent) and technical consultancy (85.7 per cent). Product (service) innovations have been introduced by 53.4 per cent of service firms. It is interesting to note that, compared to the manufacturing sector, innovation strategies in services seem to be more polarized towards either the introduction of product or process innovations: only 25.6 per cent of service firms have introduced both product and process innovations as contrasted with 62.7 per cent found in the manufacturing sector.

6.4   THE SOURCES OF INNOVATION IN INDUSTRY

The multiform nature of innovative activities and their sectoral specificity have been underlined by a vast amount of literature in recent years (Pavitt, 1984; Kline and Rosenberg, 1986; von Hippel, 1988; Archibugi et al., 1991; Evangelista, 1996). As anticipated in Chapter 5, innovation surveys allow us for the first time to actually measure the relative importance of the various technological sources used by manufacturing and service firms through a common yardstick, namely the expenditures sustained by firms for undertaking a wide range of technological activities.

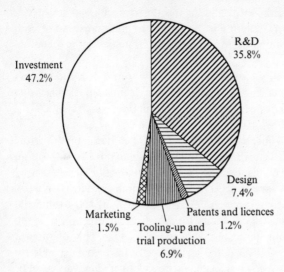

Figure 6.1   Breakdown of innovation costs in the Italian manufacturing sector (1992)

Figure 6.1 shows the breakdown of expenditure incurred by Italian manu-facturing firms in 1992 to introduce innovations. The picture which emerges from the figure is very clear-cut. Industrial innovative processes consist, first and foremost, of the purchase and use of 'embodied' technologies (innovative machinery and plants), which accounts for 47 per cent of total expenditure on innovation, and, secondly, of efforts to generate and develop new knowledge inside firms, as measured by the percentage of innovative spending for R&D activities (35.8 per cent). The other components play a relatively minor role: expenses incurred for design and trial production each account for 7 per cent of total expenditure on innovation, while just 2 per cent and 1.5 per cent of the latter are allocated, respectively, to the purchase of patents and licences and to marketing activities related to the introduction of technological innovations. These data confirm the findings of the first ISTAT–CNR innovation survey. Also, during the period 1981–85, more than half of the firms' total innovation expenditures in the manufacturing sector have been allocated to the acquisition of new machinery and equipment, followed by the activities of design and engineering of new products and processes (25.2 per cent of total innovation costs), R&D expenditures (17.9 per cent) and marketing (5.4 per cent).[7]

Figure 6.2 shows that also in services investment is the most important component of innovation, representing 46.0 per cent of total innovation expenditure, a figure very close to the one found in the manufacturing sector. R&D activities absorb 23.7 per cent of total innovation costs and software

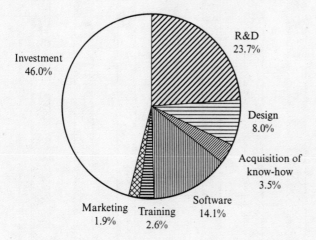

Figure 6.2   Breakdown of innovation costs in the Italian service sector (1995)

activities represent 14.1 per cent of total innovation expenditure. The other components of innovation expenditure (design, acquisition of know-how, training and marketing) play a relatively minor role, covering altogether 16.1 per cent of total innovation expenditure. Despite the fact that the breakdown of innovation costs used in the manufacturing and service questionnaires are not exactly the same, a clear and somewhat unexpected similarity in the overall structure of innovation expenditure can be identified between manufacturing and services. Investment and R&D represent in both sectors more than two-thirds of total innovation expenditures.[8]

The distribution of innovation expenditure shown in Figures 6.1 and 6.2 does not reflect only the distinctive profile of innovation activities in the Italian manufacturing industry – with its accentuated specialization in medium- and low-technology sectors (Archibugi and Pianta, 1992). This is clearly shown in Figure 6.3 which reports the breakdown of innovation costs in the manufacturing sectors of main European countries.[9] The data shown in the figure confirm the following:

1. R&D activities account for no more than one-third of total firms' innovation expenditure in both the manufacturing and service sectors.
2. The largest part of firms' innovation financial efforts, both in manufacturing and services, consists of the adoption and diffusion of technologies embodied in capital goods.

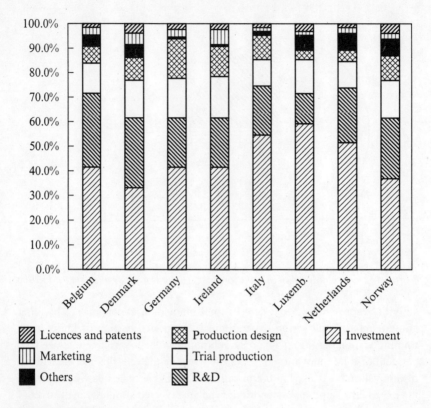

Note: *see footnote 9.

Source: Evangelista et al., 1997.

Figure 6.3   Breakdown of innovation costs across European countries (average values on 8729 innovating firms)*

3. Other innovative activities, such as design, the acquisition of patents, licences and know-how, play a secondary role with respect to the total innovation expenditures (see Evangelista et al., 1998).

The importance of the different sources of innovation in business strategies is strongly influenced by firm size. This is true especially in the manufacturing sector and in relation to the importance of R&D and innovative investment. Small firms in the manufacturing sector show a high propensity to innovate by acquiring machinery and plants against the greater propensity of large firms to internally generate new technologies. Table 6.7, referring to the Italian manufacturing sector, shows that for firms with fewer than 50 employees, R&D

activities accounted (in 1992) for 15 per cent of total innovation expenditure against approximately 47 per cent in the case of firms with more than 1000 employees. Data on investment show an opposite pattern. Innovative investments of firms with less than 200 employees account for more than 50 per cent or more of total innovation expenditures. The other components of innovation also do not appear systematically correlated to firm size. All that emerges is the greater importance of design activities in intermediate size categories, with percentages over 10 per cent of total innovation expenditures in firms with 100–200 and 500–1000 employees. What seems to emerge is, therefore, a sort of division of labour in the innovation process with large firms more concentrated in the process of generation of new knowledge and small firms whose innovative activities consist of using and adopting new vintages of capital. This again is a pattern, which holds across most European countries, as shown in a recent work that has analysed the data provided by the CIS (Evangelista et al., 1998).

Table 6.7   Innovation expenditure by firm size (percentage values) (Italian manufacturing sector, 1992)

Classes of employees	R&D	Patents and licences	Design	Tooling-up and trial production	Marketing	Innovative investment
20–49	14.9	1.5	9.4	7.7	1.9	64.6
50–99	16.3	1.3	8.4	8.5	1.7	63.8
100–199	19.8	1.7	12.8	9.0	2.2	54.5
200–499	27.6	2.2	9.1	9.6	2.2	49.3
500–999	26.0	1.6	13.4	8.1	1.3	49.6
1000 and over	46.7	0.8	4.8	5.7	1.2	40.8
Total	35.8	1.2	7.4	6.9	1.5	47.2

Note: Rows add up to 100%.

This pattern holds also across different types of industry and technological regimes, as shown in Table 6.8, which reports the breakdown of innovation costs across firm size classes within four groups of sectors aggregated according to the Pavitt's taxonomy. In all sectoral grouping R&D emerges as a much more important technological source among large firms than small firms and the opposite applies to investment. It is, nonetheless, interesting to note that in the *science-based* sectors small firms somewhat compensate for their lower R&D

propensity by performing more informal technological activities such as design and engineering.

Table 6.8   Innovation expenditure by industry and firm size (percentage values) (Italian manufacturing sector, 1992)

Classes of employees	R&D	Patents and licences	Design	Tooling-up and trial production	Marketing	Innovative investment
Science-based						
20–99	36.2	2.2	15.5	11.9	2.8	31.3
100–499	45.2	3.4	8.2	8.3	2.9	32.1
500 and over	64.1	2.1	9.0	10.8	1.0	13.0
Total	60.7	2.2	9.2	10.6	1.3	16.0
Scale-intensive						
20–99	10.9	2.(0	6.4	6.4	1.4	72.9
100–499	17.1	2.4	10.8	9.4	1.8	58.4
500 and over	30.3	0.2	3.3	3.0	0.9	62.3
Total	26.2	0.7	4.7	4.3	1.1	62.9
Specialized suppliers						
20–99	25.0	1.0	16.0	12.8	2.7	42.5
100–499	31.5	1.5	140	10.9	2.2	39.9
500 and over	43.5	1.7	16.8	10.6	2.1	25.3
Total	35.4	1.5	15.7	11.2	2.3	33.9
Supplier-dominated						
20–99	11.1	1.0	6.7	6.5	1.6	73.1
100–499	16.4	1.0	8.9	8.7	2.1	62.9
500 and over	44.3	0.3	4.6	3.6	3.2	44.0
Total	25.7	0.7	6.4	5.9	2.4	58.9

Note: Rows add up to 100%.

Table 6.8 also shows the presence of quite differentiated innovative patterns across industries. In *science-based* sectors (which include office machinery, pharmaceuticals, electronic components and apparatus, precision instruments and aerospace), firms allocate on average more than 60 per cent of their innovation costs to R&D while investments absorb a much smaller share of innovation expenditures (16 per cent). *Specialized suppliers'* sectors (which include the bulk of the machinery sectors plus some specialized transport industries) show a more balanced distribution of innovation costs between R&D and investment, each absorbing roughly one-third of total innovation expenditures. Furthermore, in these sectors, the importance of design is much higher than the manufacturing average. *Scale-intensive* sectors (including among others automobiles, metals, chemicals, paper and printing) are clearly characterized by an embodied technological pattern. Two-thirds of total innovation expenditures are allocated in these industries to the acquisition of new machines and equipment. This pattern is also shared by the *supplier-dominated* sectors including textile, clothing and footwear, leather, wood and furniture and food and tobacco. These industries are characterized by allocating few resources to innovation activities, and by concentrating their innovative efforts towards the acquisition of technologies embodied in fixed productive capital.

Marked sectoral differences in innovation patterns are also found in the service sector as shown in Table 6.9. The high heterogeneity, which charac-terizes the services sector, is, in fact, also one of the aspects more emphasized by the very young literature on innovation in services (Miles, 1993, 1996; Evangelista and Sirilli, 1998; Sirilli and Evangelista, 1998). Excluding the somewhat anomalous cases of R&D and engineering service industries (whose economic activities on the whole can be thought of as innovation), service sectors for which R&D plays an important role are post and telecommunica-tions (25.4 per cent) and computer and software (18.3 per cent). Industries that devote substantial shares of their innovation expenditure to software are advertising (62.5 per cent), other financial services (39.2 per cent), trade and repair of motor vehicles (39.1 per cent), banking (36.5 per cent) and insurance (29.0 per cent). Industries innovating mainly through the acquisition of new machinery and equipment are land transportation (93.4 per cent), shipping and sea transportation (89.2 per cent), waste disposal (89.0 per cent) and other business services (73.0 per cent). Overall, investment represents a large chunk of innovation expenditure across most industries. Hotels and restaurants, technical consultancy, advertising, retail trade and post and telecommunications devote above-average shares of innovation expenditure to marketing. Computer and software services, legal and accounting services, and insurance stress the importance of the design component. Innovation expenditures devoted to training show above-average shares in legal and accounting services, cleaning,

Table 6.9 Breakdown of innovation costs by industry in the service sector (1995)

Service sectors	Breakdown of innovation costs (% values)							
	R&D	Design	Know-how	Software	Training	Marketing	Investment	Total
Trade/repair of motor vehicles	2.1	11.0	0.4	39.1	6.1	0.4	40.9	100
Wholesale trade	4.5	3.7	2.1	18.4	3.3	2.3	65.8	100
Retail trade	1.0	4.8	4.3	22.0	2.0	4.8	61.1	100
Hotels and restaurants	2.1	4.8	1.5	25.3	3.2	11.5	51.6	100
Land transportation	1.5	1.1	0.5	2.1	0.5	0.5	93.8	100
Shipping/sea transportation	0.8	3.5	0.5	5.0	0.7	0.5	89.2	100
Travel/transport	4.3	7.1	4.0	19.6	2.6	1.2	61.2	100
Post and telecommunications	25.4	0.6	1.5	5.4	0.0	4.2	63.0	100
Banking	3.3	10.9	8.3	36.5	5.8	1.6	33.6	100
Insurance	9.1	18.5	6.4	29.0	5.2	1.1	30.7	100
Other financial	0.6	10.7	0.3	39.2	2.2	0.3	46.7	100
Computing and software	18.3	32.9	9.1	12.8	4.5	1.8	20.6	100
R&D	83.9	6.7	0.7	1.0	0.9	0.2	6.5	100
Legal, accounting	10.1	21.6	5.6	18.6	13.7	2.0	28.3	100
Engineering	70.6	5.5	3.0	5.8	2.5	0.3	12.3	100
Technical consultancy	53.8	1.8	0.2	6.1	4.6	7.0	26.5	100
Advertising	5.4	8.2	1.9	62.5	1.7	7.0	13.3	100
Security	0.3	0.0	1.2	19.9	3.9	1.0	73.8	100
Cleaning	3.5	1.6	2.7	21.2	9.5	1.1	60.4	100
Other business services	0.0	5.2	4.1	15.7	0.7	1.2	73.0	100
Waste disposal	0.0	5.8	0.0	1.5	2.2	1.4	89.0	100
Total	23.7	8.1	3.5	14.1	2.6	1.9	46.0	100
Manufacturing sector (1992)	36.0	7.0	1.0	(*)	(*)	2.0	47.0	100

Note: (*) Items not included in the questionnaire used for the manufacturing sector.

trade and repair of motor vehicles, banking and insurance. Finally, acquisition of know-how is more important in computing and software, banking, insurance and legal and accounting services.

6.5 THE OUTPUT GENERATED BY INNOVATION

In the previous section we focused on the inputs of innovation activities and more specifically on the nature of innovation activities carried out by manufacturing and services' firms. This is only one way to analyse technological change in industry (the consistency of a variety of innovation indicators is explored in Hollenstein, 1996 and Calvert et al., 1996, using CIS data). Innovation activities can also be measured according to output indicators. The Italian innovation survey and CIS offer a significative indicator of innovation output, namely the part of a firm's total sales due to innovation. This does not measure the economic impact of innovation (such as the productivity-based indices reviewed in Griliches, 1995), but rather it provides direct information on how a firm, an industry or even an economic system as a whole have changed their production output in relation to innovation.

Table 6.10 shows the distribution of total sales in the Italian manufacturing sector in 1992 according to the nature of the innovations introduced broken down by industries.[10] Looking at the Italian manufacturing sector as a whole as much as 62.5 per cent of the sales have not been affected at all by innovation. If we exclude the office machinery sector, where non-innovated turnover accounts for 19.1 per cent only, even in high-technology industries there is a remarkable share of non-innovating sales. The most remarkable result is represented by chemicals and pharmaceuticals, with a share of non-innovating sales which reaches 70 per cent.

The data provided by the ISTAT–CNR innovation survey also allow us to decompose innovative sales between process innovations, incremental product innovations and significantly new products. Also these data (shown in Table 6.10) highlight, first and foremost, the gradual and incremental nature of firms' innovative activities. 18.2 per cent of turnover was innovated by introducing process innovations and 10.7 per cent through the introduction of incremental improvements of pre-existing products. Only the remaining 8.6 per cent of turnover of the Italian manufacturing sector referred to totally new products.

A further qualification of the quality of innovations can be assessed by taking into account the degree of novelty of the products introduced. The results are reported in Table 6.11 which shows the percentages of the total sales of the Italian manufacturing industry in 1992 related to the introduction of new products distinguishing between those which are: (i) new for the firm; (ii) new for the Italian market; and (iii) new in absolute terms. Again the figures in the

Evidence from the Italian industry

Table 6.10   Distribution of total sales according to the type of innovation introduced (percentage values)* (Italian manufacturing sector, 1992)

Industrial sectors	not innovated	% of sales innovated by process innovations	innovated by incremental product innovations	innovated by significantly new products	Total sales
Office machinery	19.1	7.9	16.4	56.6	100
Electrical machinery	50.9	13.6	20.3	15.2	100
Radio, TV, telecommunications	43.2	20.4	23.0	13.4	100
Aerospace	37.7	24.7	12.6	25.0	100
Chemicals (excluding pharmaceuticals)	69.2	12.9	11.4	6.5	100
Pharmaceuticals	70.1	8.5	8.7	12.7	100
Synthetic fibres	58.3	13.5	19.4	8.9	100
Mechanical machinery	56.7	11.9	19.0	12.4	100
Precision instruments	57.9	9.4	18.6	14.1	100
Motor vehicles	53.4	7.4	24.6	14.6	100
Other transport	41.3	19.5	23.2	16.1	100
Rubber and plastic	64.1	15.0	13.2	7.7	100
Metals	53.3	37.9	6.0	2.8	100
Printing and publishing	63.1	28.2	3.6	5.1	100
Paper	69.7	15.2	9.7	5.4	100
Food, drink, tobacco	78.3	13.0	5.8	2.9	100
Textile	74.9	13.2	6.7	5.3	100
Clothing	86.5	8.7	2.6	2.3	100
Leather and footwear	82.1	7.1	4.8	6.0	100
Wood	84.4	9.2	3.0	3.4	100
Metal products	73.0	14.6	6.9	5.5	100
Mineral/non-mineral products	77.2	11.5	7.0	4.3	100
Other manufacturing	73.9	11.7	8.0	6.4	100
Oil	63.4	18.3	10.2	8.0	100
Total	62.5	18.2	10.7	8.6	100

Note: (*) including the sales of non-innovating as well as innovating firms.

Source: Evangelista et al. (1997).

table show that it is a very small fraction of economic output which is affected by technological activities. For the Italian manufacturing sector as a whole sales linked to the introduction of products which are new in absolute terms represent only 1.2 per cent of total manufacturing sales in 1992, while products which are new for the Italian market, or new only for the firm, represent 3.8 per cent and 3.6 per cent of total Italian manufacturing turnover. The incremental nature of technological change seems a feature which characterizes not only traditional

Table 6.11   Sales according to the degree of novelty of the product innovations introduced (percentage values)* (Italian manufacturing sector, 1992)

Industrial sectors	New for the firm	New for the Italian market	New in absolute terms
Office machinery	17.2	24.0	15.5
Electrical machinery	5.5	8.5	1.2
Radio, TV, telecommunications	8.7	2.8	1.9
Aerospace	2.3	15.7	7.0
Chemicals (excluding pharmaceuticals)	4.1	2.3	0.2
Pharmaceuticals	4.9	5.1	2.7
Synthetic fibres	5.0	3.6	0.2
Mechanical machinery	6.2	2.9	3.3
Precision instruments	8.6	3.0	2.5
Motor vehicles	1.5	9.3	3.8
Other transport	6.1	7.6	2.4
Rubber and plastic	3.7	2.2	1.8
Metals	1.0	1.6	0.2
Printing and publishing	2.9	1.8	0.5
Paper	4.2	1.0	0.2
Food, drink, tobacco	1.6	1.2	0.1
Textile	2.6	1.4	1.3
Clothing	1.3	0.5	0.5
Leather and footwear	2.3	1.4	2.3
Wood	1.8	1.4	0.2
Metal products	3.1	1.4	1.0
Mineral and non-mineral products	2.6	0.9	0.7
Other manufacturing	3.8	1.7	1.0
Oil	4.1	3.1	0.7
Total	3.6	3.8	1.2

Note: (*) Including the sales of non-innovating as well as innovating firms.

Source: Evangelista et al. (1997).

industries but also some of the most typical science-based sectors such as radio, TV and telecommunications and chemicals. Equally rather low shares are found in specialized industries such as mechanical machinery and precision instruments. The little impact that innovation has on firms' output might reflect the relatively backwardness of the Italian productive system also in industrial sectors characterized by high technological opportunities.[11] However we believe that first and foremost such results suggest that the pace of technological change in an economic system is probably slower than generally believed. This is confirmed by Calvert et al. (1996), who, after using the CIS data-set, also found a rather limited impact of innovation on output in the main European countries.

6.6   SOURCES OF INFORMATION, OBJECTIVES AND HAMPERING FACTORS TO INNOVATION

Finally, in this section we look at a set of more qualitative aspects of firms' innovation strategies, that is at the importance attached by manufacturing firms to different sources of technological information (Table 6.12) at different

Table 6.12   Sources of technological information in manufacturing and services

Sources	Innovating firms for which the source is very important	
	% of total innovating firms in manufacturing	% of total innovating firms in services
Internal sources: (Production/delivery, R&D, marketing department)	62.6 (1)	36.7 (1)
External sources:		
Clients or customers	44.4 (2)	33.7 (2)
Suppliers of equipment and components	36.0 (3)	30.2 (3)
Fairs and exhibitions	32.7 (4)	13.7 (7)
Competitors	23.3 (5)	21.1 (5)
Consultancy firms	15.1 (6)	26.9 (4)
Conferences, seminars, spec. journals, etc.	13.1 (7)	17.4 (6)
Universities and higher educational institutes	4.1 (8)	3.7 (8)
Private research institutes	4.0 (9)	2.3 (10)
Public research institutes (excluding universities)	2.7 (10)	2.3 (10)
Other external sources	2.5 (11)	8.3 (8)
Agencies for technological transfer	2.3 (12)	–
Patents, licences etc.	2.1 (13)	5.1 (9)

Note: Ranking in brackets.

objectives of innovation activities (Table 6.13) and different obstacles (Table 6.14) linked to the introduction of innovation. Firms were asked to attach to each specific factor a score equal to O (in case the factor was deemed not to be relevant at all) or, if perceived as relevant, a score between 1 to 4 according to its degree of importance (that is from 1: of little importance, to 4: crucial). Tables 6.12, 6.13 and 6.14 show the percentages of firms, which have indicated the factors listed in the tables as 'very important' (that is scores 3 or 4). The last columns in the tables show the importance of the same factors (where applicable) for service firms in the period 1993–95. This allows us to make a comparison of the importance of different information sources, objectives and obstacles to innovation in services and manufacturing.

Table 6.13 Objectives of innovation in manufacturing and services

	Innovating firms for which the objective is very important			
Objectives	% of total innovating firms in manufacturing		% of total innovating firms in services	
Improving service quality	86.2	(1)	76.1	(1)
Increasing or maintaining market share	81.2	(2)	59.5	(2)
Reducing production run	68.6	(3)	–	
Lower production costs	66.0	(4)	47.4	(4)
Improving working conditions	60.3	(5)	42.6	(5)
Improving production flexibility	60.2	(6)	39.1	(6)
Extending the service range	54.1	(7)	48.1	(3)
Reducing environmentally impact	40.1	(8)	11.0	(7)
Other objectives	5.8	(9)	6.8	(8)

Note: Ranking in brackets.

Table 6.14 Obstacles to innovation in manufacturing and services

	Innovating firms for which the obstacle is very important[*]			
Obstacles	% of total innovating firms in manufacturing		% of total innovating firms in services	
Innovation costs too high	41.5	(1)	21.9	(2)
Lack of appropriate sources of finance	41.4	(2)	22.9	(1)
Pay-off period of innovation too long	35.1	(3)	13.9	(3)

continued

Table 6.14 continued

Obstacles	Innovating firms for which the obstacle is very important[*]	
	% of total innovating firms in manufacturing	% of total innovating firms in services
Constraints due to legislation, norms and standards	22.8 (4)	12.6 (4)
Lack of co-operation with other firms	16.2 (5)	–
Risk of being imitated by competitors	15.1 (6)	2.2 (15)
Lack of skilled personnel	14.0 (7)	11.6 (5)
Uncertainty on the timing of innovation	13.4 (8)	–
Perceived risk too high	13.3 (9)	7 3 (10)
Innovation costs hard to control	12.9 (10)	8.6 (9)
Lack of information on markets	12.6 (11)	5.9 (12)
Lack of appropriate external technical services	12.2 (12)	5.6 (13)
Lack of customer's response	11.6 (13)	10.6 (6)
Innovation potential (R&D, design, etc.) insufficient	10.8 (14)	9.9 (7)
Resistance to change within the firm	9.9 (15)	9.7 (8)
Lack of information on technologies	8.9 (16)	6.7 (11)
Lack of technological opportunities	7.0 (17)	5.4 (14)

Note: Ranking in brackets.
[*]Both innovating and non-innovating firms have been taken into account.

6.6.1 Sources of Information for Innovation

Table 6.12 shows that internal sources such as production and delivery departments of firms are the most important channels through which manufacturing firms get technological information. In particular 62.6 per cent of innovating firms in the manufacturing sector have indicated the internal sources as 'very important'. Among the external sources clients and customers and suppliers of equipment, materials and components are mentioned as 'very important' information sources by more then 30 per cent of the firms. Research institutes (both public and private ones) and patents and licences play, on the contrary, a marginal role being perceived as 'very important' sources of information by a minority of manufacturing firms.

Internal sources are confirmed to be very important also in the service sector.[12] The same holds true for clients and customers and suppliers of equipment, material and components. Private and public research institutes play a very marginal role as providers of technological information to firms also in the service sector. On the whole data presented in Table 6.12 suggest that both in manufacturing and services the most relevant technological information are either generated through processes of 'learning by doing' (especially taking place within the production/delivery departments) or acquired from external sources through both upstream and downstream user-producer interactions. It is also interesting to note that clients and customers rank very high, both in manufacturing and in services, suggesting that information flows generated through user-producer interaction represent an important technological source, both in services and manufacturing.

6.6.2 Objectives of the Innovations

Table 6.13 shows the importance attached by manufacturing firms to different objectives pursued with the introduction of innovation. Improving the quality of the products and increasing or maintaining market shares emerge as the most important objectives pursued by manufacturing firms introducing technological innovations: more than 80 per cent of firms indicate such objectives as 'very important'. Also reducing production costs is an important objective in firms' innovation strategies as indicated by the high percentage of firms indicating such an objective as 'very important' (60 per cent of innovating firms in manufacturing). Overall, however, innovation activities in manufacturing appear to pursue a variety of objectives at the same time.

Table 6.13 also shows that firms in both manufacturing and services pursue the same kind of innovation strategies. In both sectors the most important objectives of innovation are the improvement of the quality of products, the increase of market share and the reduction of production costs.

6.6.3 Obstacles to Innovation

Table 6.14 investigates the importance of different factors, which hamper or hinder the introduction of innovations in firms. The table clearly shows that economic factors are considered the most important hampering factors to innovation. In particular, for more than 40 per cent of manufacturing firms the lack of appropriate sources of finance and the high costs of innovation are regarded as a very important obstacles to the introduction of innovation. The presence of overlong pay-off periods of innovation are regarded as 'very important' obstacles by 35.1 per cent of manufacturing firms. It is interesting to note that the constraints due to legislation, norms regulation and standards emerge as the fourth most important hampering factors. Conversely factors linked to the lack of information, technological opportunities and appropriability conditions, very much emphasized in the most recent literature, are not regarded as 'very important' in almost all manufacturing firms. The importance of economic and financial obstacles to innovation is confirmed also among service firms.

6.7   CONCLUSIONS

The descriptive analysis carried out in this chapter has shed some light on a variety of important dimensions of firms' technological activities in manufacturing and services. These can be summarized as follows:

- Innovation is a phenomenon that affects only a part of the economic system. Roughly one-third of Italian firms have introduced at least one technological innovation in the periods 1981–85, 1990–92 and 1993–95. In particular only a very small fraction of small firms are involved in innovation activities. This is a pattern that holds across most European countries, and both in manufacturing and services. Data on innovation output have shown the very cumulative nature of technical progress. Over a three-year period, the percentages of sales linked to the introduction of new products represent only a small portion of total turnover, both at the level of the manufacturing industry as a whole and also in industries characterized by high technological opportunities.
- Both in manufacturing and services the majority of firms innovate through the introduction of process innovations. Product and process innovations are, however, strongly.interlinked in firms' innovation strategies.
- Firms rely on a variegated range of innovation sources. Although R&D represents an important technological source, and is the single most important disembodied source of innovation, it absorbs just above one-third of total innovation expenditures. The largest part of firms' innovation financial efforts is linked to the adoption and diffusion of technologies embodied in capital goods.
- When introducing innovations, manufacturing and service firms use various sources of information. Technological information is drawn mainly from in-house production/delivery departments, clients and customers and outside suppliers of equipment, materials and components. Public and private research institutions, as well as patents and licences, play a very marginal role both in manufacturing and services.
- Both in manufacturing and services the most important objectives of firms' innovation strategies consist of improving the quality of products and services, increasing market shares and reducing production costs. The

most important obstacles to introducing innovation faced by firms are of an economic nature – heavy costs and too high risks.

NOTES

1. The second ISTAT–CNR innovation survey has covered all Italian manufacturing firms with more then 19 employees. For the most recent survey in the service sector a stratified random sample of 6005 firms drawn from a population of 19 300 firms has been used. The figures for the service sector reported in the tables contained in this chapter are those obtained after reproportioning the data of the stratified sample to all the population of Italian service firms.
2. It should be noted that the first and second ISTAT–CNR innovation surveys in the manufacturing sector are not directly comparable. The first innovation survey has been carried out in two stages: in the first stage a very simple and short questionnaire was sent to all the population of Italian manufacturing firms with more than 19 employees. In the second stage a much longer and quantitative questionnaire, very similar to the ones used in the following surveys, has been sent only to the firms which, on the basis of the first screening, resulted in being innovative. The use of this second questionnaire has led to a reduction in the number of innovating firms, which dropped from 16 701 to 8220 firms, a figure which is very close to the one found with the second ISTAT–CNR innovation survey.
3. An analysis of the CIS data-set has shown a clear negative correlation between response rates and percentage of innovating firms across countries (STEP-ISRDS, 1996).
4. In the two logit equations estimated, the dependent variables are either equal to 1, if the firm has introduced innovation in the period 1990–92 (equation 1) or performed R&D (equation 2), or 0 if it has not. In both equations the total sample included in the survey has been taken into account.
5. The value of the Concordant test is similar to that of R^2 in a standard regression. Both regressions show an acceptable capacity to interpret the phenomenon. Firms' behaviour is predicted by the model in 70 per cent of the cases in equation 1 and 77.5 per cent of cases in equation 2.
6. 8 per cent of the firms have introduced a product and/or a process innovation and at the same time have indicated that it is difficult to apply such a distinction for some of the innovations introduced.
7. In comparing the results of the first and second innovation survey in manufacturing it is quite surprising to see the difference in the relative importance played by design activities. This might be explained by the larger set of innovation items taken into account by the most recent innovation survey, which has included activities such as 'trial production' and the 'acquisition of know-how'. It is likely that in the first survey the latter activities were captured by the design item.
8. If the somewhat anomalous case of the R&D services is excluded, the role of investment becomes even more important, rising to 53 per cent of total innovation expenditures in the service sector while the R&D component shrinks to 13.7 per cent of the total.
9. In Table 6.2 and Figure 6.3 'micro-aggregations' of the original data carried out by EUROSTAT have been used. This was done in order to protect confidentiality. The results represent, however, a very accurate estimation of the 'true' values, which will be later produced by EUROSTAT. Estimations on the percentage of innovating firms in Europe shown in Table 6.2 have been computed using the raising factors (weights) provided by EUROSTAT in order to reproportionate the national samples to the populations from which the samples have been drawn. The above procedure has not been used for the analysis of the data on innovation costs shown in Figure 6.3 because of the large number of missing values in the relevant questionnaire section. The reproportioning to the statistical population would have yielded highly distorted estimates. The average values reported in Figure 6.3 are, therefore, calculated summing up the percentages of the manufacturing firms that in each country have filled out the innovation cost section of the questionnaire. This implies that all

firms have been attributed the same weight. A more detailed analysis of the Community Innovation Survey and data on innovation costs is contained in Evangelista et al., 1998.

10. The corresponding figures for the service sector are not available. This is due to the large percentage of service firms (more than 50 per cent of the total), which have not been able to provide a figure on the impact of innovation on sales.

11. For a comparison at the industry level of inputs and outputs innovative indicators see Sterlacchini, 1996.

12. The questionnaire used for the service sector identifies different kinds of internal information source. The most important information sources indicated by service firms have been the production and delivery departments. The other internal sources, that is R&D, marketing and other internal sources, have been perceived by service firms as less important.

7. Embodied and disembodied innovation strategies and the production structure of firms

7.1 INTRODUCTION

Chapter 6 described the basic dimensions of innovation processes in manufacturing and services.

This chapter begins with a more in-depth analysis of the multivariate universe of firms' innovation activities in manufacturing, also exploring how innovation strategies of firms relate to their productive structure and performance. Moreover in particular, the analysis aims at investigating the existence of systematic relationships *within* and *between* two sets of indicators, that is those reflecting firms' embodied and disembodied innovative activities as well as product and process innovations, and the three additional productive indicators drawn from the ISTAT industrial survey: the size of production units, the capital intensity of production processes and labour productivity. In this chapter the data will not be aggregated to any level.

As already mentioned in Chapter 5 the joint examination of innovation- and production-related variables at the firm-level obliges us to use the innovation data referring to the period 1981–85. The next section describes the characteristics of this integrated database along with the technological and production-related indicators, which will be used in this and the following chapters.

Section 7.3 investigates how the overall innovative efforts of firms are related to different innovative strategies aiming at generating new technological knowledge or using such knowledge through investment in fixed productive capital. The issue regarding the complementary or substitutive nature of disembodied and embodied technological activities is also explored. Section 7.3 thus addresses the following issues:

• Is total firms' innovative intensity associated with any particular technological source and product/process innovation mix?

Or in other words:

- Do the most innovative firms show any particular pattern in terms of the importance played by R&D, design activities and investment as well as in terms of the importance of product and process innovations?
- Are R&D and design activities complementary or substitutive with respect to innovative investment?

Section 7.4 investigates in what ways firms' innovative activities are associated with firm size, the capital intensity of production processes and level of labour productivity. Section 7.5 synthesizes the main patterns in innovation strategies and production structures applying a factor analysis to the complete set of indicators of our database while section 7.6 summarizes the main empirical findings of this chapter.

7.2   CHARACTERISTICS OF THE INTEGRATED ISTAT–CNR DATABASE

In order to build an integrated data-set comprising both technological and production related variables, innovation data on 8220 manufacturing firms referring to the period 1981–85 have been matched with those on sales, employment, fixed investment and value added drawn from the Istat 1985 Gross Industrial Product survey.

The matching of the two sets of data led to a loss of almost 1000 innovating firms, which were not present in both databases, so that 6839 firms in all were matched. Further cleaning of the data-set led to the dropping of five more firms.[1]

The final data-set thus consists of data on 6833 innovative firms.[2] Table 7.1 provides the list and the description of the technological and production-related indicators used in the empirical analysis carried out in this and the following chapters.

Production indicators are those built using data drawn from the Italian Industrial Survey and refer to year 1985. They are intended to measure basic characteristics of production activities. These are: (i) the size of the production units (as measured by the sales and number of employees); (ii) the level of investment in machinery and equipment per employee (used as a proxy for the capital intensity and level of mechanization of production processes); and (iii) the value added per employee (used as a proxy for labour productivity).

Innovation indicators are those measuring the *intensity* and *composition* of technological activities carried out by Italian manufacturing firms in the period 1981–85. They have in turn been grouped into two categories:

Table 7.1   List of production and innovative indicators used in the empirical analysis

Type of indicator	Label	Description	Used as a proxy for:
Production indicators	SALES	Sales	Firm size
	INVMAC	Investment in machinery per employee	Capital intensity of production
	VA	Value added per employee	Labour productivity
Innovative intensity indicators	INCOST (*)	Total innovation costs per employee	Total innovative intensity
disembodied	R&D	R&D expenditure per employee	
	D&E	Design and engineering expenditure per employee	Disembodied innovative intensity
	RD&DE	R&D and D&E	
embodied	INV	Innovative investment expenditure per employee	Embodied innovative intensity
	MKT	Innovative expenditure per employee in marketing***	
Innovative composition indicators**			
disembodied	%R&D	% of R&D expenditures in total innovation costs	Relative importance of disembodied
	%D&E	% of D&E expenditures in total innovation costs	technological activities
embodied	%INV	% of innovative investment in total innovation costs	Relative importance of embodied technological activities
	%MKT	% of innovative expenditure in marketing in total innovation costs	
product	%PROD	% of product innovations in total innovations introduced	Relative importance of product innovations
process	%PROC	% of process innovations in total innovations introduced	Relative importance of process innovations

Notes: * R&D + D&E + INV + MKT = INCOST.
**%R&D + %D&E + %INV + %MKT = 100%; %PROD + %PROC = 100%.
*** This cost item includes only marketing expenditure linked to innovation.

Innovative intensity indicators measure the *intensity* of innovative activities and are constructed as the ratios between the different innovation expenditures (total innovation costs, R&D, design, innovative investment and marketing[3]) and the number of employees in a manner similar to the 'capital intensity indicator' described above. These indicators can thus be read as the amount of resources that firms have spent for each employee to carry out different types of technological activities.

Innovative composition indicators measure the *internal composition* of technological activities and are constructed as the shares of different innovation expenditures to total innovation costs. The *product/process innovation propensity* of firms is proxied by the shares of product and process innovations, that is the number of product and process innovations divided by the total number of innovations introduced. The sum of the shares of different innovation components is equal to 100 per cent.

The distinction between intensity and composition indicators described above allows us to differentiate between quantitative measures of embodied innovative efforts and quantitative measures of the disembodied/embodied *innovation mix* (the relative weight of the different innovative components), independently of the amount of resources spent on the two major components of innovation activities.

As in Chapter 6, the technological indicators built from R&D and design expenditures will measure the *disembodied* components of firms' innovative activities. This is consistent with the definitions of disembodied and embodied innovation activities put forward in Chapter 1. Conversely embodied innovative activities will be measured by investment linked to the acquisition of (technologically) new process technologies.[4]

In the econometric estimates carried out in this and the following chapters log-transformed values have been used in the case of all *innovative-intensity* and *production-related* indicators. This is justified by the (almost) log-normal distribution of these two sets of indicators.

7.3   PATTERNS OF INNOVATION IN FIRMS

7.3.1   Intensity, Sources and Output of Firms' Innovation Activities

In this section we start to analyse whether the extent of firms' involvement in innovation is linked to any particular technological source and product/process innovation mix.

Table 7.2 shows the correlation matrix between total innovation costs per employee (INCOST) and firms' expenditures on R&D, design, investment and marketing (again per employee). Log-transformed values have been used in the case of the innovative-intensity indicators due to the (almost) log-normal distributions of such indicators. The elasticity coefficients between the different innovation expenditure items and total innovation costs have also been reported (in brackets).[5]

Table 7.2   *Total innovation costs and embodied and disembodied innovation expenditures (correlation and elasticity coefficients)*

| | Full sample (6833 firms) | | | |
	R&D (log)	D&E (log)	INV (log)	MKT (log)
INCOST (log)	0.413 (0.201) P = 0.000	0.493 (0.293) P = 0.000	0.869 (0.846) P = 0.000	0.393 (0.118) P = 0.000

Note: The first row shows the correlation coefficients and the third row the statistical significance. Elasticity coefficients are shown in brackets.

An analysis of correlation coefficients in Table 7.2 shows that investment represents the innovation component more strongly associated to firms' total technological efforts. The correlation coefficient between embodied innovative expenditures (INV) and total innovation costs INCOST, equal to 0.87, is by far the highest among those reported in the correlation matrix. Firms' expenditure on R&D, design and marketing show much weaker links with firms' total innovative expenditures per employee, with coefficients of 0.41, 0.49 and 0.39. Elasticity coefficients confirm the greater responsiveness of investment with respect to total firms' innovative efforts.

The stronger association between innovative investment and total innovation costs is, however, partly due to the fact that a large portion of firms in the dataset do not carry out any R&D or design activity. This is confirmed by Table 7.3, which reports, for the aggregate sample and broken down by firm size, the percentages of firms carrying out each of the four different types of innovative activities covered by the survey. In particular the table shows that R&D is performed by only 33 per cent of total innovating firms, while firms carrying out design and engineering activities represent 57 per cent of the total. This contrasts with the much more diffused use of innovative investment as a technological source, with 93 per cent of firms declaring that they have innovated through investment. Table 7.3 also shows that most of the firms not performing any disembodied technological activity are small in size. In particular, among the firms with less than 50 employees, only 24 per cent carry out R&D activities as against nearly 60 per cent of the firms in the highest firm size class. No differences across firm size classes emerge with respect to innovative investment, which confirms this as being an innovative source widely used across firms of different sizes.

Table 7.3   Distribution of firms according to the type of technological activity performed across firm size classes (1981–85)

Firm size Number of employees	Number of firms	R&D	% of firms performing		
			Design and engineering	Investment	Marketing
0–49	3018	24.8	49.5	92.1	29.9
50–99	1594	32.9	55.3	93.9	36.0
100–199	1071	36.3	61.4	93.6	38.1
200–499	725	47.9	69.2	96.0	44.0
500 and above	425	59.1	84.7	94.1	53.6
Total manufacturing	6833	32.8	57.0	93.3	35.6

In the light of the characteristics of the database described above, correlation and elasticity coefficients between total innovation costs and the different types of innovation expenditure have been computed taking into account the sub-sample of firms performing both R&D and design activities: in other words firms innovating only through the acquisition of new machinery and equipment have been excluded. It should also be noted that the average innovative intensity of the group of R&D and design-performing firms is much higher than the rest of the sample. The new estimates are reported in Table 7.4. Even taking into account this selected sample of more innovative firms, innovative investment in new machinery and equipment continue to be the innovation component more closely linked to total firms' innovation efforts. Also R&D and design expenditures become more strongly associated with total firms' innovation expenditures. On the whole Tables 7.3 and 7.4 show that firms which are more innovative use in a complementary way a wider range of technological sources to innovate.

Table 7.5 allows us to verify how firms' innovation expenditures are associated with the propensity of firms to introduce process and product innovations. It is interesting to note first of all that total innovation expenditures per employee (INCOST) are associated with larger shares of process innovations (and therefore smaller shares of product innovations). Even if the correlation coefficient between these two variables is quite low, the result is nonetheless surprising. This finding contrasts, in fact, with the general view according to which high innovative profiles are usually associated with product-oriented strategies.[6] The negative relationship between innovation-intensity and the propensity of firms to introduce product innovations might, however, reflect the large presence of small firms in our data-set. It has been shown in Chapter 6 that being innovative for such firms means by and large introducing process innovation embodied in new capital equipment.[7]

Table 7.4   Total innovation costs and embodied and disembodied innovation expenditures (correlation and elasticity coefficients)

	R&D and D&E performing firms (1738 firms)			
	R&D (log)	D&E (log)	INV (log)	MKT (log)
INCOST (log)	0.760 (0.488) P = 0.000	0.748 (0.453) P = 0.000	0.836 (0.728) P = 0.000	0.566 (0.211) P = 0.000

Note: The first row shows the correlation coefficients and the third row the statistical significance. Elasticity coefficients are shown in brackets.

Table 7.5   Embodied and disembodied innovative intensity indicators and product/process innovation shares (correlation coefficients)

	INCOST (log)	R&D (log)	D&E (log)	INV (log)	MKT (log)
%PROD	−0.096 P = 0.000	0.175 P = 0.000	0.228 P = 0.000	−0.255 P = 0.000.	−0.152 P = 0.000
%PROC	0.096 P = 0.000	−0.175 P = 0.000	−0.228 P = 0.000	0.255 P = 0.000.	0.152 P = 0.000

Note: The first row shows the correlation coefficients and the second row the statistical significance.

The other correlation coefficients reported in Table 7.5 confirm this hypothesis: once total innovation costs are broken down into their four innovation components, a more varied picture emerges. A negative association between the various innovative intensity indicators and the share of product innovations is confirmed only in the case of innovative investment (−0.25), which measures firms' innovative efforts in using new technologies through investment in fixed capital. R&D and design expenditures per employee are, on the contrary, positively associated with product innovations.

7.3.2   The Relationships Between Embodied and Disembodied Innovation Activities

In the previous section we have been shown that firms' innovation efforts are linked first of all to the acquisition of technologies embodied in fixed capital. It remains for us to clarify whether disembodied and embodied technological activities are complements or substitutes in firms' innovation strategies. These relationships will again be investigated looking at the log-linear correlations and elasticity coefficients among the different innovation indicators contained in our data-set.

Table 7.6a shows the correlation matrix between embodied and disembodied innovation expenditure per employee using the full sample of firms.

The highest correlation coefficient in Table 7.6a is the one between R&D and marketing expenditures. This shows that high R&D-intensity firms also devote consistent resources to market research associated with the development and launching of new products. On more interpretative grounds, this result suggests that marketing activities represent a necessary investment undertaken by R&D-performing firms in order to assure large volumes of sales which in turn allow firm to recover the high fixed costs in R&D. This is a thesis contained in the recent works by Sutton (1991).

The second strongest statistical correlation is that between the two disembodied components of firms' innovation expenditures, that is R&D and design (D&E). This suggests that these two different innovative sources are, in fact, complementary in firms' innovation strategies. In other words that knowledge-generating activities require to be complemented by more incremental and adaptive innovation efforts often taking place at the shop-floor level, and through processes of 'learning by doing'.

Both R&D and design activities are also positively associated with firms' expenditure on innovative investment, suggesting that innovative efforts aimed at generating new technological knowledge and those aiming at using such knowledge through production investment are also complements rather than substitutes.

The level of complementarity between embodied and disembodied techno-logical activities shown in Table 7.6a is not particularly strong. This again might be affected by the large number of firms in our data-set, which innovate only through investment.

The validity of this hypothesis is confirmed by Table 7.6b reporting the same correlation matrix as in Table 7.6a computed on the sub-sample of R&D and design-performing firms. The table shows that when such a group of more innovative firms is taken into account, the complementary links between the different innovative components increases significantly, and especially the link between embodied and disembodied technological activities. This evidence

Table 7.6   The relationship between embodied and disembodied innovation expenditures (correlation and elasticity coefficients)

a – Full sample (6833 firms)

	R&D[*] (log)	D&E[*] (log)	INV[*] (log)	MKT[*] (log)
R&D (log)	1			
D&E (log)	0.350 (0.290) P. = 0.000	1		
INV (log)	0.104 (0.206) P. = 0.000	0.128 (0.210) P. = 0.000	1	
MKT (log)	0.401 (0.246) P. = 0.000	0.416 (0.212) P. = 0.000	0.164 (0.051) P. = 0.000	1

(b) – R&D and D&E performing firms (1738 firms)

	R&D[*] (log)	D&E[*] (log)	INV[*] (log)	MKT[*] (log)
R&D (log)	1			
R&D (log)	0.653 (0.692) P. = 0.000	1		
INV (log)	0.409 (0.556) P. = 0.000	0.405 (0.583) P. = 0.000	1	
MKT (log)	0.496 (0.287) P. = 0.000	0.441 (0.271) P. = 0.000	0.39 (0.166) P. = 0.000	1

Notes: The first row shows the correlation coefficients and the third row the statistical significance. Elasticity coefficients are shown in brackets.
[*]Used as independent variables for the computation of the elasticity coefficients.

indicates also that firms, which devote large resources to the generation and development of new products require to make substantial investment in new production processes. This might simply suggest that after innovations have been designed they need to be produced. This, most of the time, requires the use of new production technologies and thus investment in new fixed productive capital. This kind of complementarity also explains the close interdependence between product and process innovations found in Chapter 6 using aggregate data.

7.4   INNOVATION, INVESTMENT AND FIRM SIZE

We can now pass on to extending the set of relationships investigated so far by looking at the way innovation patterns are related to some basic dimension of the productive structure of firms, here synthesized by the size of the firm (SALES), the capital intensity of production processes (INVMAC) and to an indicator of economic performance such as labour productivity (VA). Moreover in particular, the object of the analysis carried out in this section is threefold:

1. Verify whether firm size, investment intensity and labour productivity are positively linked to each other capturing the presence of economies of scale and increasing returns in production.
2. Verify whether investment in total fixed productive capital (equipment, machinery and plants) and investment in knowledge are complementary or substitutive in nature and what their impact is on labour productivity.
3. Explore the relationship between firm size and the innovation performance of firms.

   These issues can be investigated looking at the correlation matrix between the *innovation-intensity* and *production-related* variables included in our data-set, reported in Table 7.7.

7.4.1   Capital Intensity of Production and Firm Size

The correlation coefficients on the left-hand side of Table 7.7 show the presence of positive and statistically significant associations among the three new production-related variables. Firm size is, in fact, positively associated to total investment in machinery per employee, and the level of labour productivity is found to be correlated with both firm size and the capital intensity of production processes. Moreover in particular, the positive relationship between SALES and INVMAC indicates that large firms are characterized by higher investment in fixed capital per employee than small firms. This in turn shows the important role played by technical and economical immobilizations in fixed productive assets and related indivisibilities as determinants of firm size. These results are consistent with a large part of the theoretical and empirical literature on economies of scale reviewed in Chapter 4. However, while this literature has remained largely descriptive in nature, with few econometric attempts estimating the direct effects of capital intensity on firm size, our results emerge from a very large and highly heterogeneous sample of firms.

Table 7.7   Innovative intensity, firm size and labour productivity (correlation coefficients)

	SALES (log)	INVMAC (log)	VA (log)	INCOST (log)	R&D (log)	D&E (log)	INV (log)	MKT (log)
SALES (log)	1.000	0.330	0.421	0.108	0.195	0.127	–0.032	0.091
INVMAC (log)		1.000	0.379	0.366	0.115	0.079	0.380	0.076
VA (log)			1.000	0.279	0.194	0.160	0.209	0.129

Note: All coefficients are significant at the level of 0.000.

The capital-intensive nature of large-scale production activities seems also to lie behind the positive associations found between labour productivity and firm size. All these three variables seem, therefore, to reflect in an effective way interlinked features of the structure and organization of firms' production activities, such as the relevance of scale factors, the capital intensity and the level of mechanization of production processes, which are in turn associated to high levels of labour productivity.

7.4.2   Investment in Machinery and Innovation Activities

Positive and statistically significant correlations are also found in Table 7.7 between investment in machinery (INVMAC) and all the innovation expenditure indicators. In particular, the positive association between investment in machinery and equipment and total innovation costs per employee suggests a clear linkage between firms' innovative efforts and investment in fixed productive capital, which in turn reveals the prevalent capital-deepening nature of technological change in firms. As expected investments in machinery show their strongest links, among the innovative variables considered, with innovative investment, that is with firms' expenditure for introducing new process technologies embodied in new capital goods. Equally interesting are the positive correlations found between total investment in machinery and equipment (INVMAC) and both R&D and design expenditures (D&E). This confirms the existence of a certain degree of complementarity between disembodied and embodied technological activities, also when embodied innovative activities are measured by total investment in machinery and equipment. The latter variable can, in fact, be thought of as a cruder proxy for embodied technological activities than innovative investment. Such complementarity indicates that firms showing higher innovative expenditures in R&D and design are also characterized by heavily investing in fixed capital and by using more capital-intensive production processes.

7.4.3 The Determinants of Labour Productivity

Table 7.7 also shows that labour productivity is positively linked to firms' innovation efforts (both embodied and disembodied) as well as to more structural aspects of production process such as the size of the firm and the capital intensity of production. Given that all these technological and productive

Table 7.8   Determinants of labour productivity (regression estimates)

	Regression 1 All sample	Regression 2 R&D and D&E performing firms
Dependent variable	VA (log) Value added per employee	VA (log) Value added per employee
Intercept	2.58	2.91
(t-value)	(89.9)	(89.9)
SALES (log)	0.102	0.065
(t-value)	(27.6)	(10.1)
INVMAC (log)	0.130	0.125
(t-value)	(23.6)	(11.2)
RD&DE (log)	0.105	0.126
(t-value)	(11.9)	(8.8)
Adjusted R-square	0.257	0.229
(F)	(789)	(173)
Significance F	0.0000	0.0000

Note: All coefficients are significant at the level of 0.0000.

dimensions of firms are related to each other and are complementary in nature, it is interesting to verify whether they continue to affect labour productivity when they are jointly taken into account. This can be verified by running the following multiple regression where labour productivity is jointly explained by three different factors namely: (i) firm size (capturing the relevance of economies of scale); (ii) investment in new machinery per employee (capturing the level of mechanization and the capital intensity of production processes); and (iii) R&D and design expenditure per employee (capturing the disembodied innovative effort of firms).

$$\text{LogVA} = c_3 + b_3 \, \text{LogSALES} + d_3 \, \text{LogINVMAC} + f_3 \, \text{LogRD\&DE} + e_3 \quad (1)$$

The regression estimates, reported in Table 7.8, show that all three independent variables show positive and statistically significant coefficients. In other words labour productivity is the joint result of the presence of economies of scale in production and of the technological content of production processes and products. Furthermore the same variables continue to be statistically significant factors associated to labour productivity, also for the sub-sample of the more innovative R&D and design-performing firms.

7.4.4   The Relationship Between Firm Size and Innovation Intensity

The relationship between firm size and innovation requires a more detailed analysis, this being the issue at the centre of a long-lasting debate and numerous empirical investigations. In Chapter 4 it was pointed out that most of the empirical analyses in this field have used traditional technological indicators such as R&D and patents, which underplay the role of embodied technological activities. Table 7.7 allows us to verify the relationship between firm size and both knowledge-generating activities such as R&D and design and firms' effort to adopt new process technologies. The correlation coefficients reported in the table show that firm size is positively associated with R&D and design expenditures per employee while innovative investment (INV) per employee shows a rather weak negative correlation with the size of the firm.

The differences in the sign and the strength of the correlation coefficients between firm size and the innovation indicators in Table 7.7 seem to be the result of the polarization in the Italian industrial structure of two quite distinct innovation patterns: the first one is represented by the bulk of small firms, which are not particularly innovative and whose innovative activities are focused on the acquisition of embodied technologies; the second one is represented by a restricted group of large firms, which are on the average more innovative than small firms and which invest both in R&D and in the acquisition of new process technologies. This explanation is confirmed when we look at the relationship between innovation and firm size using more aggregated data.

Table 7.9 shows the average innovative intensity of three main firm size groups: firms with sales below 99 billions of lire, firms with sales between 100 and 499 billions of lire and firms with sales equal or above 500 billions of lire. At this level of aggregation of data, all innovative-intensity indicators increase with firm size, with the two indicators measuring R&D and design expenditures per employee showing the higher differences between small and large firms. The table also confirms that innovative investment per employee varies to a lesser degree across the three main classes and that large firms *vis-à-vis* small ones show a higher propensity towards product innovations. Furthermore large firms are characterized by more capital-intensive production structures and show a higher level of labour productivity.

Table 7.9　Innovative intensity by firm size (average values)

Firm size (billions of lire)	Innovative intensity[*]					Product/process innovation shares		Capital intensity[*]
	INCOST	R&D	D&E	INV	MKT	%PROD	%PROC	INVMAC
Up to 99	2.74	0.33	0.48	1.80	0.13	43.5	56.5	4.6
100 to 500	3.45.	0.68	0.83	1.81	0.13	42.6	57.4	5.9
Over 500	5.06	1.04	1.50	2.21	0.31	63.4	36.6	7.8
Total	3.62	0.63	0.87	1.93	0.19	45.0	55.0	5.9

Note:　[*] millions of lire per employee.

The use of aggregate data seems, therefore, to provide some broad support to the so-called neo-Schumpeterian hypothesis (discussed in Chapter 4), arguing for a technological supremacy of large firms *vis-à-vis* small- and medium-sized firms. The aggregate picture emerging in Table 7.9, as well as the correlation coefficient shown in Tables 7.7, might, however, hide marked sectoral differences in the relationship between innovation and firm size. As discussed in Chapter 4 the conditions of technological opportunity and appropriability, which are specific to the different industries and technological regimes, have been identified by the most recent literature as the true determinants of firms' innovation performance (Cohen and Levin 1989; Malerba and Orsenigo, 1995, 1996; Cohen, 1995; Klevorick et al., 1995).

In order to isolate the importance of firm size for innovation, independently from the presence of such sectoral technological specificities, Table 7.10 reports two indicators of firms' innovation performance (that is total innovation cost and R&D expenditure per employee) broken down by firm size and 21 industrial sectors.

At this level of sectoral aggregation, the results appear much more varied compared with the aggregate picture that emerged in Table 7.9. A clear positive relationship between firm size and innovation is found in six sectors. They are those where innovation costs per employee are higher. The neo-Schumpeterian hypothesis seems, therefore, to hold in what might be called the Schumpeterian industries only, that is in the industries that spend more on innovation and where higher technological opportunities are expected to be found while the opposite seems to be true for the less innovative sectors. In the traditional industries such as metal products, food, sugar and drinks, textiles, leather, footwear and clothing, firms of small or medium size spend more on innovations than large firms, even when large firms spend proportionally more on R&D.

7.5 THE MAIN DIMENSIONS OF FIRMS' INNOVATIVE PATTERNS: THE RESULTS OF THE FACTOR ANALYSIS

The previous sections have already hinted, through the use of bivariate statistics, at the existence of a complex set of relationships between the composite nature of firms' innovation strategies and their productive profiles. Factor analysis can help in summarizing and highlighting the different dimensions of innovation and productive variables taken into account in this chapter. When the original variables are sufficiently correlated with each other, the new variables extracted by the factor analysis are able to represent in a much more synthetic way the interlinked phenomena measured by the original variables. The statistical effectiveness of such a technique can be measured by the extent to which the new factors are able to reduce the original total variance, that is to reduce the multidimensional nature of the phenomena investigated. On more interpretative grounds, factor analysis is particularly effective when the factors extracted are few and they can be meaningfully interpreted by looking at the way they are linked to (and consequently able to synthesise) the original variables.

7.5.1 Results of the Factor Analysis

The variables used in the factor analysis are listed in Table 7.11. A new variable, '%RD&DE', consisting of the sum of '%R&D' and '%D&E', has been introduced, expressing the relative importance of R&D and design in firms' innovative activities. In this analysis, we have used data for the 4400 firms in our data-set, which have carried out at least one of the two disembodied technological activities (either R&D or design). This is in order to keep a large part

Table 7.10   Innovation intensity and firm size by industry (part 1)

Industrial sectors	Firm size (sales in billions of lire)	Number of firms	Innovation cost per employee (millions of lire)	R&D expenditure per employee (millions of lire)
Petrochemicals	up to 10	3	3.7	0.0
	from 10 to 100	3	3.7	0.0
	over 100	11	3.7	0.6
Rubber and plastic	up to 10	236	2.8	0.3
	from 10 to 100	150	2.8	0.3
	over 100	3	15.3	6.1
Chemicals	up to 10	128	3.3	0.9
	from 10 to 100	214	4.3	1.5
	over 100	67	2.4	0.6
Synthetic fibres	up to 100	5	2.6	0.0
	over 100	4	2.2	0.3
Mechanical machinery	up to 10	769	2.7	0.3
	from 10 to 100	364	2.7	0.4
	over 100	33	2.9	0.6
Office machinery computing	up to 10	3	4.0	0.4
	from 10 to 100	5	12.2	7.1
	over 100	3	14.5	4.9
Electrical and electronics	up to 10	272	2.5	0.3
	from 10 to 100	215	3.0	0.5
	over 100	39	5.1	1.4
Motor vehicles	up to 10	70	2.6	0.2
	from 10 to 100	72	2.4	0.3
	over 100	13	6.6	1.0
Other transport	up to 10	36	2.1	0.2
	from 10 to 100	41	2.2	0.4
	over 100	11	7.1	0.2
Precision instruments	up to 10	76	2.8	0.5
	over 10	34	5.9	1.2
Non-metals, minerals	up to 10	344	3.7	0.1
	from 10 to 100	140	4.0	0.2
	over 100	65	3.8	0.3

Table 7.10   Innovation intensity and firm size by industry (part 2)

Industrial sectors	Firm size (sales in billions of lire)	Number of firms	Innovation cost per employee (millions of lire)	R&D expenditure per employee (millions of lire)
Food	up to 10	97	3.3	0.1
	from 10 to 100	147	3.8	0.1
	over 100	24	1.9	0.1
Sugar and drinks	up to 10	57	3.4	0.0
	from 10 to 100	91	3.2	0.1
	over 100	29	1.4	0.2
Textiles	up to 10	383	2.4	0.1
	from 10 to 100	219	2.2	0.1
	over 100	8	0.9	0.3
Leather	up to 10	58	1.1	0.1
	from 10 to 100	39	1.8	0.0
	over 100	7	0.6	0.0
Footwear and clothing	up to 10	241	0.9	0.0
	from 10 to 100	95	0.6	0.0
	over 100	7	0.6	0.0
Wood, furniture	up to 10	389	1.8	0.1
	from 10 to 100	80	2.3	0.3
Paper, printing	up to 10	222	2.7	0.0
	from 10 to 100	124	2.8	0.0
	over 100	23	3.0	0.2
Metals	up to 10	32	2.1	0.1
	from 10 to 100	76	3.2	0.1
	over 100	29	2.4	0.2
Metal products	up to 10	629	2.5	0.1
	from 10 to 100	229	1.9	0.1
	over 100	6	1.8	0.2
Others	up to 10	99	1.6	0.1
	over 10	31	2.5	0.4

of the sample and exclude all firms which have innovated only through investment.

Table 7.11   List of variables used in the factor analysis

SALES (log)	Sales per firm
INVMAC (log)	Investment in machinery per employee
VA (log)	Value added per employee
INCOST (log)	Total innovation costs per employee
R&D (log)	R&D expenditure per employee
D&E (log)	D&E expenditure per employee
INV (log)	Innovative investment per employee
%RD&DE	Share of R&D and D&E expenditure in total innovation costs
%PROC	Share of process innovations in all innovations introduced

Note: The indicators listed above are computed as sectoral average values.

The use of factor analysis has turned out to be quite effective in synthesizing the different dimensions of innovative activities and the other three variables reflecting production-related characteristics of firms analysed in this chapter.

As shown in Table 7.12, out of the eight original variables three principal components have been extracted, altogether explaining 68.3 per cent of the total initial variance. The three factors (after 'rotation') highlight two quite distinct dimensions of innovative activities plus a third one reflecting some basic aspects of the productive structure of firms. Their meaning can be deduced by looking at the correlation coefficients between the original variables and the three new factors extracted (Table 7.12).

- The *first factor* represents the 'total innovative effort of firms'. The high correlation between such a factor and the three main innovation intensity indicators confirms the presence of a certain degree of complementarity between embodied and disembodied technological activities in firms' innovation strategies. Increases of the resources devoted to innovation activities are accompanied, by and large, by increasing efforts both in generating new technological knowledge and in using it through the acquisition of new technologies embodied in new equipment and machinery.
- The *second factor* shows the 'embodied versus disembodied' composition of innovative activities and process versus product innovative output of firms. Larger shares of R&D and design expenditures in total innovation costs are associated with larger shares of product innovations in total innovations introduced. Conversely process innovations are linked with a predominant role of investment.

- The *third factor* summarizes interrelated aspects of the 'productive structure of firms', such as firm size, total investment in machinery per employee and labour productivity. This reflects the presence and importance of economies of scale in production, the capital intensity of production processes, the level of mechanization – all factors related to labour productivity.

The results of the factor analysis show that the overall firms' innovative efforts (factor 1) are largely independent of the basic productive and structural dimensions of firms summarized by factor 2. Firm size and labour productivity are, in fact, determined principally by the presence of scale factors associated with high levels of capital intensity and mechanization of production processes. This confirms that firm size in itself is not a sufficient factor for a firm to be innovative, though it is more likely to find highly innovative performances among large firms than among small firms.

Table 7.12   Results of the factor analysis

Factor	Eigenvalue	% of variance explained	Cumulative %
1	2.9238	32.5	32.5
2	1.83296	20.3	52.8
3	1.3896	15.4	68.3

Rotated factor matrix

	Factor 1 Innovation intensity	Factor 2 Embodied/ Disembodied	Factor 3 Production structure
INCOST (log)	0.925	0.291	0.173
R&D (log)	0.601	–0.273	0.235
D&E (log)	0.810	–0.227	–0.018
INV (log)	0.658	0.668	0.155
%RDDE	0.195	–0.885	–0.034
%PROC	–0.015	0.618	–0.004
SALES (log)	–0.046	–0.073	0.808
INVMAC (log)	0.209	0.313	0.678
VA (108)	0.190	–0.040	0.754

Notes: Varimax rotation 1, extraction 1, analysis 1 – Kaiser normalization.

The composition of innovative activities, both in terms of the relative importance of embodied and disembodied components of innovation and product and process innovations, emerges also as a dimension of firms' innovative strategies largely independent of both the capital intensity of production and firm size, on the one hand, and the overall innovative intensity of firms, on the other.

Finally embodied innovative efforts are confirmed as being partly independent from total investment in machinery. The latter indicator, commonly used as a proxy of the capital intensity of production processes, does not completely overlap with what firms regard as their efforts to introduce and adopt technologies through the acquisition of technologically new machinery and equipment. While this might reflect wide differences in the firms' subjective evaluation of what should be regarded as 'innovative investment', this result also reflects the fact that total investment in machinery represents only a crude proxy for embodied technological change.[8]

7.6   CONCLUSIONS

In this chapter we have looked at the role of embodied and disembodied technological change and process and product innovations in firms' innovative conducts. The way in which firms' innovative patterns are linked to some basic features of the productive structure of firms has also been investigated. The main findings of this chapter can be summarized as follows:

- Innovative investments have emerged as the component of innovation costs most strongly associated and responsive to total firms' technological efforts. The importance of investment is confirmed also taking into account the more innovative sub-sample of firms performing R&D and design activities.
- Embodied and disembodied innovative activities emerge as complements rather than substitutes in firms' innovation strategies. No trade-off is found between investment in knowledge-generating actives such as R&D and design and investment in fixed productive capital.
- Firm size, capital intensity and labour productivity are strongly interlinked with each other, so identifying interrelated determinants of firms' production structures such as: (i) the importance of economies of scale in production, (ii) the capital intensity of production processes, and (iii) the levels of labour productivity.
- At an aggregate level of the analysis, firm size has emerged as an important determinant of firms' innovative patterns, defining both the intensity of embodied and disembodied technological expenditures and the relative importance of product and process innovations.

- On the whole, the econometric estimations carried out in this chapter have emerged as rather weak though always statistically significant. This could be for the following reasons:

1. The presence of a substantial 'statistical noise' in the data-set, due to the highly subjective nature of the data provided by the firms, especially those concerning innovation costs.
2. The presence of important sectoral specificities in both the technological and productive feature of firms investigated and in the way they are interlinked.

Data problems of quality are insurmountable. However the use of more aggregated values can be helpful in overcoming some of the problems mentioned above, as has been shown in the previous section in the analysis of the relationship between firm size and all innovative variables. We use this approach in Chapter 7. The aspects mentioned in 2 will be addressed in Chapters 8 and 9, which will examine the appropriateness of using sectoral average values and look in greater detail at the difficult sectoral patterns in innovation.

NOTES

1. This was because of the presence of evident anomalies of data in the variables considered, due either to errors in filling in the questionnaire or to mistakes in the subsequent entry of the data.
2. An obvious problem in matching the two data-sets was that the time-frames used in each case differed. The Gross Industrial Product Survey is an annual survey, while the Innovation survey data cover the quinquennial period 1981–85. To make the data comparable, figures of innovation costs have been divided by five.
3. In this item only marketing expenditure linked to innovation is included.
4. It might be argued that most of the engineering activities consist of incremental efforts to improve production-related technologies and devices, which take place at the shop-floor level, and consequently are 'production-related'. Nevertheless we still decided to treat such activities as disembodied, because of their ultimate knowledge-based nature. These activities involve an upgrading of the stock of knowledge and know-how of the labour force and can still be seen as distinct from the activities consisting of the acquisition and use of technologies embodied in new equipment and plant.
5. Correlation coefficients and elasticity indexes give complementary information on the nature and strength of the relationships investigated. The correlation coefficients measure whether a given variable (in this case the indicator of total innovative intensity) moves in the same or opposite direction as another given variable, and how strict is the correspondence in the movements of the two variables. However, in order to measure the extent (in percentages) to which a variable changes in its level relative to the changes in the other variables, we have to look at the elasticity indexes.
6. See, for example, Cohen and Klepper (1992).
7. This result might also reflect the overall technological profile of the Italian manufacturing industry, specialized in industrial sectors and product segments where technological activities rely upon the technical improvement or substitution of production processes.
8. The relatively weak correlation found between innovative investment and total investment in machinery and equipment can also be the result of the fact that data for investment in our data base refer to 1985 whereas data on innovation costs refer to the period 1981–85.

8. Innovation strategies and the productive structure of firms: do industrial sectors matter?

8.1 INTRODUCTION

In Chapter 7 innovation strategies of firms and their productive structure were investigated using unaggregated firm level data. The implicit assumption was that there were no sectoral-specific differences in each of the technological and production-related variables taken into account and in the way they were linked with each other.

Over the last few years a large amount of literature has shown that innovation processes are indeed sector-specific. Industries differ in the opportunities offered by technological advancements, in the extent and ways in which firms can appropriate the results of their innovative activities, in the technological source used and in the importance played by innovation in firms' innovation strategies and performances (Pavitt, 1984; Klevorick et al., 1995; Malerba and Orsenigo, 1995). Accordingly industrial sectors have been often used to identify the presence of different technological regimes, and the latter in turn have been associated to specific technological fields, production activities and classes of products. Much more rarely, however, the nature and extent of such intersectoral differences in innovation have been investigated with proper statistical tools and quantitative data.

In this chapter we drop the assumption of technological uniformity across industry and investigate the extent to which sectors differ in the following aspects: (i) in the nature and intensity of firms' innovation activities; (ii) in the level of complementarity between embodied and disembodied technological activities; and (iii) in the technological determinants of labour productivity.

In the next section, an analysis of variance on the whole set of variables contained in our data-set will be carried out using different levels of sectoral aggregation and cut-off points in terms of firm size. This is to enable a clearer identification of the major inter-industry sources of variety in firms' innovation strategies, production structures and performances.

In Section 8.3 we verify the existence of sectoral specificities in firms' innovation strategies looking at: (i) the technological sources used by firms when they increase their innovative efforts; (ii) the level of complementarity between embodied and disembodied technological activities; and (iii) the way innovation patterns are linked to the productive structure of firms and their performances. These issues will be addressed by running the same econometric estimations as in Chapter 7, including dummy variables for 21 industrial sectors (least squares dummy variables regressions – LSDV).

8.2 DIFFERENCES IN THE TECHNOLOGICAL AND PRODUCTIVE PROFILES OF INDUSTRIAL SECTORS

The evidence presented in Chapter 6 has already shown, on a purely descriptive basis, the existence of marked sectoral differences in the innovation patterns, namely in the percentage of innovating firms and in the nature of innovation activities in the different industries. Yet a more rigorous statistical investigation is needed to explore the extent to which the different variables used in Chapter 7 define sufficiently coherent sector-specific innovative patterns.

This issue bears important methodological implications. The methodological and theoretical consistency of any analysis based on sectorally aggregated data, like the one that will be carried out in the next two chapters, relies on the implicit assumption that industrial sectors are sufficiently coherent aggregations of firms. If intersectoral differences were found to be not statistically significant, industrial sectors would not represent appropriate units of analysis to study firms innovation activities and highlight major technological patterns in industry. Of course the extent and statistical significance of such differences are likely to be affected by both the level of sectoral aggregation chosen and the types of variable taken into account. These issues are empirically investigated in this section carrying out an analysis of variance (one-way analysis) across industries on all the indicators contained in our data-set.

One-way analysis of variance allows us to test the hypothesis that the differences between the industrial sectoral means are different from 0, against the hypothesis that such differences are not significantly different from 0.[1]

Table 8.1 reports, for each variable of our database, F-values obtained by applying ANOVA at the 2- and 3-digit levels of a NACE industrial classification. An index measuring the percentage of inter-firm variance explained by calculating the sum of squares of the observations from their sectoral means instead of from the overall manufacturing mean is also shown in the table. This index can be interpreted as an R-square in a regression where the dependent variable (in our case any of the variables shown in the table) is explained by the simple fact that a firm belongs to a specific sector.

Table 8.1   Analysis of variance at different levels of sectoral aggregation (R-square and F-ratios)

Variables		30 sectors Full sample	108 sectors Full sample
SALES	RSQ	0.16	0.18
	F	45.54	14.52
INVMAC	RSQ	0.06	0.10
	F	15.18	7.36
VA	RSQ	0.11	0.15
	F	29.78	11.34
INCOST	RSQ	0.04	0.07
	F	11.03	5.22
R&D	RSQ	0.08	0.10
	F	20.92	7.29
D&E	RSQ	0.08	0.09
	F	20.58	6.4
INV	RSQ	0.05	0.09
	F	12.43	6.78
RD&DE	RSQ	0.11	0.13
	F	30.06	9 75
%R&D	RSQ	0.10	0.12
	F	27.33	9.05
%D&E	RSQ	0.14	0.17
	F	37.99	13.58
%INV	RSQ	0.17	0.21
	F	49.85	18
%RD&DE	RSQ	0.19	0.23
	F	54.36	19.11
%PROC	RSQ	0.09	0.12
	F	22.17	7.98

Note: All coefficients are significant with probability levels at least equal to 0.0000.

The very high F-values in the table confirm the existence of significant differences in the sectoral average values in all variables of our database, when taking into account both 30 and 108 sectors. It is also clear by the analysis of both F- and R-square levels that industrial sectors differ from each other to a different extent according to technological and production dimensions taken into account. Thus industrial sectors seem more dissimilar in terms of firm size

(SALES) and value added per employee (VA) than in terms of investment in machinery per employee (INVMAC).[2] Among the innovative variables, total innovative intensity (INCOST) shows the lowest R-square value. Much higher levels of both F and R-square values are found when firms' expenditures on R&D, design and engineering (D&E) and investment (INV) are taken into account. This suggests that differences across sectors in innovative patterns become much more clear-cut when one looks in more detail at the internal structure of the innovation process in firms.

Overall these results suggest that industrial sectors show a much clearer technological definition and coherence (low intrasectoral variance compared to a high intersectoral one) when the different components of innovative activities within total innovative expenditure are distinguished, and particularly when the relative importance played by embodied and disembodied components of technological activities are taken into account. Interestingly enough intersectoral differences in the propensity of firms to innovate through product or process innovation do not appear considerable, compared to other technological features of firms.[3]

Table 8.1 also shows that increasing the level of sectoral disaggregation, that is passing from 30 (2-digit) sectors to 108 (3-digit) sectors, also helps (as expected) in identifying more clear-cut sectoral technological and production profiles. R-square values increase with respect to all variables, even if a very large intrasectoral variance still remains unexplained.[4]

8.2.1   Sectoral Differences and the 'Small Firm Factor'

To what extent does the exclusion of different proportions of small firms in the sample lead to more homogeneous and consistent sectoral profiles? Or, in other words, what is the contribution of small firms to the large intrasectoral variance in firms' innovation conducts found in the previous section? Table 8.2 allows us to shed some light on this particular issue comparing the results of the ANOVA analysis applying three different cut-off points in the dataset in terms of firm size (that is excluding firms with less than 5, 25 and 50 billion lire respectively), and maintaining the 2- and 3-digit sectoral classifications used in the previous section.

An analysis of the F- and R-squares coefficients across the columns of Table 8.2 shows that small firms contribute significantly to the intrasectoral variance observed in Table 8.1. R-squares increase considerably when the cut-off point is higher, so that it is like putting on a filter in the data-set, which is able to diminish the variance added by small firms. In some cases, as with the R&D and design (D&E) innovative intensity indicators, R-square values increase by as much as three times the corresponding values obtained using the entire sample of firms.

Evidence from the Italian industry

Table 8.2   Analysis of variance at different levels of sectoral aggregation and cut-off in firm size (R-square and F-ratios)

Variables		108 sectors Sales over 5 billion	108 sectors Sales over 25 billion	108 sectors Sales over 50 billion	30 sectors Sales over 5 billion	30 sectors Sales over 25 billion	30 sectors Sales over 50 billion
SALES	RSQ	0.19	0.22	0.28	0.17	0.16	0.18
	F	9.50	3.60	2.59	29.90	9.92	4.80
INVMAC	RSQ	0.13	0.22	0.23	0.07	0.12	0.16
	F	5.90	3.60	1.90	11.30	6.09	4.20
VA	RSQ	0.13	0.14	0.15	0.08	0.08	0.09
	F	5.90	2.10	(**)1,1	14.00	4.08	2.70
INCOST	RSQ	0.08	0.15	0.18	0.05	0.09	0.11
	F	3.50	2.19	(*)1,44	7.80	4.40	2.70
R&D	RSQ	0.11	0.23	0.29	0.09	0.21	0.27
	F	4.99	3.80	2.64	14.10	11.86	7.80
D&E	RSQ	0.12	0.20	0.29	0.11	0.18	0.25
	F	5.50	3.20	2.60	17.30	9.70	7.30
INV	RSQ	0.10	0.14	0.16	0.05	0.07	0.08
	F	4.20	2.05	(*)1,26	8.10	3.16	1.89
RD&DE	RSQ	0.16	0.28	0.35	0.13	0.25	0.33
	F	7.50	4.98	3.56	22.40	15.18	10.30
%R&D	RSQ	0.14	0.20	0.23	0.12	0.18	0.15
	F	6.60	3.21	1.96	19.80	8.20	3.80
%D&E	RSQ	0.18	0.19	0.26	0.15	0.14	0.17
	F	9.20	2.94	2.25	26.00	7.20	4.30
%INV	RSQ	0.24	0.25	0.29	0.20	0.20	0.18
	F	12.60	4.26	2.63	36.50	10.60	4.70
%RD&DE	RSQ	0.25	0.27	0.32	0.21	0.21	0.22
	F	13.60	4.67	3.11	39.60	11.90	6.22
%PROC	RSQ	0.13	0.19	0.25	0.10	0.12	0.12l
	F	5.57	2.78	2.10	15.40	5.91	2.83

Note: All coefficients are significant with probability levels at least equal to 0.0000 with the exception of:* significant at 0.05 and** non-significant.

A first explanation of this finding might be related to the very nature of innovation activities of small firms: compared to large firms, small firms could use, alternatively, a wider range of technological sources, and this independently from the specific industry in which they operate. In other words, the boundaries of technological regimes could be much looser for small firms than for large firms and this in turn could indicate a higher flexibility characterizing small firms also with reference to innovation. However there might be other two reasons behind the high inter-firm variance in innovation found among small firms. One explanation lies in the occasional and non-systematic nature of technological activities in small firms, which is going to be reflected in all the variables and indicators of our database.[5] A second important source of inter-firm variance among small firms might be due to the less rigorous and more subjective procedures followed by small firms, *vis-à-vis* large firms, in quantifying innovative phenomena such as the cost of innovation, especially in the absence of a proper budgeting of innovation activities. Both these aspects considerably increase the statistical inter-firm variance, which structurally characterizes the collection of innovation data based on questionnaires and unselected samples of firms.

8.3 SECTORAL DIFFERENCES IN FIRMS' INNOVATION STRATEGIES

In this section the presence and the extent of sector specificities in firms' innovation strategies and in the determinants of labour productivity are examined in greater detail. More specifically, we verify the existence of sectoral specificities in the following relationships:

a. in the ways firms' innovation activities are linked to the use of any specific technological source (that is embodied and disembodied technological activities) (see equations 1, 2 and 3 below);
b. in the level of complementarity between firms' embodied and disembodied technological activities (see equations 4 and 5 below);
c. in the importance of capital intensity as a determinant of economies of scale in production (see equation 6 below);
d. in the role played by firm size, capital intensity and firms' innovation efforts in determining labour productivity (see equation 7 below).

These relationships will be estimated running the regressions 1–7 listed below with the use of sectoral dummy variables for 21 industrial sectors (LSDV). This will allow us to control for differences in both the intercepts and slopes of each of the following regressions.[6] Because of the use of log-transformed values, the slope coefficients b can be interpreted as the elasticity of the dependent variables *vis-à-vis* the ones reported in the right-hand side of the equations.

$$\text{LogR\&D} = c_1 + b_1 \text{ LogINCOST} + e_{1p} \tag{1}$$

$$\text{LogD\&E} = c_2 + b_2 \text{ LogINCOST} + e_2 \tag{2}$$

$$\text{LogINV} = c_3 + b_3 \text{ LogINCOST} + e_3 \tag{3}$$

$$\text{LogR\&D} = c_4 + b_4 \, \text{LogINV} + e_4 \qquad\qquad (4)$$

$$\text{LogD\&E} = c_5 + b_5 \, \text{LogINV} + e_5 \qquad\qquad (5)$$

$$\text{LogSALES} = c_6 + b_6 \, \text{LogINVMAC} + e_6 \qquad\qquad (6)$$

$$\text{LogVA} = c_7 + b_7 \, \text{LogSALES} + d_7 \, \text{LogINVMAC} + f_7 \, \text{LogRD\&DE} + e_7 \quad (7)$$

Estimations of the equations 1–7 have been reported in Tables 8.3 to 8.5. Only sectoral 'slope coefficients' b will be shown in the tables, since intersectoral differences in the levels of all the innovative and productive variables of our data-set (expressed by the sectoral intercepts) have already been investigated in the previous section through the analysis of variance. Dummies for one of the sectors had to be dropped to avoid a situation of perfect multicollinearity among the right-hand side variables of the equations. The sectoral dummy omitted has been chosen on the basis of the closeness of the respective sectors to the manufacturing average in terms of its own slope and intercept. This allows us to interpret the b coefficients reported in the tables as approximate differences from the manufacturing average (see Kennedy, 1984, 1992; Suits, 1984). Since we are also interested in looking at the true 'sectoral elasticity coefficients', the latter have also be estimated and reported in the tables. These are the b coefficients which would be obtained by running separate regressions for each of the industries taken into account.[7]

We can now proceed to examine the results of the LSDV regression estimates, and interpret them in the light of the empirical issues listed above.

8.3.1   Sectoral Specificities in the Technological Sources used by Firms

Table 8.3 shows regression estimates of equations 1, 2 and 3. In this case the slope coefficients can be interpreted as the elasticity of firms' innovative disembodied and embodied efforts with respect to total innovation costs. The analysis of the sectoral elasticity coefficients (second column) allows us to verify the extent to which firms' innovation activities rely on different technological sources in different sectors, while 'b' coefficients (first column) allow us to check for the statistical significance of such intersectoral differences in the relationship examined. Dummies for the class 'rubber and plastic' have been omitted, so constituting the benchmark for the other sectors. Significance levels associated to the t statistics have also been indicated showing the probability levels, that is the probability of b coefficients being equal to the reference sector – here used as a proxy for the 'manufacturing average'.

Firstly we note that the use of dummy variables has improved the R-square compared to the pooled regressions (also reported in brackets at the bottom of

Table 8.3): from 0.17 to 0.35 in the first regression, from 0.24 to 0.30 in the second regression and from 0.75 to 0.80 in the third one. This suggests the presence of sectoral specificities in the relationships examined. We then look in more detail at the types of technological activity carried out by firms when they increase the amount of resources devoted to innovation. This can be done by comparing the sectoral elasticities' coefficients across the three regression estimates (equations 1, 2 and 3). In Chapter 7 we have seen that innovative investments show a higher correlation with respect to total innovation costs than the two disembodied innovation expenditures. It is evident from Table 8.3 that this continues to hold at the level of the main industrial sectors. Sectoral elasticity coefficients of innovative investment with respect to total innovation costs are much higher than those shown in the other two regression estimates. In almost all sectors, increases in innovation expenditures are accompanied by almost proportional increases of innovation investment, with the highest elasticity coefficients found among traditional consumer-good sectors and process-based industries such as energy, metals and chemicals. Elasticity coefficients above the average are also found in industries such as synthetic fibres, metal and non-metal processing industries. In the latter industries, increases in the firms' innovative efforts are associated with substantial investment in new machinery and plant. Moreover, inter-industry differences in the elasticity coefficients appear as highly significant.

More varied patterns emerge from the other two regression estimates (equations 2 and 3). Firms' innovation patterns based on R&D and design expenditures characterize the mechanical, chemical and electronic sectors. The first regression shows R&D elasticity coefficients above the average in the case of office machinery, chemicals, precision instruments, electrical appliances and components, motor vehicles and other transport. These are industries characterized by high technological opportunities, where a deeper involvement in innovation requires an increase in the innovative efforts aimed at generating or developing new technologies. However only in the first three sectors among those listed (namely office machinery, chemicals and precision instruments) do firms' innovation patterns seem clearly associated with R&D, as evidenced by their high elasticity coefficients. On the other hand, all traditional consumer-good sectors and process-based industries are characterized by very low elasticity coefficients of R&D expenditure with respect to total innovation costs. This confirms that in these sectors firms' innovation strategies are quite independent of the actual involvement in R&D activities. Here, too, inter-industry differences in the elasticity coefficients appear in most cases as highly significant.

Higher coefficients are found in the second regression, which estimates the elasticity between D&E expenditure and total innovation costs. Compared to R&D, design expenditures emerge, in fact, as a much more reactive innovative

Table 8.3 Elasticity of embodied and disembodied innovation expenditures with respect to total innovation costs (LSDV estimations)

Independent variables	Equation 1 Dependent variable: R&D (log)		Equation 2 Dependent variable: D&E (log)		Equation 3 Dependent variable: INV (log)	
	b coefficient (LSDV estimate)	Sectoral elasticity coefficient (1)	b coefficient (LSDV estimate)	Sectoral elasticity coefficient (1)	b coefficient (LSDV estimate)	Sectoral elasticity coefficient (1)
Sectoral dummies						
Energy and Gas	−0.204**	0.009	0.091	0.399***	0.068	0.931***
Metals	−0.092*	0.121***	−0.115**	0.193***	0.058	0.920***
Non-metals, minerals	−0.180***	0.033*	−0.160***	0.149***	0.122***	0.985***
Chemicals	0.310***	0.523***	0.038	0.346***	−0.205**	0.658***
Synthetic fibres	−0.104	0.109	−0.242*	0.066	0.190	1.053***
Metal products	−0.081***	0.132***	−0.049*	0.259***	0.039	0.902***
Machinery	0.060*	0.273***	0.173***	0.481***	−0.128***	0.735***
Office machinery and computing	0.745***	0.958***	0.128	0.436***	−0.411***	0.452***
Electrical products and components	0.127***	0.340***	0.282***	0.590***	−0.224***	0.638***
Motor vehicles and components	0.092*	0.305***	0.134**	0.442***	−0.037	0.826***
Other transport	0.092*	0.305***	0.277***	0.585***	−0.160***	0.703***
Precision instruments	0.299***	0.512***	0.359***	0.668***	−0.270***	0.592***
Food	−0.133***	0.080***	−0.217***	0.091***	0.132***	0.995***

Sugar, drinks	-0.183***	0.030	-0.160***	0.148***	0.103**	0.966***
Textiles	-0.125***	0.088***	-0.212***	0.096***	0.098***	0.961***
Leather	-0.161**	0.052	-0.167**	0.141**	0.067	0.929***
Footwear, clothing	-0.138***	0.074*	-0.120**	0.188***	-0.027	0.835***
Wood, furniture	-0.119***	0.094***	-0.120***	0.188***	0.051	0.914***
Paper, printing	-0.192***	0.021	-0.218***	0.090***	0.091**	0.954***
Rubber and plastic	ref.	0.213***	ref.	0.308***	ref.	0.863***
Other manufacturing	0.104*	0.317***	-0.119**	0.189***	-0.058	0.805***
INCOST (log)	0.213***		0.308***		0.863***	
constant	-0.090*		-0.105*		-0.047*	
	Adjusted R-square:		Adjusted R-square:		Adjusted R-square:	
	0.351 (0.170)§		0.305 (0.249)§		0.810(0.755)§	
	F: 90.9		F: 131.4		F: 713.1	
	Significance F: 0.000		Significance F: 0.000		Significance F: 0.000	

Notes:
(1) These are obtained running separate regressors for each industry.
§ R-square obtained by running a pooled regression without the inclusion of sectoral dummies.
* significant at 0.1; ** : significant at 0.01; *** : significant at 0.001.

component for a larger group of sectors. Precision instruments, electronic components, other transport and machinery are the sectors that show the highest elasticity coefficients and, thus, a clearer 'design orientation' of their innovative efforts. As for the other two regression estimates, the intersectoral differences in the elasticity coefficients appear statistically significant in most of the cases.

8.3.2 Sectoral Differences in the Complementarity between Embodied and Disembodied Innovative Activities

We now verify the extent to which the level of complementarity between disembodied and embodied innovative activities of firms changes from sector to sector.

Table 8.4 reports the results of equations 4 and 5, estimating the elasticities of R&D and design expenditures with respect to innovative expenditure in investment. The table is structured as Table 8.3, with *b* coefficients representing the differences of each of the sectoral elasticity from the one holding for the manufacturing industry as a whole and the second column showing the actual elasticities within the sector.

Also in the case of equations 4 and 5, the inclusion of the dummy variables for both intercepts and slopes improves the fit of the pooled regressions.[8] Furthermore Table 8.4 shows that the two disembodied components of innovation costs and innovative investment emerge to be complementary in nature across all industries.

The analysis of the sectoral elasticity indexes again shows traditional and metal-processing sectors having a lower complementarity between embodied and disembodied technological activities compared with the manufacturing average value, represented here by the metal products sector. All the rest of the sectors, including mechanical, electronic and electrical sectors, show an elasticity of disembodied relative to embodied expenditures above the average. It is, therefore, mainly in the industries characterized by higher technological opportunities and higher innovative profiles, mainly in the electronic *filiere*, where embodied and disembodied technological sources emerge as complements. Conversely industries usually characterized by low technological performances demonstrate much weaker levels of such complementarity. This is because innovative activities for the latter sectors rely, as already pointed out, mainly on the acquisition of technologies embodied in fixed capital.

Table 8.4 also shows that there are only slight differences in the regression estimates of equations 4 and 5. The sectors which show high and significant complementary relationships between R&D and innovative investment are the same as those that show high and significant elasticity coefficients between design expenditures and innovative investment: they are office machinery,

Table 8.4   The relationship between embodied and disembodied innovation expenditures (LSDV estimations)

Independent variables	Equation 4 Dependent variable: R&D (log)		Equation 5 Dependent variable: D&E (log)	
Sectoral dummies	b coefficient (LSDV estimate)	Sectoral elasticity coefficient (1)	b coefficient (LSDV estimate)	Sectoral elasticity coefficient (1)
Energy and Gas	−0.198*	−0.138	0.340***	0.410***
Metals	−0.012	0.048	−0.060	0.010
Non-metals, minerals	−0.058*	0.001	ref.	0.070***
Chemicals	0.122***	0.182***	0.121***	0.190***
Synthetic fibres	0.020	0.080	−0.074	−0.004
Metal products	ref.	0.060***	0.037	0.106***
Machinery	0.032	0.092***	0.069*	0.139***
Office machinery and computing	1.460***	1.519***	0.641*	0.710**
Electrical Products and components	0.110***	0.170***	0.269***	0.339***
Motor vehicles and components	0.135**	0.195***	0.129*	0.198***
Other transport	0.158**	0.217***	0.273***	0.342***
Precision instruments	0.387***	0.447***	0.388***	0.457***
Food	0.000*	0.060**	−0.016*	0.054*
Sugar, drinks	−0.075*	−0.016	−0.029*	0.040
Textiles	−0.030	0.029	−0.050*	0.020
Leather	−0.056	0.004	−0.046	0.024
Footwear, clothing	−0.059	0.001	−0.045	0.025
Wood, furniture	−0.037	0.022	−0.020	0.049
Paper, printing	−0.070*	−0.010	−0.092**	−0.023
Rubber and plastic	0.030	0.090***	0.102**	0.172***
Other manufacturing	0.108*	0.167***	−0.032	0.038
INV (log)	0.060***		0.070***	
constant	0.035**		0.095	
	Adjusted R-square: 0.150 (0.107)§ F: 30.3 Significance F: 0.000		Adjusted R-square: 0.175 (0.163)§ F: 36.5 Significance F: 0.000	

Notes:
(1): These are obtained running separate regressions for each industry.
§: R-square obtained by running the two pooled regressions without the sectoral dummies.
*Significant at 0.1; **: significant at 0.01; ***: significant at 0.001.

precision instruments, and other transport. The exceptions are represented by energy and non-metal minerals, which show elasticity coefficients not significantly different from zero in the first regression estimate, while showing a clear complementarity between D&E and innovative investment in the second regression. Such a difference reflects the importance that innovative activities consisting of the improvement of production processes through design and engineering activities play in these 'production-intensive' industries. The much higher elasticity coefficients found in regression 4 in the case of the office machinery sector are, on the other hand, due to the crucial role played by R&D in firms' innovation strategies in this sector.

There are also industries whose elasticity coefficients do not significantly differ from the ones that hold at the level of the manufacturing sector as a whole. This is the case with all traditional consumer-good sectors. This might partially be the result of the high level of sectoral aggregation used and of the large number of firms concentrated in these sectors, which end up representing the dominant innovation pattern in the manufacturing sector as a whole.

8.3.3   Sectoral Differences in the Relationship between Firm Size and Capital Intensity

Table 8.5 shows the LSDV regression estimates of equation 6, which allow us to test the importance of capital intensity of production processes as a determinant of firm size.

The sectoral elasticity coefficients in the table show that capital intensity is an important determinant of firm size in all sectors, with the exception of synthetic fibres. Taking into account sectoral specificities in the relationships between firm size and capital intensity leads to a substantial increase of the R-square compared to that obtained by running a simple regression. The share of variance explained by the regression rises from 10 per cent to 22 per cent.

A heterogeneous group of industries including traditional consumer-good sectors, such as textiles, footwear and clothing, wood and furniture, other process-based industries such as metals, non-metals and minerals, synthetic fibres, sugar and drinks, rubber and plastics and machinery and precision instruments show elasticity coefficients below the average. Elasticity coefficients above the average are found in energy and gas, office machinery, electronic components and motor vehicles. However, in most of the cases, sectoral differences in the elasticity coefficients do not emerge as statistically significant. This indicates that roughly the same positive relationship between firm size and the capital intensity of production processes holds across all industries.

Table 8.5   Firm size and capital intensity (LSDV estimations)

Independent variables	Equation 6 Dependent variable: SALES (log)	
Sectoral dummies	b coefficient (LSDV estimate)	Sectoral elasticity coefficient (1)
Energy and Gas	0.074	0.560*
Metals	−0.231*	0.255*
Non-metals, minerals	−0.072	0.414***
Chemicals	ref.	0.485***
Synthetic fibres	−0.016	0.470
Metal products	−0.088	0.398***
Machinery	−0.160*	0.325***
Office machinery and computing	1.162***	1.648***
Electrical products and components	0.080	0.565***
Motor vehicles and components	0.059	0.544***
Other transport	−0.052	0.433*
Precision instruments	−0.108	0.378**
Food	0.073	0.559***
Sugar, drinks	−0.108	0.377***
Textiles	−0.262**	0.223***
Leather	0.026	0.511**
Footwear, clothing	−0.047	0.439***
Wood, furniture	−0.054	0.431***
Paper, printing	−0.159*	0.326***
Rubber and plastic	−0.165*	0.320***
Other manufacturing	0.031	0.516***
INVMAC(log)	0.485*	
constant	9.261	
	Adjusted R-square: 0.225 (0.163)§ F: 49.4 Significance F: 0.000	

Notes:
(1): These are obtained running separate regressions for each industry.
§: R-square obtained by running a pooled regression without sectoral dummies.
* Significant at 0.1;**: significant at 0.01;***: significant at 0.001.

Table 8.6   The determinants of labour productivity (LSDV estimations)

Equation 7 Dep. var. LogVA	Elasticity coefficients					
	SALES (log)		INVMAC (log)		RD&DE (log)	
Sectoral dummies	b coefficient (LSDV estimate)	Sectoral elasticity coefficient (1)	b coefficient (LSDV estimate)	Sectoral elasticity coefficient (1)	b coefficient (LSDV estimate)	Sectoral elasticity coefficient (1)
Energy and Gas	0.122*	0.134**	−0.128	−0.066	−0.350	−0.215
Metals	ref.	0.012	ref.	0.062*	ref.	0.134
Non-metals, minerals	0.123***	0.135***	0.021	0.083***	−0.044	0.090
Chemicals	0.041	0.053***	0.091*	0.153***	−0.073	0.062*
Synthetic fibres	−0.064	−0.052	0.232	0.294*	0.093	0.228
Metal products	0.067**	0.079***	0.065*	0.127***	−0.063	0.071
Machinery	0.069**	0.081***	0.036	0.098***	−0.072	0.063*
Office machinery and computing	0.190**	0.202***	−0.161	−0.099	−0.298*	−0.164
Electrical products and components	0.013	0.025*	0.095**	0.157***	−0.053	0.081*
Motor vehicles and components	−0.001	0.011	0.152**	0.214***	0.080	0.214**
Other transport	0.042	0.054*	0.146*	0.208***	−0.113	0.021
Precision instruments	0.068*	0.080*	−0.023	0.039	−0.043	0.091
Food	0.130***	0.142***	0.057	0.119***	0.106	0.241*
Sugar, drinks	0.067*	0.079***	0.089*	0.151***	−0.171	−0.037
Textiles	0.125***	0.137***	0.077*	0.139***	0.020	0.154*
Leather	0.219***	0.231***	0.140*	0.202***	−0.053	0.081

Footwear, clothing	0.159***	0.171***	0.157***	0.219***	0.225	0.360*
Wood, Furniture	0.168***	0.180***	0.011	0.073**	-0.071	0.064
Paper, printing	0.093***	0.106***	0.049	0.111***	0.087	0.221*
Rubber and plastic	0.090**	0.102***	0.018	0.080***	-0.050	0.084
Other manufacturing	0.187***	0.199***	0.042	0.104*	0.111	0.245**
SALES (log)	0.012					
INVMAC (log)			0.062*			
RD&DE (log)						
constant					0.134	
Adjusted R-square: 0.322 (0.257)§						
F: 40.04						
Significance F: 0.0000						

Notes:

(1) These are obtained running separate regressions for each industry.

§: R-square obtained by running a pooled regression without the sectoral dummies.

*Significant at 0.1; **: significant at 0.01; ***: significant at 0.001.

8.3.4   Sectoral Differences in the Sources of Labour Productivity

Finally Table 8.6 presents the regression results of equation 7, which tries to capture major differences across sectors in the importance played by different determinant factors of labour productivity (as measured by value added per employee). As for the previous regressions the coefficients of the dummy variables can be read as estimates of the elasticity indexes of labour productivity with respect to the three independent variables included in the equation.

A first look at the three different sets of sectoral elasticity coefficients confirms that the levels of value added per employee continue to be positively associated with the capital intensity of production processes in most of the sectors. The negative coefficients found in the case of energy products and office machinery are statistically not significant.

With the exception of synthetic fibres, firm size also tends to be positively and significantly associated in most of the sectors with labour productivity, with the highest elasticity coefficients found in heterogeneous sectors such as leather, office machinery and food.

Generally positive, even if statistically less significant, are the associations between value added per employee and firms' innovative efforts in R&D and D&E. Elasticity coefficients statistically not different from zero are found in sectors where disembodied technological activities do not play a significant role and consequently are not expected to have an impact on firms' performances. These are sectors such as metals, metal products, plastics, synthetic fibres, food, sugar and drink.

On the whole the results of this last regression estimate suggest that, as emerged in Chapter 7, inter-firm differences in the levels of the value added per employee are related in the first place to differences in the productive structure of firms as expressed by the size of production units, the capital intensity and the level of mechanization of production processes. Technological factors seem to play a less important role at least when such relationships are estimated in a static framework like the one adopted here.

8.4   CONCLUSIONS

The aim of this chapter was twofold: (i) to quantify and qualify intersectoral differences in firms' technological profiles and their productive structure; (ii) to verify whether the relationships and regularities found in Chapter 7 between the different components of firms' innovation strategies were holding also at the level of the main industrial sectors. The empirical evidence presented in this chapter can be synthesized as follows.

The ANOVA analysis carried out in sections 8.2 and 8.3 has shown that industrial sectors differ from each other in a wide range of technological dimensions. This finding has, therefore, provided empirical support for the importance and methodological consistency of studying the relationships investigated in the previous and present chapter at the firm-level, taking average sectoral values as the unit of the analysis. Furthermore it has been shown that the use of average sectoral values allows a substantial reduction of the statistical noise associated with the use of firm-level data, and particularly with the large presence of small firms in our data-set.

As far as sectoral specificities in the nature and strength of the relationships investigated in Chapter 7 are concerned, a first general finding is that all the regularities and patterns found in the previous chapter have been confirmed by controlling for sectoral specificities. Few additional qualifications are, however, worth stressing:

- Firms' innovative efforts are associated in different sectors with different innovative components. Two kinds of sectoral pattern can be identified: traditional consumer-good sectors and process-material industries, which show an above-average elasticity of embodied expenditures with respect to total innovation costs, while the disembodied component yields a higher elasticity with respect to total firms' innovation expenditures in sectors characterized by higher technological opportunities.
- The complementary relationship between embodied and disembodied technological activities is confirmed and considerably strengthened, when sectoral specificities are taken into account. More innovative sectors show a higher level of complementarity between disembodied and embodied technological activities.
- The capital intensity of production processes is confirmed to be a fundamental factor associated to firm size. This holds in all industrial sectors.
- Embodied and disembodied innovation activities as well as firm size have been found to play a different role in different sectors as factors associated to labour productivity.
- Finally only in a few cases have the differences in the coefficients not resulted in being significantly different from the manufacturing average. This suggests that most of the sectors differ from each other at least in some of the technological dimensions and relationships taken into account in this study.

NOTES

1. Such a statistical technique works by subdividing the observed variance in the phenomenon investigated into two components: (i) the variability of the observations within a group about the group mean (in our case the industrial sector); and (ii) the variability of the group means themselves. Two different indexes of variability are computed: the within-groups sum of squares and the between-groups sum of squares. An F-statistic can be computed as the ratio between the two variance indicators, testing for the hypothesis that all groups (industrial sectors in our case) have the same average.
2. The large intersectoral differences in firm size (sales) is affected by the presence of a few outlier firms in sectors such as motor vehicles, office machinery and energy.
3. This last result can partly be explained by the limitations of the indicator used. An index based on the number of innovations does not allow us to weight the actual technological content of the innovations introduced.
4. Note that the F-values cannot be compared across columns, since they are affected (with an inverse relationship) by the number of observations.
5. The annual surveys of R&D activities carried out by ISTAT show that a large percentage of small firms conduct R&D activities on an occasional and temporary basis while the bulk of large firms carry out R&D programmes on a more systematic and permanent basis.
6. The inclusion of dummy variables for both intercepts and slope in each of the previous equations is equivalent to the estimation of as many sectoral independent regressions as the number of dummies included. This is what is usually called an 'unrestricted estimation' of the regression coefficients.
7. These coefficients have been obtained by estimating the same LSDV regression without omitting any sectoral dummies and omitting the intercept and the independent variable (Kennedy 1984; Suits, 1984).
8. In the case of equation 4, the R-square increases from 0.10 to 0.15, suggesting the presence of significant sectoral differences both in the absolute level of R&D expenditures and in the way they are associated with innovative investment. In the case of equation 5 the increase of the R-square is only 1.5 per cent.

9. Innovative patterns and technological regimes of production: a sectoral analysis

9.1 INTRODUCTION

Chapter 8 has shown that industrial sectors do differ in terms of firms' innovation conducts, investment patterns, firm size and labour productivity. However the actual ways in which industrial sectors differ, both in their technological patterns and prevalent production structures, deserve a more detailed investigation, which will be carried out in this chapter using data aggregated at a sectoral level.

The use of sectoral data also changes the interpretative meaning of the different relationships investigated in Chapters 7 and 8. A cross-sectoral analysis instead of reflecting differences in firms' innovative behaviours, investment decisions and performances is more likely to highlight sector-specific differences in technology and production structures, as condensed into the features of 'sectorally representative firms'. The use of sectoral data also has the advantage of reducing most of the statistical noise in the data-set brought by small firms and which is at the basis of the rather low correlation coefficients obtained in Chapters 7 and 8 where firm-level data were used.

In the following section the variety of innovation patterns in industry will be explored looking at the ways industrial sectors combine innovative efforts aimed at generating and developing new technologies, and innovative activities consisting of the use of technologies embodied in new production processes. In Section 9.3 we look at the relationship between firm size and innovation performances across industries and also explore other fundamental factors explaining intersectoral differences in firm size.

As in the previous two chapters the statistical analysis is based on the interpretation of the correlation coefficients between the different variables contained in our integrated data-set, using average sectoral values on 108 industrial sectors.[1] More descriptive evidence on the technological and productive profiles of industries will be also provided through two-dimensional plots of a reduced number of variables and sectors corresponding to a 2-digit industrial classification.

9.2   EMBODIED AND DISEMBODIED INNOVATION PROFILES OF INDUSTRIES

In this section we look at the variety of sectoral innovation patterns investigating whether total innovative intensity of sectors is associated with any particular innovation mix, as defined by the relative importance of R&D, design and investment, as well as by the relative importance of product and process innovations in the sectoral innovative output. The correlation matrix reported in Table 9.1 explores this issue. The first set of correlation coefficients in this table shows that the share of R&D and design expenditures in total innovation costs (%R&D, %D&E) are both positively associated with total innovation costs per employee (INCOST) while the latter variable is negatively correlated with the share of innovative investment (%INV). These results show, in other words, that, compared to less innovative sectors, more innovative industries are characterized by devoting a higher share of their innovation expenditures to R&D and design activities. The second set of correlation coefficients suggests that higher expenditures on R&D and design are in turn associated to innovation output with a higher percentage of product innovations. Product innovations show however, only a weak positive association with the overall innovative intensity of the sectors.

Table 9.1   Innovative intensity and product/process innovation shares across sectors (correlation coefficients – 108 sectors)

	INCOST (log)	%R&D	%D&E	%INV	%MKT
INCOST(log)	1.0	0.555	0.641	0.858	0.411
	–	P = 0.000	P = 0.000	P = 0.000	P =0.000
%PROD	0.21	0.246	0.231	–0.256	0.110
	P = 0.036	P = 0.012	P = 0.019	P = 0.008	P = 0.268
%PROC	–0.21	–0.246	–0.231	0.256	–0.110
	P = 0.036	P = 0.012	P = 0.019	P = 0.008	P = 0.268

Note: The first row shows the correlation coefficients and the second row the statistical significance.

A more direct visualization of the way the embodied/disembodied mix in the sectoral innovation patterns changes in accordance with the overall innovative intensity of the sectors is shown in Figure 9.1. The figure shows the position of 30 industrial sectors according to two innovative variables: total innovation costs per employee (INCOST) and the percentage of innovation costs devoted to R&D and D&E (%RD&DE).

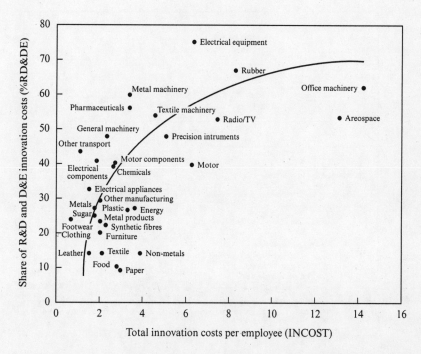

Figure 9.1   Innovative intensity and the share of R&D and D&E expenditures

The absence of sectors in the bottom-right side of the figure expresses the fact that high levels of innovation costs per employee are always associated with shares of R&D and design activities above a threshold level of 40 per cent of total innovation costs. In other words, it is difficult to find sectors among the highly innovative industries, which do not devote a substantial part of their technological activities to the generation and development of new technologies. Conversely it is rare to find highly innovative sectors, which innovate exclusively by acquiring new capital goods. It is, however, interesting to note that even in a typical science-based sector such as aircraft-aerospace, innovative investments represent an important part of total innovation costs (47 per cent).

Less innovative sectors, that is all the traditional sectors such as leather, textiles, footwear, metal products, and also some *scale-intensive* sectors such as food, paper, synthetic fibres, are concentrated in the first quadrant. These sectors show low innovation costs per employee and also rather small shares of R&D and design activities (below 30 per cent). This means that firms in these sectors innovate mainly through the acquisition and use of new machinery and equipment.[2]

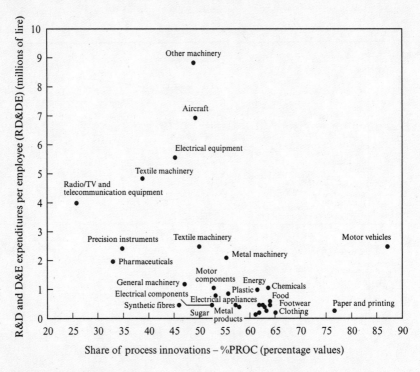

Figure 9.2 Disembodied innovative intensity and the share of process innovations

Figure 9.2 allows us to visualize the ways in which embodied and disembodied innovation expenditures are combined with different propensities to introduce product and process innovations. The figure shows the share of process innovations relative to the total number of innovations introduced on the horizontal axis, while the vertical axis measures total disembodied expenditures per employee (RD&DE). From the distribution of the sectors in the figure it emerges that 'product-oriented' innovative patterns mainly characterize industries which spend substantial resources for R&D and design activities. More particularly, Figure 9.2 shows a clear polarization between a group of sectors devoting high financial resources to knowledge-generating activities (top-left side of the figure), including office machinery, aircraft, rubber, electric and electronic components, radio and TV, and another group of sectors concentrating their innovative activities on the introduction of process innovations. Among the latter we find low innovative sectors such as food, other industries, wood and furniture, leather, footwear and clothing, and some process-based industries whose innovative patterns are characterized by heavy investment in process innovation, as in the case of paper and printing, chemicals, food, energy products, and non-metals and minerals. The motor vehicles' sector assumes a peculiar position, with a very high share of process innovations accompanied by a level of innovative expenditures on R&D and design close to the manufacturing average. This pattern is likely to reflect a high level of vertical integration both in production and in the innovation process, which characterizes the motor vehicles' sector. In this industry firms develop internally a large part of the technologies embodied in new products and in their production processes.

9.2.1 The Complementarity between Embodied and Disembodied Innovative Activities across Industries

We can now proceed to investigate the nature of the relationships existing between embodied and disembodied innovative activities across sectors. This can be done by looking in Table 9.2 at the correlation coefficients between the different kinds of innovation expenditure (R&D, design, innovative investment and marketing) and total investment in plants, equipment and machinery (INVMAC). Table 9.2 provides a similar picture to the one obtained in Chapter 7 using firm-level data. Innovative expenditures on R&D and design (D&E) appear, in fact, also across sectors to be complementary to embodied innovative activities. A positive relationship between total investment in productive capital (INVMAC), on the one hand, and R&D and D&E expenditures per employee, on the other, confirms that at least some of the most innovative sectors invest heavily in fixed productive capital and are characterized by capital-intensive production processes. This in turn suggests that no trade-off between what are regarded as the major components of 'tangible' and 'intangible' investments seems to emerge across industries (see Chapter 2).

However, while design activities show a higher degree of complementarity with both innovative investment and total investment in machinery, much weaker links are found between R&D and the two types of investment activities. The stronger link between design activities and investment suggests that sectors which invest in technologically new production processes, normally find it necessary to complement such innovative efforts with design activities, which usually take place at the shop-floor level, outside formal R&D departments. This in turn reflects the necessity for firms in process-based industries to keep improving the design and performances of their own production equipment. On the other hand, the weaker association between R&D and investment might suggest that, for at least some of the highly R&D-intensive sectors, investment activities and process innovations may not represent an important technological source.

Table 9.2   The relationship between embodied and disembodied innovation activities across sectors (correlation coefficients – 108 sectors)

	R&D (log)	D&E (log)	INV (log)	INVMAC (log)	MKT (log)
R&D (log)	1				
D&E (log)	0.704	1			
	P. = 0.000				
INV (log)	0.137	0.372	1		
	0.166	P. = 0.000			
INVMAC (log)	0.196	0.268	0.656	1	
	P. = 0.046	P. = 0.006	P. = 0.000		
MKT (log)	0.567	0.557	0.163	0.294	1
	P. = 0.000	P. = 0.000	P. = 0.099	P. = 0.002	

Notes: The first row shows the correlation coefficients and the second row the statistical significance.

More generally, the correlation matrix reported in Table 9.2 hints at the presence of a large variety of innovative patterns as far as the importance of embodied and disembodied innovative activities is concerned. Figure 9.3 gives an idea of the range of different sectoral innovation patterns measured in terms of innovative expenditures on R&D and design per employee (shown on the vertical axis) and innovative investments per employee (measured on the horizontal one). Excluding a consistent group of low innovative sectors close to the origin, quite a few innovative patterns can be identified. Office machinery and aerospace have not been shown in the figure being outliers as far as their levels of both embodied and disembodied innovative expenditure. Along the horizontal axis we found a group of sectors which, despite devoting low resources to R&D and design, are rather innovative through using technologies embodied in new machinery and equipment. The embodied profile of these industries is also characterized by a high capital intensity of production processes and by innovative activities oriented towards process innovations. This is a pattern that characterizes process-based industries such as non-metals and minerals, synthetic fibres, food and energy. An opposite pattern characterizes industrial sectors such as machinery (metal and textile machinery), pharmaceutical and even more clearly rubber and electronic equipment, which all show a rather high disembodied innovative intensity though maintaining low levels of innovative investment per employee. In both these last two groups of industries knowledge-generating activities are not combined with high levels of investment in fixed productive capital.[3] A more mixed technological pattern

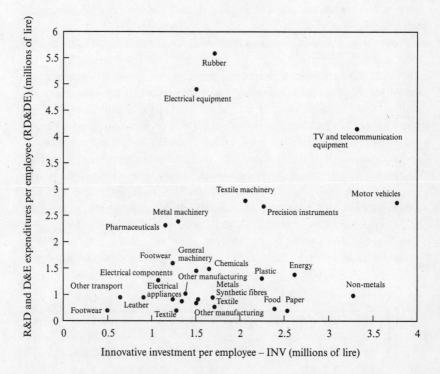

Figure 9.3   Disembodied and embodied sectoral innovative patterns

characterizes industries such as TV and telecommunications, office machinery and aerospace (these last two are not shown in the figure). These innovative industries show both very high innovative investment and expenditures on R&D and design.

The disembodied and embodied technological patterns highlighted in Figure 9.3 are worth exploring in more detail looking, on the one hand, at the different role played by R&D and design among the most innovative industries and, on the other, looking at the relative importance of innovative investment with respect to total investment in fixed productive capital.

As far as the relationship between the two main disembodied technological sources is concerned, here it is enough to mention that despite the fact that R&D and design do complement each other in most sectors, there are also a few industries in which firms focus either on R&D or design to generate new products. To mention only the most emblematic cases, typical *Science-based* sectors such as pharmaceuticals, chemicals, office machinery and rubber, show a clear propensity towards R&D activities, while sectors such as textiles, metals, general machinery and even aerospace-aircraft show a clear technological orientation towards design.[4]

As far as the nature of investment patterns is concerned, it is worth exploring more in depth the ways in which total investments in fixed productive capital (INVMAC) are combined with more 'technologically driven' investment across industries (INV). This relationship raises the crucial issue concerning the definition and measurement of embodied technological activities. We have seen in Part I of this book that embodied technological activities have usually been measured by total investment in fixed capital or investment in machinery and equipment. It is likely, however, that the innovative content of such investment varies systematically across industries in relation to the specific nature of production activities and innovation strategies in the different industries. Figure 9.4, reporting the position of 30 industrial sectors with respect to these two variables, provides a visual confirmation of such an hypothesis. The layout of the different sectors in the figure confirms that for a quite large number of industries there is, in fact, an almost fixed proportion of innovative

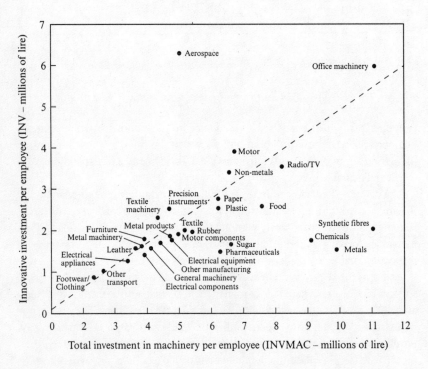

Figure 9.4   Total investment in machinery and innovative investment

investment with respect to total investment in machinery. For the manufacturing industry as a whole such a percentage is close to 30 per cent. However the absence of a perfect linearity between the two variables reveals that investment in machinery does not represent a perfect proxy of embodied technological activities.[5] In particular, in capital intensive industries such as synthetic fibres, metals, chemicals, food, sugar and drink and tobacco, a substantial part of investment in fixed capital does not seem to embody new technologies. This implies that using total investment in machinery and plant stands the risk of highly overestimating the innovative performance of these sectors. The aircraft-aerospace sector shows an opposite pattern. Though this sector is characterized by a relatively low level of investment in machinery, it shows surprisingly high innovative efforts in technologically new production investments. This can be explained by the important role played in this sector by investment in research equipment and infrastructure linked to development of new prototypes.

9.3 INNOVATION PERFORMANCES AND FIRM SIZE ACROSS INDUSTRY

In this section we investigate whether, and the extent to which, innovation performances and firm size are associated across industries. Table 9.3 shows the correlation coefficients between firm size and different types of innovation expenditure (per employee) (total innovation costs, R&D, design, innovative investment and marketing).

Table 9.3 Innovative intensity and firm size across sectors (correlation coefficients – 108 industrial sectors)

	INCOST (log)	R&D (log)	D&E (log)	INV (log)	MKT (log)
SALES (log)	0.184	0.258	0.115	0.036	0.406
	P = 0.033	P = 0.008	P = 0.246	P = 0.714	P = 0.000

Note: The first row shows the correlation coefficients and the second row the statistical significance.

Table 9.3 shows that firm size is positively associated with total innovation costs per employee, although the correlation is rather low (0.18). Stronger links are found between firm size and R&D and marketing (MKT) expenditures per employee. As suggested by most of the neo-Schumpeterian literature reviewed in Chapter 4 and also by most recent contributions by Sutton, the presence of economies of scale and barriers to entry associated to R&D activities and marketing can explain these positive correlations, which were also found in Chapter 7 using firm-level data (Sutton, 1991; Cohen, 1995).[6] Design and engineering activities are, on the contrary, only weakly associated with firm size reflecting the importance that such source of innovation has for small firms, especially those located in highly specialized sectors such as machinery and precision instruments. The weak, and statistically not significant, positive correlation between innovative investment and firm size is more difficult to be interpreted. This result is likely to reflect the fact that both small and large firms innovate through investing in new process technologies embodied in fixed capital.

The correlation coefficients contained in Table 9.3 are not able, however, to reflect the variety of ways in which sectoral innovation performances are combined with the average firm size of industries. This is shown in Figure 9.5 where industrial sectors are positioned according to the average size of the firms in each industry and their (average) R&D and design expenditures per employee.[7] Industries appear rather scattered in the figure. Sectors such as rubber, electronic components and equipment and radio/TV components show a medium-average firm size associated with a high innovative intensity. Beside these high R&D sectors, there are sectors such as textile machinery, metal machinery and precision instruments that, even though dominated by small firms, show high innovation expenditure per employee, especially devoted to the design and engineering of new products. Sectors such as synthetic fibres, metals, sugar and drink, and chemicals show an opposite pattern. They are characterized by medium-large firms and medium-low disembodied innovative activities. As already seen, in these sectors firms innovate mainly through investment in machinery and process innovations.

The absence of a clear-cut cross-sectoral relationship between firm size and innovative intensity in Figure 9.5 suggests that, apart from the presence of economies of scale and barriers to entry in R&D, there are other more fundamental factors, which explain actual differences in firms' size across industries. In Chapter 4 we have seen that contributions in the evolutionary literature have emphasized the role played by technological opportunity and appropriability conditions which are identified as the most important determinants of cross-industry differences in market structure and in the size distribution of firms. With the data at our disposal we are not able to test the importance of such factors. We are able, however, to highlight the role played by other production-related technological determinants of firm size. In Chapters 7 and 8 it was found that a strong positive relationship existed between firm size, investment in machinery per employee and labour productivity. It was argued that the linkages between these variables were able to reflect the importance of technological-related economies scale in production.

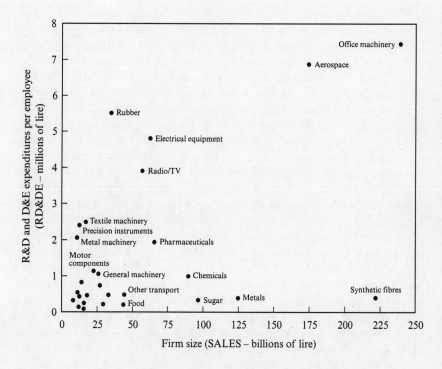

Figure 9.5   R&D and D&E expenditures per employee and firm size

Table 9.4   Firm size, capital intensity and productivity across sectors (correlation coefficients – 108 industrial sectors)

	SALES (log)	INVMAC (log)	VA (log)
SALES (log)	1.000	0.453	0.444
		P = 0.000	P = 0.000
INVMAC (log)		1.000	0.658
			P = 0.000
VA (log)			1.000

Note: The first row shows the correlation coefficients and the second row the statistical significance.

The correlation coefficients in Table 9.4 show that, also across sectors, firm size is positively correlated with total investment in fixed capital per employee, and the latter variable is strongly associated with labour productivity.[8] Even more clearly than at the firm level, these three variables thus seem to reflect the existence of different 'technological regimes of production', which can be defined by interdependent factors such as the importance of economies of scale, the level of technical and financial immobilization in fixed capital, and the level of mechanization of production processes. A synthetic visualization of these different technological regimes of production is provided by Figure 9.5, which reports the average values of firm size and capital intensity (as measured by investment in machinery per employee) across the main manufacturing sectors.

In Figure 9.5 we first identify a large group of sectors characterized by a low firm size and a low investment intensity. These are mainly consumer goods and mechanical-engineering industries. This pattern reflects the low levels of physical immobilization and mechanization, which characterize the technologies used in these sectors and the low opportunities to exploit economies of scale both in production and R&D activities. At the other extreme of the regression line, there are industrial sectors characterized by a high capital intensity such as energy, chemicals (production and transformation of), metals, synthetic fibres, motor vehicles and office machinery.[9] Sectors, combining the presence of large firms with a high investment intensity, include electronic components, pharmaceuticals, sugar and drink, rubber, paper and printing, food, and TV and other telecommunication components. A surprising pattern is shown by the aerospace-aircraft industry, where the presence of large firms is combined with a relatively low capital intensity of production processes. However, in interpreting this last pattern, the high level of innovative investments per employee of this industry should be kept in mind (see Figure 9.3).

9.4   CONCLUSIONS

The empirical evidence provided in this chapter has shown the presence of a large variety of sectoral innovative patterns. Industrial sectors have been found to differ in the following three innovative dimensions: (i) in the total innovative expenditures per employee; (ii) in the relative importance of embodied and disembodied technological activities; and (iii) in the role played by product and process innovations.

Despite the variety of innovation patterns some clear cross-sectoral regularities have nonetheless emerged:

- More innovative sectors are characterized by spending higher resources on disembodied technological activities (R&D and design) and show a higher propensity towards product innovation. Conversely less innovative sectors largely concentrate their innovative efforts on the acquisition and use of technologies embodied in new machinery and equipment. Despite this polarization, the most typical high-technology sectors such as office machinery and aerospace are characterized by heavily investing in both R&D and productive investment.

• Positive relationships have been found between total innovation expenditure per employee and firm size across sectors. This relationship is due almost exclusively to the R&D component. The result reflects the importance of economies of scale and barriers to entry in R&D in industries characterized by high technical opportunities.

• Industrial sectors have also been found characterized by quite different technological regimes in production: these can be identified by major differences in the levels of immobilization in fixed capital, level of mechanization and presence of economies of scale in production. These aspects largely explain differences in the average firm size across industries.

NOTES

1. Firm-level data have been aggregated at the level of a 3-digit NACE industrial classification. Correlation matrixes will be computed using log-transformed values in the case of all the innovative intensity and production variables. This is due to the close log-normal distribution of such variables.
2. This is consistent with the analysis of section 8.2 in the previous chapter.
3. A statistically significant negative correlation between capital intensity and both the share of D&E expenditure (%D&E) and the share of product innovations (%PROD) is, in fact, found across industries.
4. These results confirm once again that technological indicators based on R&D are likely to underestimate the actual innovative efforts of a wide range of industries, and in particular of those sectors where innovation is based on the accumulation of highly specific technological know-how and capabilities.
5. This is confirmed by the value of the elasticity coefficient of innovative investment with respect to total investment in machinery. A 10 per cent increase in total investment in machinery is accompanied by only a 7.5 per cent increase in innovative investment.
6. Compared with the low level of the other correlation coefficients, the strong relationship between firm size and innovative expenditure in marketing is quite striking, though consistent with the firm-level results of Chapter 7. This, however, might reflect the fact that firms in sectors dominated by large-scale production and characterized by more concentrated markets are likely to spend larger resources for the promotion, launching and commercialization of their products, and this is reflected in higher innovative expenditure on such activities. This finding is fully consistent with the recent works and models proposed by Sutton (1991).
7. Because of the use of normal values, office machinery and computing and motor vehicles fall outside the scatterplot.
8. Even stronger correlation coefficients have been found using a two-digit sectoral aggregation of data.
9. Motor vehicles, office machinery and energy sectors are clearly outliers, being characterized by average values of firm size and investment intensity much higher than the rest of the manufacturing sectors. The use of log values has positioned the latter sectors closer to the other sectors.

10. Embodied and disembodied patterns of technological change and production structure: a sectoral taxonomy

10.1 INTRODUCTION

The purpose of this chapter is to take jointly into account the multidimensional nature of innovative activities and production structures in industry which have been hinted at and reported in various parts of the previous chapters, and summarize them in a sectoral taxonomy.

The underlying idea behind this taxonomic exercise, which closes the empirical section of this book, is that taking into account both embodied and disembodied dimensions of technological change not only allows an effective identification of the different sectoral innovative patterns, but it also allows a better understanding of the complex links between the diversified nature of innovative conducts of firms and the structural characteristics of production of industries. The evidence presented in Chapter 9 has given certain preliminary hints, which support such a hypothesis. However the scattered and largely descriptive evidence presented in Chapter 9 needs to be investigated on a more analytical basis and somehow summarized. To this end, in section 10.2 a factor analysis will be carried out to single out some few dimensions by which sectoral differences in technology and production characteristics of industries can be summarized. The distribution of sectors according to such new technological and productive dimensions will then be described in greater detail in the taxonomy presented in section 10.3. Section 10.4 provides a more interpretative reading of the taxonomy while section 10.5 compares our findings with previous attempts to categorize sectoral innovation patterns in industry.

10.2 THE EMBODIED AND DISEMBODIED INNOVATION PATTERNS ACROSS INDUSTRY

In order to reduce the number of technological and productive dimensions (and relationships) investigated in Chapter 9, a factor analysis has been carried out on a large set of variables, which emerged in Chapter 9 as the most effective in defining the technological and productive profiles of industrial sectors.

Table 10.1   List of variables used in the 'sectoral' factor analysis

SALES (log)	Sales per firm
INVMAC (log)	Investment in total machinery and plant per employee
VA (log)	Value added per employee
R&D (log)	R&D expenditure per employee
D&E (log)	D&E expenditure per employee
INV (log)	Innovative investment expenditure per employee
%RD&DE	Share of R&D and D&E expenditure in total innovation costs
%PROD	Share of product innovations in all innovations introduced

Note: The indicators listed above are computed as sectoral average values.

As already described in Chapter 7, the statistical effectiveness of such a technique can be measured by the extent to which the new factors are able to reduce the original total variance. On more interpretative grounds, factor analysis is particularly effective when the factors extracted are few and they can be meaningfully interpreted by looking at the way they are linked to (and consequently are able to synthesize) the original variables. If effective in both respects, the new factorial values can then be used instead of the original variables for analytical and descriptive purposes, as shown in the following section.[1]

The variables used in the factor analysis are those listed in Table 10.1. Sectoral average values for 108 industrial sectors, corresponding to a three-digit NACE industrial classification, have been used.

Table 10.2 shows that the factor analysis has been quite effective in summarizing the original set of technological and productive characteristics of industries contained in our data-set. The two factors extracted explain more than two-thirds of the original total variance (67.5 per cent). The rotated factor matrix (also shown in Table 10.2) allows us to interpret the technological and economic meaning of such factors.

The 'first factor' summarizes interrelated aspects linked to *disembodied* technological patterns and *product-oriented* innovation activities: this interpretation is based on the high and positive correlation coefficients between factor 1 and the technological indicators measuring the following dimensions of sectoral innovative patterns: (i) the disembodied innovative intensity of industries, measured by the expenditures on R&D and design per employee (R&D and D&E); (ii) the disembodied innovative propensity of industries measured by the shares of total innovation costs devoted to R&D and design (%RD&DE); and (iii) the product/process innovation propensity (%PROD).

Table 10.2   Results of the factor analysis (108 sectors)

Factor	Eigenvalue	% of variance explained	Cumultive %
1	2.9398	36.7	36.7
2	2.4596	30.7	67.5

Rotated factor matrix

	Factor 1 Disembodied innovation intensity and product innovation	**Factor 2** Embodied innovation intensity and economies of scale
R&D (log)	0.853	0.276
D&E (log)	0.832	0.172
%RD&DE	0.942	-0.156
%PROD	0.646	−0.125
INV (log)	−0.191	0.714
SALES (log)	0.241	0.646
INVMAC (log)	−0.073	0.926
VA (log)	0.117	0.794

Note: Varimax rotation 1, extraction 1, analysis 1 – Kaiser normalization.

The 'second factor' reflects the importance of *embodied* innovative activities and the relevance of *scale* factors in production. This is because of the high and positive correlation between this factor and the technological and productive dimensions measured by innovative investment per employee (INV), the capital intensity of production processes (INVMAC), firm size (SALES) and labour productivity (VA).

By and large these results confirm the findings of the factoral analysis carried out in Chapter 7, where firm-level data were used. An important difference is, however, that at the sectoral level the complementarity between embodied and disembodied innovative activities becomes weaker. Compared to the firm-level analysis, where the total innovative intensity of firms was found to be associated with larger efforts in embodied innovative activities and larger shares of process innovations, across sectors the overall technological intensity of industries is associated with disembodied patterns, that is the more innovative sector shows higher expenditure on R&D and design and larger shares of product innovations. Conversely high shares of innovative investment and process innovations are associated with poor innovative performances. Such differences between firm-and sectoral-level results can be explained by the large influence that the innovative profile of small firms and traditional sectors have on the econometric estimates when data on individual firms are used. The embodied pattern which specifically characterizes both traditional sectors and small firms (as shown in the previous chapters), together with the very large number of small firms in our data-set, heavily affects most of the econometric estimates that use the full sample of firms.

Figure 10.1 shows the plot of the 108 industrial sectors according to their position with respect to the two new technological and productive factors. This

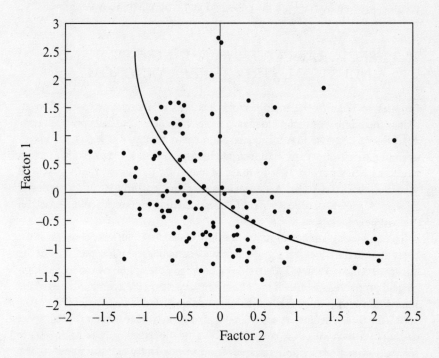

Figure 10.1   Scatterplot of the sectors according to the two factors

allows us to interpret the relationship between factor 1 (that is disembodied sources of innovation and importance of product innovations) and factor 2 (representing embodied sources of innovation and size-related factors), by studying the distribution of sectors in these two dimensions. The figure shows a large variety of sectoral innovative and productive patterns. A large number of sectors are positioned along a concave curve, which seems to show the presence of an inverse relationship (trade-off) between the two factors.

This suggests that for most of the sectors an increase in embodied innovative intensity (which is associated with a larger scale of production, a higher capital intensity in production and a larger share of process innovation), is accompanied by lower R&D and design expenditures and by a smaller presence of product innovations (with respect to process ones). Some trade-off thus seems to exist between disembodied and product-oriented innovative patterns, on the one hand, and embodied, process- and scale-based technological patterns across sectors, on the other.

However the clustering of some sectors in the bottom left and upper right quadrants also suggests that there are quite a few exceptions to this rule. These consist of a group of very low innovative sectors, in the first case, and a few sectors showing both a high disembodied and embodied innovative intensity.

10.3 SECTORAL PATTERNS OF INNOVATION AND INDUSTRIAL STRUCTURE: A TAXONOMY

In order to identify the main sectoral patterns of innovation, as well as to reduce the number of sectors to manageable and meaningful categories, a factor analysis was repeated on a reduced number of sectors (30 industries corresponding to a 2-digit NACE industrial classification) with the first two factors extracted being very similar to those obtained on the basis of 108 industrial sectors (see Table 10.3). A cluster analysis was performed on this reduced number of sectors in order to identify homogeneous groups of sectors based on the two new factors.[2]

The clustering statistical procedure has yielded 11 clusters, chosen on the basis of both the statistical significance and technological interpretability of the clusters formed. Table 10.4 provides a detailed description of the technological and productive profile of the 11 clusters, reporting the average values of the innovation and production variables contained in our data-set. Figure 10.2 shows the different clusters according to their approximate position with respect to the two technological axes already used (average values of the main innovation and production variables used in this study are also shown). The different groups of sectors can labelled and described as follows:

Table 10.3 Results of the factor analysis (30 sectors)

Factor	Eigenvalue	% of variance explained	Cumultive %
1	3.9044	48.8	48.8
2	2.1834	27.3	76.1

Rotated factor matrix

	Factor 1 Embodied innovation intensity and economies of scale	**Factor 2** Disembodied innovation intensity and product innovation
R&D (log)	0.429	0.834
D&E (log)	0.271	0.885
%RD&DE	0.186	0.958
%PROD	−0.079	0.754
INV (log)	0.706	0.183
SALES (log)	0.828	0.084
INVMAC (log)	0.936	−0.012
VA (log)	0.860	0.135

Note: Varimax rotation 1, extraction 1, analysis 1 – Kaiser normalization.

10.3.1   Technology Users and Traditional Sectors

Cluster 4 is found in the bottom-left part of Figure 10.2 (footwear, clothing, leather, wood furniture, metal products and other manufacturing). These are low innovative intensity sectors, characterized by both a low disembodied and embodied innovative intensity and a large prevalence of small firms. R&D and design expenditures per employee are very low and also innovative investment per employee is below the average. In these sectors, firms innovate almost exclusively by purchasing and using technologies embodied in new machinery and equipment. Almost 80 per cent of innovative activities rely upon this technological source and 62.4 per cent of the innovations introduced are process innovations. These sectors are also characterized by a low level of value added

Table 10.4 Productive and technological profiles by sectoral clusters (average values)

Cluster	No. cluster	No. firms	% of total sales	% of total innovation cost	Firm size		Investment intensity	Labour productivity	Innovative intensity (m. of innovation costs per employee)				Innovative composition (percentage values)			
					EMPL	SALES	INVMAC	VA	INCOST	R&D	D&E	INV	%R&D	%D&E	%INV	%PROC
Investment intensity	1	17	10.5	0.9	779	1469	25.92	107.22	3.66.	0.52	0.46	2.63	14.2	12.4	71.8	61.3
	2	1139	13.2	11.8	172	28	6.58	48.26	3.18.	0.15	0.22	2.69	4.7	6.8	84.7	64.5
	3	903	26.4	11.9	308	69	8.32	47.99	2.25.	0.34	0.35	1.44	15.1	15.8	63.8	59.4
Traditional	4	2511	12.2	8.8	103	11	3.71	38.56	1.78	0.12	0.22	1.37	6.8	12.5	76.8	62.4
R&D and D&E innovators	5	1437	14.8	13.3	225	24	3.34	41.12	2.16	0.34	0.60	1.13	15.9	27.7	52.2	50.3
	6	423	2.1	4.0	116	12	3.65	41.76	4.29	0.73	1.56	1.77	17.1	36.4	41.2	46.5
	7	141	2.8	9.1	470	47	4.50	44.38	7.24	2.50	2.62	1.54	34.6	36.1	21.3	42.7
R&D and investment intensive sectors	8	227	5.9	8.8	381	61	6.82	57.56	5.37	1.51	1.37	2.12	28.2	25.4	39.5	29.8
	9	15	1.1	6.8	1798	174	4.63	47.08	13.32	0.31	6.68	6.32	2.3	50.2	47.4	49.5
	10	9	7.4	14.3	13093	1936	6.43	44.29	6.38	0.98	1.50	3.79	15.3	23.5	59.4	86.8
	11	11	3.6	10.3	3413	786	17.11	107.15	14.40	4.99	3.85	3.56	34.7	26.8	24.7	49.4
Total		6833	100.0	100.0	213	35	5.90	46.76	3.62	0.63	0.87	1.93	17.4	24.1	53.3	55.0

Notes:
Cluster 1   Energy
Cluster 2   Synth fibres, non-metals, food, paper and printing
Cluster 3   Chemicals, plastic, metals, sugar, drinks
Cluster 4   Textiles, metal products, footwear, clothes, furniture, others
Cluster 5   Other transportation, general machinery, electrical components, electrical appliances, motor vehicle components
Cluster 6   Metal machinery, textile machinery, precision instruments
Cluster 7   Rubber and plastics, electronic equipment and components
Cluster 8   Radio/TV, telecomunication equipment, pharmaceuticals
Cluster 9   Aircraft and aerospace
Cluster 10 Motor vehicles
Cluster 11 Office machinery

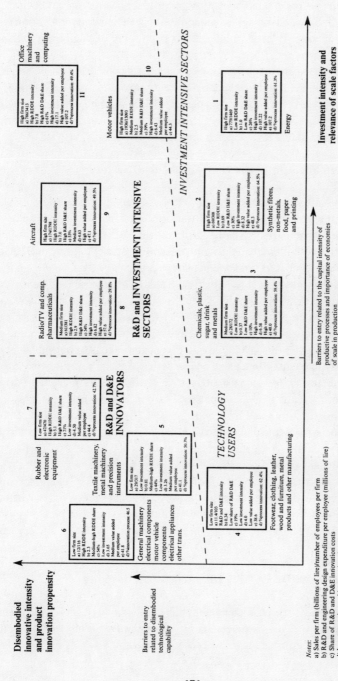

Figure 10.2   Disembodied and embodied innovative patterns and industrial structure: a taxonomy

171

per employee, probably related both to a low technological content of final products and to a low capital intensity of the production processes. The limited possibility of taking advantage of economies of scale either in production and innovation activities largely explains the large presence of small firms in these low innovative sectors.

This innovative pattern condenses the evidence that has already been pointed out in both Chapters 8 and 9, where the same group of sectors was found to be relying on process innovation and on the acquisition of embodied technologies (see Chapter 9), and was characterized by a low level of complementarity between embodied and disembodied innovative activities (Chapter 8).[3]

10.3.2   Investment-intensive (Fully Embodied) Sectors

In this group of sectors, investment activities play an important role both as a factor defining the structure and organization of production activities and as a form of innovative activity. The key technological feature of these sectors is that innovative activities are mainly embodied in investment in new machinery and equipment, while R&D and design play a marginal role. Process innovations are the prevalent innovation typology, with shares of process innovations far above the manufacturing average. There are, however, significant intersectoral differences among the *investment-intensive sectors* in the intensity and technological content of investment activities, as well as in the importance played by economies of scale. Synthetic fibres, non-metals, food and paper in cluster 2 are more capital-intensive and scale-based than the sectors in cluster 3, which contain sectors such as chemicals, plastics, metals, and sugar, drink and tobacco. As far as innovative patterns are concerned, chemicals, plastics, metals, and sugar, drink and tobacco (in cluster 3) carry out also some R&D and design activity, while the more capital-intensive and scale-based sectors in cluster 2 show higher innovative investment per employee and a large share of process innovations (64.5 per cent).

Such an aggregated description of the embodied pattern characterizing clusters 2 and 3 is consistent with the firm-level evidence presented in Chapter 8, where it was shown that innovation performances in these process-based industries are linked to investment in technologically new machinery and equipment.

10.3.3   R&D and D&E (Fully Disembodied) Innovators

Clusters 5, 6 and 7 are characterized by the combination of high expenditure on R&D and design per employee, large percentages of product innovations, small production units and low levels of investment per employee.

Cluster 6 (textile and metal machinery, precision instruments) includes all the most innovative mechanical-engineering sectors. Firm size and investment intensity are very low in these groups of industries. The relatively high innovative intensity of these sectors is due above all to the importance of design activities, which are oriented towards product innovations (representing 53.5 per cent of total innovations). Compared to industries in cluster 6, those in cluster 7 show higher R&D and design expenditures per employee and an even higher share of product innovations (57.3 per cent). The higher innovative intensity and the rather sophisticated technological content of the products of these industries might also explain the high average value added per employee found in these sectors, which include among others electronic apparatus and components.

Cluster 5, composed of some electrical and general mechanical sectors, consists of the less innovative sectors among the *R&D and D&E innovators*. Industrial sectors in this group have R&D and design expenditures per employee just above the manufacturing average and a rather low level of value added per employee associated with both a low capital intensity and around average R&D and design expenditures per employee. Innovative activities also seem to rely on a more balanced product/process mix. The share of product innovations is just above 50 per cent.

10.3.4   R&D and Investment-intensive Innovators

In clusters 8, 9, 10 and 11, high expenditures on R&D and design are accompanied by medium or high levels of investment in machinery per employee and a medium or large scale of production. The combination of high embodied and disembodied innovative expenditures is reflected in quite different product/process innovation mixes.

In the top-right part of the figure we find the office machinery industry (cluster 11). Large firms, high expenditures on R&D, design and investment are the characteristics of this typical science-based sector. The value added per employee in this industry is also very high, being related to the high technological content of products and processes as well as to the high capital intensity of this sector. Despite the fact that product innovations represent the prevailing innovative typology, the share of process innovations is relatively high, reaching almost 50 per cent of total innovations introduced by the firms in this sector.

A similar pattern, but with less extreme values, is shown by clusters 9 and 8, where a high disembodied innovative intensity is associated with medium- and large-sized firms and a rather high capital intensity. In these sectors, innovative activities aimed at producing new technological knowledge represent a large part of total innovative expenditures. As far as the relevance of product and process innovations is concerned, a clear difference exists between the two patterns. Innovation activities in cluster 8, which includes pharmaceuticals and radio and TV and telecommunication equipment, are clearly oriented towards the introduction of product innovations. The latter represents more than 70 per cent of total innovations introduced, which is the largest share of product innovations among all the clusters reported in the figure.

The automobile industry (cluster 10) is an outlier among the *R&D and investment-intensive sectors*, and this is with respect both to its production features (especially firm size) and its innovative characteristics (importance of process innovations). The very large average firm size in this sector reflects the importance of economies of scale in this industry. Investment expenditures on machinery per employee are high, but the importance of economies of scale is related not only to the amount of fixed capital invested but also to the organizational complexity of the productive processes in this industry. R&D and design expenditures and their shares in total innovation costs are also above the average but do not reach the levels of other more typically R&D-intensive sectors. An important role is also played by process innovations, which represent 86.8 per cent of the total innovations introduced in this sector. Such a high percentage of process innovations, the largest among the clusters identified in the figure, reflects the aforementioned capital-intensive and process-based nature of innovative patterns in this sector.

R&D and investment-intensive sectors bear the major 'responsibility' for the positive relationship between innovative intensity and firm size found at both firm and sectoral level respectively in Chapters 7 and 9. In particular in Chapter 9 we have seen that most of these sectors are, in fact, characterized by combining high embodied and disembodied innovative expenditures with large-scale production structures. This is a pattern symmetrically opposed to the one characterizing the *technology user sectors*, which is dominated by small firms with low innovative performances.

10.4   A MORE INTERPRETATIVE ANALYSIS OF THE SECTORAL TAXONOMY

Our taxonomy, along with defining the main sectoral innovation profiles, can be read in a more interpretative light. Moreover in particular, the taxonomic exercise contained in this chapter allows us to put into a more interpretative perspective the complex set of relationships linking sectoral-specific innovation patterns to the productive structure of firms and industries. The taxonomy highlights in fact three types of technological barriers to entry and economies of scale which can in turn be seen as different determinants of observable differences across industries in firm size and market structure and namely:[4]

1. those related to the presence of economies of scale and financial barriers to entry in R&D activities (measured on the vertical axis of Figure 10.2);
2. those related to the cumulative and tacit nature of the process of accumulation of technological know-how, which are associated with less formalized innovation activities (such as design and engineering and professional skills) (measured, as the previous ones on the vertical axis of Figure 10.2);
3. those related to the presence of high economies of scale in production, which are associated with large amounts of fixed capital and embodied technological patterns (measured on the horizontal axis of Figure 10.2).

The empirical evidence presented in this and Chapter 9 shows that the three different types of barrier to entry and economies of scale work to a different extent for different sectors.

The importance of barriers to entry of the first kind can explain market structure conditions in sectors where scale factors and investment requirements are high, such as in the case of *investment-intensive sectors*. On the other hand, the presence of small firms in all traditional sectors (technology users and traditional sectors) seems to be the result of the absence of economies of scale and barriers to entry of both a static (embodied) and dynamic (disembodied) nature.

The presence of barriers to entry and appropriability conditions related to the tacit and cumulative nature of technological change characterizes the innovative and productive profiles of many specialized machinery and precision instruments' sectors. Our evidence seems to suggest that the large presence in these sectors of small firms is explained above all by the absence of scale economies in both R&D and production activities and by the highly specialized and customized nature of most of these markets.

Finally, in the *R&D and investment-intensive sectors*, the joint presence of static and dynamic economies of scale in production and R&D are the key factors which favour large firms and concentrated market structures.

Our empirical analysis shows, therefore, that the extent to which disembodied technological activities are combined with more embodied innovative efforts plays a key role in determining in which cases the innovation performances of industrial sectors are accompanied by large-scale and capital-intensive production activities. Such an explanation might be complementary to the one provided by the evolutionary contributions in which intersectoral differences in market structures and firm size are seen as the results of sectoral differences in the levels of the technological opportunities and conditions of appropriability of innovation (Nelson and Winter, 1982; Levin et al., 1987; Dosi and Orsenigo, 1989). On the other hand, our taxonomy is rather consistent with the contribution of Sutton, which has distinguished between the effects of economies of scale in production (which are related to embodied technological activities) and economies of scale and barriers to entry linked to R&D and advertising expenditures (Sutton, 1991).[5]

10.5   THE CONSISTENCY OF OUR FINDINGS WITH PREVIOUS TAXONOMIC EXERCISES

We can now ask about the extent to which our taxonomy fits with previous attempts to categorize sectoral technological profiles and trajectories. The first reference point in this respect is the sectoral taxonomy proposed by Pavitt in 1984. We also discuss the level of consistency of our 'static' technological profiles with the dynamic framework envisaged by the product cycle model.

10.5.1   Pavitt's Taxonomy

It is clear that our contribution is very much in line with Pavitt's work. Most of the sectoral aggregations presented in Figure 10.2 can, in fact, be read into the Pavitt taxonomy. The focus and targets of our analysis are, however, somewhat different: compared to Pavitt's contribution our analysis has been characterized by putting a stronger emphasis on the distinction between embodied and disembodied technological change and by investigating in more detail the interdependencies between R&D, design and investment. We have also looked in more detail at the relationship between embodied and disembodied patterns of technological change and the basic characteristics of productive structure of industries (what we have named 'technological regimes of production').

The results of our taxonomy can, therefore, be seen as an integration and qualification of Pavitt's work. It is worth then stressing the elements of originality of our findings with respect to the ones contained in the taxonomy proposed by Pavitt:

1. The first point concerns the actual importance of embodied technological activities in sectoral innovation patterns. Pavitt's taxonomy tends to confine the importance of embodied technological activities to the 'supplier-dominated' technological trajectory which characterizes mainly services and traditional consumer-good sectors in manufacturing. Our evidence shows that the acquisition of technologies embodied in new machinery and equipment plays a significant role in a much larger section of the manufacturing industry, that is at least in three of the four sectoral aggregations

reported in Figure 10.2, and namely among *technology users, investment-intensive sectors*, and *R&D and investment-intensive sectors*. Altogether these three groups of sector cover more than two-thirds of industrial output and employees of the Italian manufacturing industry. The only sectors which do not seem to rely upon investment and embodied technologies are those labelled as *R&D and D&E innovators*. Compared to Pavitt's taxonomy our work thus tends to re-emphasize the importance of investment and the 'production domain' in firms' innovation conducts.

2. The second point has to do with the importance given to different technological determinants of industrial structure, as measured by the relative importance of large and small firms in innovation activities and industrial output. The role played by economies of scale in production and the capital-intensive nature of production activities are acknowledged by Pavitt as factors, among others, explaining sectoral differences in market structure and technological trajectories. However at least an equal emphasis is given to appropriability conditions linked to the accumulation of disembodied technological assets, that is to technological capabilities which have the characteristic of being firm-specific in nature and associated with dynamic learning economies in production and innovation. Our evidence tends to re-emphasize the importance of the basic characteristics of the production domain and its technical and technological dimensions. The importance of technical economies of scale, the specific nature of production processes, the level of financial immobilization in fixed productive capital, and the organizational complexity of production systems, are identified in our taxonomy as primary sources of the sectoral differences in market structures. The market structure characteristics of the specialized machinery sectors are emblematic cases in this respect. Our evidence suggests that the large presence of small firms and low concentrated market structures in these industries (*R&D and D&E innovators* in Figure 10.2) is primarily based on interrelated productive aspects such as the low opportunity to exploit economies of scale, the low levels of mechanization and the highly customized nature of these products and markets.

3. Finally our taxonomic exercise tends to emphasize, more than does Pavitt's, the complementary nature of embodied and disembodied technological activities, product and process innovations and static and dynamic economies of scale and barriers to entry. These complementarities are condensed into the technological and productive profiles of the most innovative firms and industries characterized by high technological opportunities, such as office machinery, aerospace and electronic and telecommunication equipment.

10.5.2 Product Cycle Approach

The relationships between sectoral technological patterns and industrial structural conditions highlighted in our empirical analysis and taxonomy are inserted into a static context. However we believe that our taxonomy can also be interpreted in a more dynamic perspective. In particular, the different patterns in Figure 10.2 could also be read within (and provide additional qualifications to) the product cycle models reviewed in Chapter 4. The latter take explicitly into account the interlinkages between the evolution of production structures and changes in the innovation patterns characterizing the long-term evolution of industries. According to both the old and revised versions of the product cycle models (Vernon, 1966; Utterback and Abernathy, 1975; Abernathy and Utterback, 1978; Gort and Klepper, 1982; Klepper and Graddy, 1990), in the mature phase of industries technology is fairly standardized, innovations are aimed at cost reduction and tend to be based on improvement of the production processes. This appears to be consistent with a rising proportion of embodied to disembodied technology in mature, scale-based and investment-intensive industries, and reflect rather well the pattern of the *investment-intensive sectors* in our taxonomy. New industries, conversely, are associated with lower levels of standardization and could be characterized by a high proportion of disembodied to embodied technological activities. This latter pattern might reflect the technological profile of most of the industries in the *R&D and D&E innovators'* cluster as well as those in the *R&D and investment-intensive* sectoral category.

However the technological characteristics and the evolutionary pattern of some sectors go contrary to what one would have expected from a reading of the product cycle approach. On the one hand, industries like most of the specialized machinery producers do not seem to have ever passed through a large-scale standardization stage, being still characterized by a large presence of small firms due to the high customization of their products and technologies. On the other hand, more recent R&D-intensive sectors like office machinery, telecommunication and radio and TV have attained in a relatively short time a significant standardization of products, processes and technologies, together with concentrated market structures. The set of technological, structural and demand-led dimensions, which characterize the dynamics of industrial sectors, has emerged even from our static analysis as a highly complex and interactive one.

10.6 CONCLUSIONS

The taxonomy presented in this chapter has identified main innovation patterns and technological regimes of production in the manufacturing industry.

Four main innovative patterns have been identified on the basis of the type of technological source used in the different industries, the type of innovation introduced (product or process) and the overall innovative performance of industrial sectors. The clustering of industries has shown: (i) the predominant role of R&D and design activities for the machinery, electrical and electronic components sectors; (ii) the central role of investment in the chemicals, food, rubber and metals industries; (iii) a combination of very high levels of R&D and investment in large-scale organizations which characterize the most representative high-technology sectors such as aerospace, office machinery, telecommunications and radio and TV apparatus.

The taxonomy presented has also shed some light on the complex links between the diversified nature of sector-specific innovative conducts and the existence of a variety of technological regimes in production. In particular it has been shown that embodied and disembodied patterns of innovation are associated with different kinds of scale factor and barrier to entry, which in turn are able to explain main differences in the average size of firms and market structures across industries. The sectoral patterns identified in our taxonomy show that large-scale and concentrated productive structures are found in those industries where disembodied technological activities are combined with more embodied innovative efforts. These are the sectors where economies of scale and barriers to entry, both in the process of generation of knowledge (R&D) and in production activities, reinforce each other.

NOTES

1. The principal steps involved in a factor analysis, and the rationale for it have been discussed in Chapter 7.
2. The essential aim of the cluster analysis consists of grouping the original observations into more aggregated groups in order to minimize the internal variance within each group and maximize intergroup variance. The grouping procedure is based on the measurement of 'distances' between the objects originally located in a multidimensional space defined by the full set of variables chosen. It should be stressed, however, that the final results of such a statistical procedure (that is, number of groups and objects composing each group) crucially depend on the set of variables chosen and the way distances between objects and groups are measured. There are, in fact, several clustering methods, depending on how the distances are estimated. In this study the complete linkage method has been used. With such a method the distance between two clusters is calculated as that between their two furthest points (observations). The use of other clustering methods (that is, single linkage and average linkage methods) have given the same results. A cluster analysis on firm-level data provided by the first ISTAT–CNR innovation survey has been carried out by Cesaratto and Mangano (1993).
3. The firm-level positive relationships found in Chapter 7 between firm size, innovative intensity and share of process innovations can be explained by the specific technological profile of this group of sectors, which is also the most numerous one (2511 firms), and is, therefore, able to influence the econometric estimates for the manufacturing industry as a whole.
4. The vertical and horizontal distances between clusters can be considered as an indicator of both technological and productive distances among sectors. These distances can be seen also as

    barriers to intersectoral movements of the firms and to diversification strategies in technology and production. What the figure suggests is that in moving from one sector to another a firm faces productive, technological and organizational barriers to entry and to exit (due to the presence of sunk costs in both technology and production assets), whose nature and importance varies according to the starting point and the direction of movement. The concept of techno-logical distance has been developed by Jaffe (1986).

5. Sutton in this regard distinguishes between investments which have an endogenous sunk cost nature (R&D and advertising) and those which are 'exogenous' (and linked to investment in fixed productive capital) in the sense that they are determined by the state of technology. Both give rise to economies of scale and barriers to entry. According to Sutton, the former have a more strategic or behavioural nature (Sutton, 1991).

11. Conclusions and policy implications

This concluding chapter synthesizes the main findings which have emerged throughout our empirical analysis and draws from them a set of implications and recommendations for theoretical and empirical research, as well as for technology policy.

The first objective of this book has been to build an integrated perspective on technological change, that is one acknowledging the importance of both disembodied and embodied technological activities. The empirical analysis, based on the results of the Italian innovation surveys, has confirmed that knowledge-generating activities in the form of R&D and design on the one hand, and investments in fixed productive capital on the other, represent the two main sources of innovation in industry. It has also been shown that the distinction between embodied and disembodied technological change is able to effectively discriminate between different sectoral patterns of innovation and regimes of production in industry. These have been summarized in the taxonomy presented in Chapter 9. The clustering of industries has clearly identified: (i) the important role of design and product innovations for the machinery sector and the producers of electrical and electronic components; (ii) the importance of investment and process innovations in the chemicals, food, rubber, and metals industries; (iii) a combination of very high levels of R&D and investment in the case of the most representative high-technology sectors such as office machinery, telecommunication equipment and aerospace.

Our taxonomy thus largely confirms the technological profiles of industries identified by Pavitt (1984). There are, however, two important differences between our taxonomy and the Pavitt's one which are worth stressing: first, our results extend the importance of the acquisition of technologies embodied in new machinery much beyond the less innovative 'supplier-dominated' sectors. Secondly, our empirical analysis puts much more emphasis on the complementary nature of embodied and disembodied technological activities, and of product and process innovation strategies. These complementarities have been found particularly evident among the most innovative firms and industries characterized by high-technological opportunities such as office machinery, aerospace and electronic and telecommunication equipment. Both these findings show that the industries usually labelled as 'knowledge-intensive' heavily invest both in R&D and technologies embodied in fixed productive capital.

In this book we have also shown that taking into account both embodied and disembodied dimensions of technological change makes it possible to shed new light on the complex relationship between technology, firm size and market structure. Our taxonomy highlights three types of different technologically-related barriers to entry and economies of scale: (i) those related to the presence of economies of scale and financial barriers to entry in R&D; (ii) those related to the cumulative and tacit nature of less formalized innovation activities such as design and engineering and professional skills; and (iii) those related to the presence of high economies of scale in production, associated to high investment in fixed capital and embodied technology.

Our taxonomy can thus bridge the gap between the three main bodies of empirical literature reviewed in Chapter 4, in which the relationships between technology, firm size and market structures are envisaged in the light of quite distinct perspectives:

1. the Structure-Conducts-Performance approach in industrial economics which emphasizes the role of embodied technology for explaining the presence of static economies of scale and barriers to entry in production;
2. the neo-Schumpeterian literature, as well as the most recent works by Sutton, which emphasize the key role of economies of scale, barriers to entry, indivisibilities and sunk costs in R&D activities;
3. the recent contributions in the neo-Schumpeterian and evolutionary literature which stresses the importance of the tacit and cumulative nature of techno-logical knowledge as the key factor explaining the persistence of asymmetries in innovative conducts and performances of firms (see Chapters 4 and 5).

The empirical evidence presented in this book shows that the three perspectives have to be seen as complementary rather than competing or alternative ones. Large firms and concentrated market structure are, in fact, found in industries where economies of scale and barriers to entry arise from high investment and financial immobilization in both R&D and fixed productive capital. On the other hand the tacit and cumulative nature of technological change is able to explain the presence of barriers to entry and the persistence of technological asymmetries across firms in highly innovative industries dominated by small and medium enterprises.

The strongest result emerging from our empirical analysis concerns however the centrality of embodied technological activities in manufacturing industry. While not denying the increasing importance of science, knowledge and information in modern industrial societies, the evidence provided in this book shows that investments in fixed capital remain the fundamental channel through which knowledge is diffused and used throughout the economic system. Investments have been found to represent a fundamental technological source among both small and large firms, low and high innovative sectors, both in manufacturing and services, and across most European countries.

This finding has very important implications for the general conceptualization of the innovation process, for the ways the latter is endogenized into economic models and studied in empirical research. Activities consisting of the adoption and diffusion of new technologies through investment in fixed productive capital should be considered as a central component of the overall process of technological change. Accordingly this study supports all those theoretical and empirical contributions which over the last few years have started to re-emphasize the importance of investment in the analysis of technological change (Scott, 1989; De Long and Summers, 1991; Antonelli et al., 1992, Wolf, 1991, 1994a, 1994b).

It is also worth stressing that putting investment at the centre of the economic analysis of technological change is going to have quite important implications in the evolution of this discipline since it reinforces and enriches the endogenous nature of technological change, especially in a macroeconomic framework. Most contributions in the so-called 'new growth theory' already reflect such concern for the endogenous and macroeconomic role of investment. It is, however, somehow puzzling that, apart from a few exceptions (Scott, 1989, Antonelli et al., 1992), the richness of the heterodox contributions contained in the classical and post-Keynesian tradition have only to a limited extent been exploited in their theoretical and interpretative implications. This is a theoretical avenue which would deserve much more intellectual investments and a good deal of empirical research.

However empirical analyses aimed at taking into account embodied technological change are still seriously hampered by the lack of appropriate data and indicators. While we have now a good range of 'disembodied technological indicators', indicators measuring firms' innovation efforts consisting of the acquisition, adoption and use of new (largely embodied) process technologies are still scarce and not internationally standardized. Gross investment in fixed capital is still the most widely used variable in empirical research.

The recent attempts undertaken in many countries to design and carry out innovation surveys aimed at collecting data on a large range of technological activities (investment included) represent a very promising step ahead in this respect. Our empirical results strongly encourage a more extensive use of such data, both for micro and macroeconomic empirical analyses.

11.1   SOME POLICY IMPLICATIONS

Three main themes emerge from our empirical analysis and are rich in implications for technology policy:

1. the key importance of diffusion in the innovation process;
2. the complementary nature of embodied and disembodied technological change in industries characterized by high-technological opportunities;
3. the strong link between technological accumulation and investment.

All of them do challenge the 'disembodied' and 'R&D-centred' approach to technology policy which permeates the theoretical literature in this field as well as most of policy practices. State intervention in the field of science and technology has traditionally been justified by the presence of market failures in the process of generation and dissemination of knowledge (due to the well-known characteristics of indivisibility and non-rival use of knowledge). Technology policy practices in most OECD countries have mirrored such an approach focusing most of the efforts in supporting knowledge-generating activities and infrastructures, and more in particular R&D programmes.

1. The evidence provided in this book strongly supports the need for a rebalancing of technology policy towards diffusion, and in particular in favour of measures which can facilitate the absorption in the economic system of new production technologies. Acknowledging diffusion as a key domain of technology policy asks, however, for a more general rethinking of the theoretical rationale and operative tools of state intervention. Furthermore diffusion is a complex and multidimensional phenomenon, which involves not only the adoption of more sophisticated vintages of capital but also complementary changes in skills and organizational arrangements. In the last few years some attempts have been made in the direction of drawing from the vast literature on technology diffusion some indications for reorienting technology policy (OECD, 1992a; Metcalfe, 1995; Smith, 1996b). We are, however, far away from having reached a comprehensive framework or a consistent set of policy guidelines.

2. The complementarity between embodied and disembodied technological change, which characterizes firms' strategies and patterns of innovation, especially in the industries characterized by high-technological opportunities, is another important theme and finding of this book. In particular it has been shown that R&D, the design and engineering of new products and processes, and investment in fixed productive capital are joint determinants of the performances of firms and industries. Also this finding supports the need to overcome the R&D-centred approach to technology policy discussed above. An effective technology policy should consist of a balanced and selective mix of measures able to strengthen the knowledge base of economic systems, enhancing the technological competencies and absorption capacity of firms and favouring the diffusion of better process technologies. We have also shown that the nature and levels of technological complementarities

varies across industries and this also should be taken into account in tailoring more selective and effective innovation policies.

3. The strong link between technological change and investment activities found in our empirical analysis also carries important implications for technology policy. The existence of a macroeconomic link between investment, technological change and economic growth has long been identified in economic theory and now rediscovered by the new-growth theory. Surprisingly enough, however, the existence of such a link has been neglected by traditional as well as more recent literature on technology policy. Macroeconomic references in the present debate on technology policy have rarely gone beyond the usual claim that favourable macroeconomic conditions are important for technology and innovation to exert their beneficial economic impact.

We do not have here the ambition to raise the issue of causality between technological change, investment and growth which would lay at the very heart of a discussion on technology policy. The message is a less ambitious one and consists of stressing the need to bring back technology policy in a macroeconomic context. This claim is based on the simple belief that macroeconomic forces linked to aggregate demand and investment do have some kind of autonomous role for explaining the dynamics of economic systems as opposed to the potential of firms' behaviour and performances. If this is accepted, then it is time to make a shift from the dominant supply-side and micro-founded approach to technology policy towards one which acknowledges the need of stimulating technological change, investment and aggregate demand within an integrated macroeconomic framework.

As a matter of fact, however, the continuous shrinking of public budgets, the reduced room for national monetary policies, and the reduced importance of public investment in infrastructure and production have not left much room for manoeuvre for policies sustaining investment and aggregate demand as a way to foster technological accumulation.

In the light of these constraints a viable and more realistic alternative to generalized expansive policies would consist of more selective measures aimed at sustaining those components of investment and demand which are likely to have a greater impact on both the accumulation of technological competencies and on economic growth and employment.

Bibliography

Abernathy, W.J. and Utterback, J.M. (1978), 'Patterns of industrial innovation', *Technology Review*, June–July, **7**, pp. 41–7.

Abramovitz, M. (1986), 'Catching-up, forging ahead and falling behind', *Journal of Economic History*, **46** (2), pp. 385–406.

Abramovitz, M. (1993), 'The search for the sources of growth: areas of ignorance, old and new', *Journal of Economic History*, **53** (2).

Abramovitz, M. and David, P.A. (1996), 'Technological change and the rise of intangible investments: the US economy's growth-path in the twentieth century', in OECD, 1996b.

Acs, Z.J. and Audretsch, D.B. (1990), *Innovation and Small Firms*, The MIT Press, Cambridge, Mass.

Aghion, P. and Howitt, P. (1992), 'A model of growth through creative destruction', *Econometrica*, **60** (2).

Amable, B. (1993), 'Catch-up and convergence: a model of cumulative growth', *International Review of Applied Economics*, **7** (1).

Amable, B. and Boyer, R. (1992), 'The R&D-productivity relationship in the context of new growth theories: some recent applied research', paper presented at the seminar on *Quantitative Assessment of Technological Change*, Brussels, January.

Amable, B. and Verspagen, B. (1995), 'The role of technology in market share dynamics', *Applied Economics*, **27**, pp. 197–204.

Amendola, G., Dosi, G. and Papagni E. (1993), 'The dynamics of international competitiveness', *Weltwirtschaftliches*, **3**.

Amendola, M. and Gaffard, J. (1988), *The Innovative Choice*, Basil Blackwell, Oxford.

Antonelli, C. (1995), *The Economics of Localized Technological Change and Industrial Change*, Kluwer Academic Publishers, Dordrecht.

Antonelli, C., Petit, P. and Tahar G. (1992), *The Economics of Industrial Modernization*, Academic Press, Cambridge.

Antonelli, G. and De Liso, N. (1997) (eds), *Economics of Structural and Technological Change*, Routledge, London.

Archibugi, D., Cesaratto, S. and Sirilli G. (1991), 'Sources of innovative activities and industrial organization in Italy', *Research Policy*, **20**.

Archibugi D. and Pianta, M. (1992), *The Technological Specialization of Advanced Coutries*, Kluwer Academic Publishers, Dordrecht.

Archibugi, D., Evangelista, R. and Simonetti, R. (1995), 'Concentration, firm size and innovation: evidence from innovation costs', *Technovation*, **15** (3), pp. 153–63.

Archibugi, D., Howells, J. and Michie, J. (1998) (eds), *National Systems of Innovation or the Globalization of Technology?*, Cambridge University Press, Cambridge.

Arrow, K. (1962), 'The economic implications of learning by doing', *Review of Economic Studies*, **29** (2), pp. 155–73.

Arrow, K.J., Karlin, S. and Suppes, P. (1959) (eds), *Mathematical methods in the social sciences*, Stanford University Press, Stanford.

Athreye, S. (1998), 'On markets in knowledge', *Journal of Management and Governance*, **1** (2), pp. 231–53.

Audretsch, D. and Yamawaki, H. (1988), 'R&D rivalry, industrial policy, and U.S. Japanese trade', *The Review of Economics and Statistics*, **70** (3).

Babbage, C. (1883), *On the Economy of Machinery and Manufactures*, (4th edn.), Charles Knight, London.

Bain, J.S. (1956), *Barriers to New Competition*, Harvard University Press, Cambridge.

Bain, J.S. (1959), *Industrial Organization*, John Wiley & Sons, New York.

Baldwin, W.L. and Scott, J.T. (1987), *Market Structure and Technological Change*, Harwood, Chichester.

Banerji, R. (1978), 'Average size plants in manufacturing and capital intensity, across country analysis by industry', *Journal of Development Economics*, **5**.

Baumol, W.J. (1982), 'Contestable markets: an uprising in the theory of industrial structure', *American Economic Review*, **72**, pp. 1–15.

Bell, M. and Pavitt, K. (1993), 'Technological accumulation and industrial growth: contrasts between developed and developing countries', *Industrial and Corporate Change*, **2**, pp. 157–210.

Bernstein, J. (1989), 'The structure of Canadian interindustry R&D spillovers, and the rates of return to R&D', *Journal of Industrial Economics*, **37** (3).

Bound, J., Cumminis, C., Griliches Z., Hall, B.H. and Jaffe, A. (1984), 'Who does R&D and who patents?', in Z. Griliches.

Burmeister, E. and Dobell, R. (1969), 'Disembodied technical change with several factors', *Journal of Economic Theory*, **1**, pp. 1–8.

Calvert, J., Ibarra, C., Patel, P. and Pavitt, K. (1996), 'Innovation outputs in European industry: analysis from CIS', paper presented to the International conference on Innovation Measurement and Policies, Luxembourg, 20–21 May.

Carlsson, B. (1989), *Industrial Dynamics*, Kluwer Academic Publishers, Boston.

Casson, M. and Creedy, J. (1993), *Industrial Concentration and Economic Inequality*, Edward Elgar, Aldershot.

Cesaratto, S. and Mangano, S. (1993), 'Technological profiles and economic performance in the Italian manufacturing sector', *Economics of Innovation and New Technology*, **2**.

Clark, J.M. (1923), *Studies in the Economics of Overhead Costs*, University of Chicago Press, Chicago.

Clarke, R. and Davies, S.W. (1982), 'Market structure and price-cost margin', *Economica*, **49**, pp. 277–87.

Cohen, W.M., Levin, R.C. and Mowery, D.C. (1987), 'Firm size and R&D intensity: a re-examination', *Journal of Industrial Economics*, **35**.

Cohen, W.M. (1995), *Empirical studies of innovative activities*, in P. Stoneman.

Cohen, W.M. and Levin, R.C. (1989), 'Empirical studies of innovation and market structure', in R. Schmalensee and R.D. Willing.

Cohen, W.M. and Klepper, S. (1992), 'Firm size and the nature of innovation within industries: the case of process and product R&D', paper presented to the International Schumpeter Society conference, Kyoto, August.

Cohen, W.M. and Klepper, S. (1996), 'A reprise of size and R&D', *Economic Journal*, 106.

Comanor, W.S. and Wilson, T.A. (1967), 'Advertising, market structure and performance', *Review of Economics and Statistics*, **49**.

Commission of the European Communities (1988), *Research on the 'cost of non-Europe'*, Studies on the Economics of Integration, Luxembourg.

Coombs, R., Saviotti, P. and Walsh, V. (1987), *Economics and Technological Change*, Macmillan, London.

Curry, B. and George, K.D. (1983), 'Industrial concentration: a survey', *Journal of Industrial Economics*, **31**.

Dasgupta, P. and Stiglitz, J. (1980), 'Industrial structure and the nature of innovative activity', *Economic Journal*, **90**, pp. 266–93.

David, P.A. (1969), *A Contribution to the Theory of Diffusion*, Stanford Center for Research on Economic Growth, memorandum no. 71, Stanford University.

David, P.A. (1975a), *Technical Change, Innovation and Economic Growth*, Cambridge University Press, Cambridge.

David, P.A. (1975b), '*The mechanization of reaping in the anti-bellum Midwest*', in P. David (1975a).

Davies, S. (1979), *The Diffusion of Process Innovations*, Cambridge University Press, Cambridge.

Davies, S. and Lyons, B. (1988), *Economics of Industrial Organization*, Longman, London.

Davies, S. and Lyons, B. (1996), *Industrial Organization in the European Union*, Oxford University Press, Oxford.

DeBresson, C. (ed.) (1996), *Economic Interdependence and Innovative Activity*, Edward Elgar, Aldershot.

DeBresson, C., Sirilli, G. and Hu, X. (1996), 'The structure of innovative interactions in the Italian economy (1981–85)', in C. Debresson.

De Long, J.B. and Summers, L.H. (1991), 'Equipment investment and economic growth', *Quarterly Journal of Economics*, **106** (2).

Denison, E.F. (1967), *Why Growth Rates Differ: post-war Experience in the Nine Western Countries*, Brookings Institution, Washington, DC.

Denison, E.F. (1974), *Accounting for United States Economic Growth 1929–69*, Brookings Institution, Washington, DC.

Denison, E.F. and Chung, W.K. (1976), *How Japan's Economy Grew so Fast: the Sources of Post-war Expansion*, Brookings Institution, Washington, DC.

Denison, E.F. (1985), *Trends in American Economic Growth*, Brookings Institution, Washington, DC.

Dodgson, M. and Rothwell, R. (1994), *The Handbook of Industrial Innovation*, Edward Elgar, Aldershot.

Domar, E.D. (1946), 'Capital expansion, rate of growth, and employment', *Econometrica*, **14** (2).

Dosi, G. (1982), 'Technological paradigms and technological trajectories: a suggested interpretation of the determinants and direction of technical change', *Research Policy*, **11**, pp. 147–62.

Dosi, G. (1984), *Technical Change and Industrial Transformation*, Macmillan, London.

Dosi, G. (1988), 'Sources, procedures and microeconomic effects of innovation', *Journal of Economic Literature*, **26**, pp. 1120–71.

Dosi, G., Freeman, C., Nelson, R., Silverberg, G. and Soete, L. (1988), *Technical Change and Economic Theory*, Frances Pinter, London.

Dosi, G. and Orsenigo, L. (1989), 'Industrial structure and technical change', in A. Heertje.

Dosi, G., Pavitt, K. and Soete, L. (1990), *The Economics of Technical Change and International Trade*, Harvester Wheatsheaf, London.

Dosi, G., Malerba, F., Marsili, O. and Orsenigo, L. (1997), 'Industrial structures and dynamics: evidence, interpretations and puzzles', *Industrial and Corporate Change*, **6** (1), pp. 3–24.

Eliasson, G. (1989), 'The dynamics of supply and economic growth', in B. Carlsson, 1989.

Englander, S., Evenson, R. and Hanazaki, M. (1988), 'R&D, innovation and the total factor productivity slowdown', *OECD Economic Studies*, **10**.

EUROSTAT (1994), *The Community Innovation Surveys: Status and Perspectives*, Luxembourg.

Evangelista, R. (1996), 'Embodied and disembodied innovative activities: evidence from the Italian innovation survey', in OECD (1996c).

Evangelista, R. and Sirilli, G. (1998), 'Innovation in the service sector', *Technological Forecasting and Social Change*, **58**, pp. 251–69.

Evangelista, R., Perani, G., Rapiti, F. and Archibugi, D. (1997), 'Nature and impact of innovation in manufacturing industry: some evidence from the Italian innovation survey', *Research Policy*, **26**, pp. 521–36.

Evangelista, R., Sandven, T., Sirilli, G. and Smith, K. (1998), 'Measuring innovation in European industry', *International Journal of the Economics and Business*, **5** (3), pp. 311–33.

Fagerberg, J. (1987), 'A technology gap approach to why growth rates differ', *Research policy*, **16** (2).

Fagerberg, J. (1988a), 'Why growth rates differ', in G. Dosi et al. (1988).

Fagerberg, J. (1988b), 'International competitiveness', *Economic Journal*, **98** (391).

Fagerberg, J. (1991), 'Innovation, catching-up and growth', in OECD (1991).

Fagerberg, J. (1994), 'Technology and international differences in growth rates', *Journal of Economic Literature*, **32**.

Fagerberg, J., Verspagen, B. and von Tunzelman, N. (eds.) (1994), *The Dynamics of Technology, Trade and Growth*, Edward Elgar, Aldershot.

Freeman, C. (1974), *The Economics of Industrial Innovation*, Penguin, Harmondsworth.

Freeman, C. (1982), *The Economics of Industrial Innovation*, Frances Pinter, London.

Freeman, C., Clark, C. and Soete, L. (1982), *Unemployment and Technical Innovation*, Frances Pinter, London.

Freeman, C. and Soete, L. (1997), *The Economics of Industrial Innovation* (3rd edn.), Frances Pinter, London.

Gibrat, R. (1931), *Les Inégalities Economiques*, Sirey, Paris.

Giersch, H. (1982), *Emerging Technologies: Consequences for Economic Growth, Structural Change, and Employment*, J.C.B. Mohr, Tubingen.

Gold, B. (1981), 'Changing perspective on size, scale, and returns: an interpretative survey', *Journal of Economic Literature*, **19**, pp. 5–33.

Gort, M. and Klepper, S. (1982), 'Time path in the diffusion of product innovations', *Economic Journal*, **92**, pp. 630–53.

Goto, A. and Suzuki, K. (1989), 'R&D capital, rate of return on R&D investment and spillovers of R&D in Japanese manufacturing industries', *The Review of Economics and Statistics*, **71** (4).

Greenhalgh, C. (1990), 'Innovation and trade performances in the United Kingdom', *Economic Journal*, **100**, pp. 105–118.

Griliches, Z. (1957), 'Hybrid corn: an exploration in the economics of technological change', *Econometrica*, **25**.

Griliches, Z. (ed.) (1984), *R&D Patents and Productivity*, Harvard University Press, Cambridge.

Griliches, Z. and Lichtenberg F.(1984), 'Interindustry technology flows and productivity growth: a re-examination', *The Review of Economics and Statistics*, **61**.

Griliches, Z. (1995), 'R&D and productivity: econometric results and measurements issues', in P. Stoneman.

Grossman, G.M. and Helpman, E. (1991), *Innovation and Growth in the Global Economy*, The MIT Press, Cambridge, Mass.

Grossman, G.M. and Helpman, E. (1994), 'Endogenous innovation in the theory of growth', *Journal of Political Economy*, October.

Hagedoorn, J. (1989), *The Dynamics of Innovation and Diffusion: A Study in Process Control*, Frances Pinter, London.

Hanel, P. (1994), 'R&D, interindustry and international flows of technology and the total factor productivity growth of manufacturing industries in Canada, 1974–1989', *Cahier de Recherche 94–04*, Université de Sherbrooke.

Harrison, B. (1994), *Lean and Mean*, Basic Books, New York.

Harrod, R.F. (1939), 'An essay in dynamic theory', *Economic Journal*, **49**.

Hassard, J. and Proctor, S. (eds) (1996), *R&D Decisions: Policy, Strategies and Disclosure*, Routledge, London.

Heertje, A. (1989), *Innovation, Technology and Finance*, Basil Blackwell, Oxford .

Heertje, A. and Perlman, M. (eds) (1990), *Evolving Technology and Market Structure*, The University of Michigan Press, Ann Arbor.

Hollenstein, H. (1996), 'A composite indicator of a firm's innovativeness: an empirical analysis based on survey data for Swiss manufacturing', *Research Policy*, **25**, pp. 633–45.

HMSO (1978), *A Review of Monopolies and Mergers Policy* (Green Paper), Cmnd. 7198, HMSO, London.

Jaffe, A. (1986), 'Technological opportunity and spillovers in R&D: evidence from firms' patents, profits and market values', *American Economic Review*, **76** (5).

Jorgenson, D. and Griliches, Z. (1967), 'The explanation of productivity growth', *Review of Economic Studies*, **34**.

Kaldor, N. (1957), 'A model of economic growth', *Economic Journal*, **67**, pp. 591–624.

Kaldor, N. and Mirrlees, J.A. (1962), 'A new model of economic growth', *Review of Economic Studies*, **29** (3).

Kamien, M.I. and Schwartz, N.L. (1982), *Market Structure and Innovation*, Cambridge University Press, Cambridge.

Kennedy, P. (1984), 'Interpreting dummy variables', *The Review of Economics and Statistics*, **66**.

Kennedy, P. (1992), *A Guide to Econometrics* (3rd edn.), Martin Robertson, Oxford.

Kleinknecht, A. and Reijnen, J.O.N. (1991), 'More evidence on the undercounting of small firm R&D', *Research Policy*, **20**, pp. 579–87.

Klepper, S. (1993), 'Entry, exit, growth, and innovation over the product life cycle', mimeo.

Klepper S. and Graddy E. (1990), 'The evolution of new industries and the determinants of market structure', *Rand Journal of Economics*, **21** (1).

Klepper, S. and Simons, K.L. (1994), 'Technological change and industry shakeouts', paper presented to the International Schumpeter Society conference, Munster, August.

Klevorick, A.K., Levin, R.C., Nelson, R.R. and Winter, S.G. (1995), 'On the sources and significance of interindustry differences in technological opportunities', *Research Policy*, **24**, pp. 185–205.

Kline, S.J. and Rosenberg, N. (1986), *The Positive Sum Strategy: Harnessing Technology for Economic Growth*, The National Academy Press, Washington DC.

Kline, S.J. and Rosenberg, N. (1986), *An Overview on Innovation*, in Landau and Rosenberg, 1986.

Levin, R., Choen, W. and Mowery, D. (1985), 'R&D appropriability, opportunity, and market structure: new evidence on the Schumpeterian hypothesis', *American Economic Review*, **75** (2), pp. 20–24.

Levin, R., Klevorick, A., Nelson, R. and Winter, S. (1987), 'Appropriating the returns from industrial research and development', *Brooking Papers on Economic Activity*, **3**, pp. 783–831.

Levin, R. and Reiss, P. (1988), 'Cost reducing and demand-creating R&D with spillovers', *Rand Journal of Economics*, **19** (4).

Link, A.N. (1981), 'Basic research and productivity increase in manufacturing: additional evidence', *American Economic Review*, **71** (5).

Lissoni, F. and Metcalfe, S. (1994), 'Diffusion of innovation ancient and modern: a review of the main themes', in M. Dodgson and R. Rothwell.

Lucas, R.E. (1988), 'On the mechanisms of economic development', *Journal of Monetary Economics*, **22** (1).

Lundvall, B. and Johnson, B. (1994), 'The learning economy', *Journal of Industry Studies*, **2** (1).

Lyons, B.R. (1980), 'A new measure of minimum efficient plant scale in U.K. manufacturing industry', *Economica*, **47**, pp. 19–34.

McGee, J. and Thomas, H. (eds) (1986), *Strategic Management Research: A European Perspective*, Wiley, New York.

Maddison, A. (1979), 'Long run dynamics of productivity growth', *Banca Nazionale del Lavoro, Quarterly Review*, **32** (128).

Maddison, A. (1982), *Phases of Capitalist Development*, Oxford University Press, New York.

Maddison, A. (1991), *Dynamic Forces in Capitalist Development*, Oxford University Press, Oxford.

Mairesse, J. (1991), 'R&D and productivity: a survey of econometric studies at the firm level', *STI Review*, **8**, OECD, Paris.

Malerba, F. (1992), 'Learning by firms and incremental change', *Economic Journal*, **102**, pp. 845–59.

Malerba, F. and Orsenigo, L. (1990), 'Technological regimes and patterns of innovation: a theoretical and empirical investigation of the Italian case', in A. Heertje and M. Perlman.

Malerba F. and Orsenigo, L. (1995), 'Schumpeterian patterns of innovation', *Cambridge Journal of Economics*, **19** (1), pp. 47–65.

Malerba, F. and Orsenigo, L. (1996), 'The dynamics and evolution of industries', *Industrial and Corporate Change*, **5**, pp. 51–87.

Mansfield, E. (1961), 'Technical change and the rate of imitation', *Econometrica*, **29**.

Mansfield, E. (1963), 'Size of firm, market structure, and innovation', *Journal of Political Economy*, **71**.

Mansfield, E. (1968), *Industrial Research and Technological Innovation: An Econometric Analysis*, Norton, New York.

Mansfield, E. (1980), 'Basic research and productivity increase in manufacturing', *American Economic Review*, **70**.

Marshall, A. (1920), *Principles of Economics*, (8th edn.), Macmillan, London.

Marx, K. [1847] (1973), *The Poverty of Philosophy*, International Publisher, New York.

Marx, K. [1857] (1973), *Grundrisse*, Penguin, Harmondsworth.

Marx, K. [1867, 1885, 1894] (1983, 1977, 1977), *Capital I, II and III*, Lawrence and Wishart, London.

Meliciani, V. (1998), *Technical Change, Patterns of Specialization and Uneven Growth in OECD Countries*, PhD thesis, Science Policy Research Unit, University of Sussex, UK.

Mensh, G.O. (1975), *Stalemate in Technology*, Ballinger Publishing Company, Cambridge, Mass.

Metcalfe, J.S. (1981), 'Impulse and diffusion in the study of technological change', *Futures*, **13**.

Metcalfe, J.S. (1994), 'Evolutionary economics and technology policy', *Economic Journal*, **104** (July), pp. 931–44.

Metcalfe, S. (1995), *The economic foundations of technology policy: equilibrium and evolutionary perspectives*, in P. Stoneman.

Miles, I. (1993), 'Services in the new industrial economy', *Futures*, **25** (6), pp. 653–72.

Miles, I. (1996), 'Infrastructure and the delivery of new services', in OECD, 1996b.

Mohnen, P. (1995), 'R&D externalities and productivity growth', paper presented to the OECD conference on *Expert Workshop on Technology and Employment: Macroeconomic and Sectoral Evidence*, Paris, 19–20 June.

Morroni, M. (1992), *Production Process and Technical Change*, Cambridge University Press, Cambridge.

Nelson, R. (1963), *Concentration in the Manufacturing Industries of the United States*, Yale University Press, New Haven.

Nelson, R. (1964), 'Aggregate production function and medium-range growth projections', *American Economic Review*, **54**, pp. 575–606.

Nelson, R. (1981), 'Research on productivity growth and productivity differences: dead ends and new departures', *Journal of Economic Literature*, **19**.

Nelson, R. and Winter, S. (1977), 'In search of a useful theory of innovation', *Research Policy*, **6** (1).

Nelson R. and Winter, S. (1978), 'Forces generating and limiting concentration under Schumpeterian competition', *Bell Journal of Economics*, **9**, pp. 524–48.

Nelson, R. and Winter, S. (1982), *An Evolutionary Theory of Economic Change*, Harvard University Press, Cambridge, Mass.

OECD (1991), *Technology and Productivity: The Challenge for Economic Policy*, OECD, Paris.

OECD (1992a), *Technology and Economy: The Key Relationships*, OECD, Paris.

OECD (1992b), *Oslo manual: OECD Proposed Guidelines for collecting and Interpreting Technological Innovation Data*, OECD, Paris.

OECD (1994), *The Measurement of Scientific and Technological Activities. Proposed Standard Practice for Surveys of Research and Experimental Development. 'Frascati Manual 1993'*, OECD, Paris.

OECD (1996a), *The Knowledge-based Economy*, Science Technology Industry, OECD, Paris.

OECD (1996b), *Employment and Growth in the Knowledge-based Economy*, OECD, Paris.

OECD (1996c), *Innovation, Patents and Technological Strategies*, OECD, Paris.

OECD-EUROSTAT (1997), *Proposed Guidelines for Collecting and Interpreting Technological Innovation Data – Oslo Manual*, OECD, Paris.

Ornstein, S.I., Weston, J.F., Intriligator, M.D. and Shrieves, R.E. (1973), 'Determinants of market structure', *Southern Economic Journal*, **39**.

Papaconstantinou, G., Sakurai, N. and Wyckoff, A. (1995), 'Technology diffusion and industrial performance: an empirical analysis for ten countries', OECD, mimeo, March.

Papaconstantinou, G., Sakurai, N. and Wyckoff, A. (1996), 'Embodied technology diffusion: an empirical analysis for ten OECD countries', STI working papers, 1, OECD, Paris.

Pashigian, B.P. (1968), 'Market concentration in the U.S. and Great Britain', *Journal of Law and Economics*, **11**.

Pashigian, B.P. (1969), 'The effect of market size on concentration', *International Economic Review*, **10**.

Patel P. and Pavitt, K. (1995), 'Patterns of technological activity: their measurement and interpretation', in P. Stoneman.

Pavitt, K. (1984), 'Sectoral patterns of technological change: toward a taxonomy and a theory', *Research Policy*, **13**.

Pavitt, K. (1986), 'Technology, innovation and strategic management', in J. McGee and H. Thomas.

Pavitt, K., Robson, M. and Townsend, J. (1987), 'The size distribution of innovating firms in the U.K.: 1945–1983', *Journal of Industrial Economics*, **35** (3).

Pavitt K. and Soete, L. (1982), 'International differences in economic growth and the international location of innovation', in H. Giersch.

Phillips, A. (1971), *Technology and Market Structure*, M.A. Heath, Lexington.

Pianta, M. (1995), 'Technology and growth in OECD countries, 1970–1990', *Cambridge Journal of Economics*, **19**.

Pianta, M. (1998), 'Technology, growth and employment: do national systems matter?' in Archibugi et al. 1998.

Pratten, C. (1971), *Economies of Scale in Manufacturing Industry*, Cambridge University Press, Cambridge.

Pratten, C. (1988), 'A survey of the economies of scale', in Commission of the European Communities.

Pratten, C. (1991), *The Competitiveness of Small Firms*, Cambridge University Press, Cambridge.

Ricardo, D. [1817] (1951), *On the Principles of Political Economy and Taxation*, Cambridge University Press, Cambridge.

Robinson, E.A.G [1931] (1958), *The Structure of Competitive Industry*, Cambridge University Press, Cambridge.

Romer, P. (1986), 'Increasing returns and long-run growth', *Journal of Political Economy*, **94** (5).

Romer, P. (1990), 'Endogenous technological change', *Journal of Political Economy*, **98**.

Rosenberg, N. (1963), 'Capital goods, technology and economic growth', *Oxford Economic Papers*, **15**.

Rosenberg, N. (1976a), 'Technological change in the machine tool industry: 1840–1910', in N. Rosenberg, 1976b.

Rosenberg, N. (1976b), *Perspectives on Technology*, Cambridge University Press Cambridge.

Rosenberg, N. (1982a), *Inside the Black Box*, Cambridge University Press, Cambridge.

Rosenberg, N. (1982b), 'Marx as a student of technology', in N. Rosenberg, 1982a.

Rosenbluth, G. (1957), *Concentration in Canadian Manufacturing Industries*, Princeton University Press, Princeton.

Sakurai, N., Ioannidis, E. and Papaconstantinou, G. (1996), 'The impact of R&D and of technology diffusion on productivity growth: evidence from ten OECD countries in the 1970s and 1980s', *STI working papers*, 2, OECD, Paris.

Salter, W.E.G. (1960), *Productivity and Technological Change*, Cambridge University Press, Cambridge.

Saviotti, P.P., Metcalfe, J.S. (eds) (1991), *Evolutionary Theories of Economic and Technological Change*, Harwood Academic Publishers, Reading.

Scazzieri, R. (1993), *A Theory of Production*, Clarendon Press, Oxford.

Scherer, F.M. (1965), 'Firm size, market structure, opportunity, and the output of patented inventions', *American Economic Review*, **5** (55).

Scherer, F.M. (1967), 'Market structure and the employment of scientists and engineers', *American Economic Review*, **57**, pp. 524–31.

Scherer, F.M. (1970), *Industrial Market Structure and Economic Performance*, Rand MacNally, Chicago.

Scherer, F.M. (1980), *Industrial Market Structure and Economic Performance*, (2nd edn.) Rand MacNally, Chicago.

Scherer, F.M. (1982a), 'Interindustry technology flows and productivity growth', *The Review of Economics and Statistics*, **64**.

Scherer, F.M. (1982b), 'Interindustry technology flows in the United States', *Research Policy*, **11** (4).

Scherer, F.M. (1984a), 'Using linked patent and R&D data to measure interindustry technology flows', in Z. Griliches.

Scherer, F.M. (1984b), *Innovation and Growth: Schumpeterian Perspectives*, The MIT Press, Cambridge, Mass.

Scherer, F.M. and Ross, D. (1990), *Industrial Market Structure and Economic Performance*, Houghton Mifflin Company (3rd edn.) Boston, Princeton.

Schmalensee, R. and Willig, R.D. (eds) (1989), *Handbook of Industrial Organization*, vols. I and II, Elsevier Science Publishers B.V., Amsterdam.

Schmookler, J. (1966), *Invention and Economic Growth*, Harvard University Press, Cambridge, Mass.

Schumpeter, J.A. [1912] (1934), *The Theory of Economic Development*, Harvard University Press, Cambridge, Mass.

Schumpeter, J.A. (1939), *Business Cycles*, McGraw-Hill, New York.

Schumpeter, J.A. (1942), *Capitalism Socialism and Democracy*, Harper, New York.

Scott, J.T. (1984), 'Firm versus industry variability in R&D intensity', in Z. Griliches.

Scott, M.F.G. (1989), *A New View of Economic Growth*, Clarendon Press, Oxford.

Shaked, A. and Sutton, J. (1987), 'Product differentiation and industrial structure', *Journal of Industrial Economics*, **35**.

Silverberg, G. and Soete, L. (eds) (1994), *The Economics of Growth and Technical Change*, Edward Elgar, Aldershot.

Sirilli, G. (1997), 'Science and technology indicators: The state of the art and prospects for the future', in *Economics of Structural and Technological Change*, in G. Antonilli and N. De Liso (eds).

Sirilli, G. and Evangelista R. (1998), 'Technological innovation in services and manufacturing: results from Italian surveys', *Research Policy*, **27**.

Smith, A. (1791), *An Inquiry into the Wealth of Nations*, (6th edn.) Strahan and Cadell, London.

Smith, A. (1976) [1776], *An Inquiry into the Wealth of Nations*, R.H. Campbell, A.S. Skinner, W.B. Todd (eds), Clarendon Press, Oxford.

Smith, K. (1996a), 'Interaction in knowledge systems: foundations, policy implications and empirical methods', *STI Review*, **16**, OECD.

Smith, K. (1996b), 'New views of innovation and challenges to R&D policy', in J. Hassard and S. Proctor.

Soete, L. and Patel, P. (1985), 'Recherche-développement, importations de technologie et croissance économique', *Revue Economique*, **36** (5).

Solow, R. (1957), 'Technical change and the aggregate production function', *The Review of Economics and Statistics*, **39**.

Solow, R. (1959), *Investment and technical progress*, in K.J. Arrow, S. Karlin, P. Suppes (eds).

STEP-ISRDS (1996), 'Patterns of innovation input, innovation costs, non-research and intangible inputs – analysis of the data from the Community Innovation Survey', mimeo.

Sterlacchini, A. (1996), 'Inputs and outputs of innovative activities in Italian manufacturing', *Quaderni di Ricerca*, Università degli Studi di Ancona, Dipartimento di Economia, **78**.

Stoneman, P. (1983), *The Economic Analysis of Technological Change*, Oxford University Press, New York.

Stoneman, P. (ed.) (1995), *Handbook of the Economics of Innovation and Technical Change*, Blackwell, Oxford.

Stoneman, P. and Ireland, N. (1983), 'The role of supply factors in the diffusion of new process technology', *Economic Journal*, **93**.

Suits, D.B. (1984), 'Dummy variables: mechanics v. interpretation', *The Review of Economics and Statistics*, **66**.

Sutton, J. (1991), *Sunk Costs and Market Structure: Price Competition, Advertising and the Evolution of Concentration*, The MIT Press, Cambridge, Mass.

Sveikauskas, L. (1986), 'The contribution of R&D to productivity growth', *Monthly Labor Review*, March.

Sylos Labini, P. (1956), *Oligopoly and Technical Progress*, Harvard University Press, Cambridge, Mass.

Terleckyj, N. (1974), *Effects of R&D on the Productivity Growth of Industries: an Explanatory Study*, National Planning Association, Washington, DC.

Ure, A. (1835), *The Philosophy of Manufactures*, C. Knight, London.

Utterback, J.M. and Abernathy, W.J. (1975), 'A dynamic model and process and product innovation', *Omega*, **3**.

Utterback, J.M. and Suàrez, F.F. (1993), 'Innovation, competition, and industry structure', *Research Policy*, **22**.

Vernon, R. (1966), 'International investment and international trade in the product cycle', *Quarterly Journal of Economics*, **80** (2).

Verspagen, B. (1991), 'A new empirical approach to catching-up or falling behind', *Structural Change and Economic Dynamics*, **2** (2).

von Hippel, E. (1988), *The Sources of Innovation*, Oxford University Press, New York.

Vivarelli, M. (1995), *The Economics of Technology and Employment*, Edward Elgar, Aldershot.

Wakelin, K. (1997), *Trade and Innovation: Theory and Evidence*, Edward Elgar, Aldershot.

Waterson, M. (1993), *Are industrial economists still interested in concentration?* in M. Casson and J. Creedy.

Winter, S. (1984) 'Schumpeterian competition in alternative technological regimes', *Journal of Economic Behaviour and Organisation*, **5**.

Wolf, E.N. (1991), 'Capital formation and productivity convergence over the long term', *American Economic Review*, **81** (3).

Wolf, E.N. (1994a), *Technology, Capital Accumulation and Long Run Growth*, in J. Fageberg et al.

Wolf, E.N. (1994b), 'Productivity growth and capital intensity on the sector and industry level: specialisation among OECD countries, 1970–1988', in G. Silverberg and L. Soete.

Index

Abernathy, W.J. 61–3, 73, 178
Abramovitz, M. 29, 44, 46
Aghion, P. 21
alienation concept 4–5, 10
Amable, B. 30, 31
Amendola, M. 30, 41, 73
America *see* United States
analytical techniques
  cluster analysis 168, 179, 181
  factor analysis 125–30, 165–74, 181
Antonelli, C. 24, 33, 34, 79, 183
Archibugi, D. 58, 84, 93, 95
Arrow, K. 19–20, 26
assets 46
  intangible 42–3, 44, 46
Audretsch, D. 30, 32, 45
Australia 46

Babbage, C. 25, 48
Bain, J.S. 49, 53
Baldwin, W.L. 55, 66
Banerji, R. 66
barriers to entry *see* entry barriers
Baumol, W.J. 50
Bell, M. 41, 46
Bernstein, J. 36
biased technological change 17–18, 26
bibliographic data 7, 42
  see also technological information
'black box' concept 26, 38–41, 45–6,
    69–70, 72
  see also technological change
Bound, J. 58
Boyer, R. 31
Burmeister 3
business cycles 14

Calvert, J. 101, 104
Canada 36, 46

capital accumulation 12, 13, 15, 23, 25,
    48
capital centralization 48, 65
capital concentration 48, 65
capital intensity
  firm size and 144–7, 149
capital investment 8, 19, 24, 32–3, 35,
    46, 53, 121–2, 152–9
  as form of technological change 72–3,
      182–3, 184, 185
capital-saving technological change 25,
    26
Cesaratto, S. 179
Chung, W.K. 29
Clark, J.M. 49, 79
Clarke, R. 65
classical economics 11–15, 25, 47, 64,
    183
  neo-classical 3, 17–22, 49
client relationships 104, 106–7
cluster analysis 168, 179, 181
Cohen, W.M. 55, 56, 58, 66, 124, 131,
    160
Comanor, W.S. 66
Community Innovation Survey (CIS)
    (EC) 74, 79, 87, 97, 101, 104,
    109–10
competitiveness 21, 30, 42, 49
  imperfect 49, 55, 56–7
  innovative 58–9, 67
  non-competitive markets 49
  perfect 54, 55, 56
computer software 42, 46
copyrights *see* patents and copyrights
costs 52, 65
  of design 94–8, 100, 109, 118, 121–2,
      139–44, 152–60, 162–3, 166–8,
      172–4, 178, 181
  fixed 50, 55, 65
  of innovation 74, 75, 79, 94–101, 105,
      107, 109, 114–17, 152–9, 172

Curry, B. 66

Dasgupta, P. 58
data collection *see* innovation surveys
David, P.A. 33, 44, 46, 60, 61
Davies, S.W. 33, 52, 60, 61, 65
DeBresson, C. 35
De Long, J.B. 31, 73, 182
demand-pull 23
    see also technology-push
Denison, E.F. 18, 29, 44
design costs 94–8, 100, 109, 118, 121–2,
        139–44, 152–60, 162–3, 166–8,
        172–4, 178, 181
diffusion *see* technology diffusion
disembodied innovative processes 22,
        37–8, 73, 76, 77, 114–31
    definition 5–6, 9, 68
    embodied innovation and 118–20,
        142–4, 149
    in industrial sectors 142–4, 149, 152–9
disembodied technological change 17,
        24–5, 42–4, 47, 54–7, 59–60, 73–7,
        181–5
    bias towards 68–72, 73, 76
    'black box' concept 26, 38–41, 45–6,
        69–70, 72
    definition 3–6, 7–8, 10, 68, 69
    embodied technological change and
        74–7, 79, 177, 184
    literature survey 27–46
    in neo-classical economics 17–22
    production function and 164–80
disembodied technological indicators
        183
    definition 7–8, 9
disembodied technology 3, 4–5, 8, 40–41
    definition 68
    literature survey 28–32
Dobell, R. 3
Dodgson, M. 45
Domar, E.D. 22
Dosi, G. 30, 39, 40, 45, 46, 58, 60, 72,
        73, 175

economic conditions 16
    increased dimension 50
    massed resources 50
    see also market structure
economic convergence 29, 49

economic growth 18, 20, 21–2, 26, 33,
        184–5
    cross-country differences 29, 73
    GDP 44
    growth accounting 44
    innovative process and 35
    knowledge-based economies 11, 20,
        30, 42–5, 69, 131
    literature survey 28–32
    new growth economics 24, 72–3, 183
economics of technological change *see*
        'black box' concept
economies of scale *see* scale
education and training 21, 26, 29, 42, 43,
        44
    investment in 79
Eliasson, G. 43
embodied innovative process 22, 37–8,
        46, 53–4, 60–63, 73, 114–31
    definition 5–6, 9, 68
    disembodied innovation and 118–20,
        142–4, 149
    in industrial sectors 142–4, 149, 152–9
embodied technological change 22–5,
        48–54, 59, 72–7, 181–5
    in classical economics 11–15
    definition 3–7, 9, 10, 68, 69
    disembodied technological change and
        74–7, 79, 177, 184
    as an investment 6, 72–3, 182–3, 184,
        185
    literature survey 27–46
    in neo-classical economics 17–22, 26
    production function and 164–80
    Schumpeter on 69
embodied technological indicators 183
    definition 7–8, 9
embodied technology
    adoption of 60–61
    definition 3, 4–5, 9, 68
    literature survey 28–32
enabling investments 42
Englander, S. 35, 36
entrepreneurial activity 54
entry barriers 49–50, 52, 53, 63, 65, 72,
        76, 79, 180, 182
    to research and development 55–7, 66,
        175–6, 182
EUROSTAT 74, 79, 87, 109–10

Evangelista, R. 57, 87, 93, 96, 97, 99, 110

factor analysis 125–30, 165–74, 181
Fagerberg, J. 29, 30
Federal Trade Commission (US) 66
firm size 70–72, 84–7, 90, 96–8, 108, 149
  economies of scale 49–53, 55–6, 63, 65, 66, 72, 76, 79, 175–6, 177, 180, 182
  innovative process and 115–16, 120–25, 126–7, 135–7, 144–7, 159–62, 163, 173–4, 182–3
  minimum efficient scale 52, 53, 65
  small 135–7, 150, 162, 175, 177, 178
  technological change and 47–67, 182–3
  see also industrial firms; industrial structure
firm-specific capabilities 72
fixed costs 50, 55, 65
Freeman, C. 4, 6, 21, 45, 54, 55

Gaffard, J. 41
George, K.D. 66
Gibrat, R. 65
Gold, B. 65, 79
Gort, M. 62, 63, 73, 178
Goto, A. 36
Graddy, E. 62, 63, 73, 178
Great Britain *see* United Kingdom
Greenhalgh, C. 30
Griliches, Z. 29, 31, 32, 35, 36, 46
gross domestic product (GDP) 44
  see also economic growth
Grossman, G.M. 21

Hanel, P. 36
Harrison, B. 51
Harrod, R.F. 22
Helpman, E. 21
high technology firms 90, 181, 184
Hollenstein, H. 101
Howitt, P. 21
human capital
  investment in 46
  knowledge embodied in 21, 24, 26, 39
  see also labour
human capital formation 44

imperfect competition 49, 55, 56–7
increased dimension economies 5
indivisibilities concept 49–50, 51, 53, 65
industrial concentration 51, 52, 53, 63, 65, 66, 67
industrial firms
  definition 43
  firm-specific capabilities 72
  high technology 90, 181, 184
  innovating firms 84, 86, 87–90, 109–10, 111–20, 177
  innovation strategies 111–31
  innovative process 5–7, 12, 14, 25, 36–40, 46, 60–63, 64, 78, 83–110
  medium/low technology 95, 169, 171–2
  monopolies 16, 54, 56
  new industrial organization 65, 66
  oligopolies 49, 56
  research and development by 87, 90, 96–8, 108, 123–5, 136–7, 150, 152–9, 165–79
  Structure-Conduct-Performance concept 49–50, 55, 65, 66, 76, 182
  technological change and 47–67
  technology diffusion 32–4, 45–6, 60–61, 72, 79, 84–91, 95, 169, 172, 174, 182–3
  technology flows 4–5, 6, 7, 10, 34–6, 37, 46, 79, 182–3
  see also firm size
industrial laboratories 17
  see also research institutes
industrial performance
  S-C-P concept 49–50, 55, 65, 66, 76, 182
industrial sectors 37, 38, 43, 50, 58, 61, 64, 79
  differences between 137, 149
  innovation strategies 132–50
  innovative process 76, 78, 79, 83–110, 151–63, 168–74
  sector specific innovation 76, 79, 99, 132, 137–48, 149, 179
  small firms 135–7, 162
industrial specialization 5, 25, 37, 38, 48, 175
industrial structure 16, 17, 42
  changes in 62–3
  improvements in 65

innovative process and 64–5, 76–8,
        83–110, 115–16, 120–25, 126–7,
        135–7, 144–7, 163, 168–74
    technology and 48, 58–9, 63–5, 66
industrialization *see* mechanization
information *see* technological
    information
information technology 4, 43
innovating firms 84, 86, 87–90, 109–10,
        111–12, 177
    indicators used to identify 112–14
    patterns of innovation 114–20
innovation costs 74, 75, 79, 94–101, 105,
        107, 109, 114–17, 152–9, 172
innovation diffusion *see* technology
    diffusion
innovation expenditure 12, 16, 19–24,
        26, 31, 33–4, 70, 79, 121–2
    distribution of 95–8
    see also research and development
        expenditure
innovation patterns 60–63, 71–3,
        114–20, 125–30, 176–7
    by industrial sectors 76, 78, 79,
        83–110, 151–63, 168–74
    production function and 76–8, 111–31
    sector specific 76, 79, 99, 132,
        137–48, 149, 179
innovation sources 93–101, 181
    firm size and 96–8
innovation strategies
    firm size and 120–25, 126–7
    in industrial sectors 132–50
    labour productivity and 111, 121,
        122–3, 124, 130, 148, 149, 162,
        166
    production function and 76–8,
        111–31, 132–50
    sector specific 76, 79, 99, 132,
        137–48, 149
innovation surveys 8, 29, 34–5, 46, 70,
        74, 79, 93, 183
    indicators used in 112–14, 183
    Italy 35, 74–8, 83–110, 112–85
    OECD countries 74, 79, 87, 109–10
innovative competition 58–9, 67
innovative output 101–4, 108, 110
innovative process 39–40, 41, 47, 183
    Arrow on 20
    in classical economics 12, 14–15

cumulative nature of 39
data collection on 54, 57, 66
definition 5–7, 9, 15–16, 68
disembodied 5–6, 22, 37–8, 68, 73,
        76, 77, 114–31, 142–4, 149,
        152–9
economic growth and 35
embodied 5–6, 9, 22, 37–8, 46, 53–4,
        60–63, 68, 73, 114–31, 142–4,
        149, 152–9
firm size and 115–16, 120–25, 126–7,
        135–7, 144–7, 159–62, 163,
        173–4, 182–3
by industrial firms 5–7, 12, 14, 25,
        36–40, 46, 60–63, 64, 78, 83–110
industrial sectors and 76, 77, 79,
        83–110, 132–50, 151–63,
        168–74,
industrial structure and 64–5, 76–8,
        83–110, 115–16, 120–25, 126–7,
        135–7, 144–7, 163, 168–74
information sources 104, 106–7, 108,
        110, 138–42
interactive 75–6, 79
licensing agreements 8, 42, 46, 70, 79,
        96, 108
manufacturing sector 83–110
market structure and 79
measurement of 7–8, 9, 57, 71–3, 79
in neo-classical economics 17–18
'new perspectives' on 38–41, 45–6
new products 101–3, 120, 160, 184
non-imitable 39
objectives of 105, 107, 109, 111–12
obstacles to 105–6, 107–8, 109
process innovation 62–3, 70, 73, 74,
        76, 91–3, 101, 108, 109, 152–9,
        166–8, 172, 174, 181, 184
product cycles 61–3
product innovation 51, 53, 74, 76,
        91–3, 101, 109, 152–9, 163,
        165–8, 172–4, 181
production function and 53–4
profits from 56–7
risks in 56, 106, 109
Schumpeter on 15–17, 26, 38, 39,
        54–5, 66
science-based sector 97–8, 99
sector specific 76, 79, 99, 132,
        137–48, 149, 179

service sector 83–110
technology and 72, 79
types of 101–3
in United Kingdom 66
in United States 66
weaknesses in 66
see also patents and copyrights;
    research and development; tech-
    nological change
institutional structure 16–17, 26
research institutes 106, 107
see also industrial structure
intangible assets/investments 42–3, 44,
    46, 79
investment 29, 30, 45, 189
capital 8, 19, 24, 32–3, 35, 46, 53,
    121–2, 152–9
in education and training 79
enabling 42
in human capital 46
in innovation 12, 16, 19–24, 26, 31,
    33–4, 70, 79, 95–8, 121–2
intangible 42–3, 44, 46, 79
in mechanization 13
in production function 31, 33
in research and development 36, 42,
    44, 46, 55–7, 79, 94–100, 109,
    114–22, 139–44, 152–63, 169,
    172–4
see also costs
investment intensity 172, 173–4, 175,
    177, 178
Ireland, N. 61
Italian industry
innovation strategies 111–31
innovation surveys 35, 74–8, 83–110,
    112–85
innovative output 101–4
manufacturing sector 83–110, 111–31
science-based sector 37, 38, 97–8, 99
service sector 83–110
supply sector 37, 43, 98, 99, 181
technological profile 116–17, 131
Italian Statistical Institute (ISTAT) 35,
    74–8, 83–110, 112–85

Jaffe, A. 180
Japan 45, 46
Johnson, B. 42
Jorgenson, D. 29

Kaldor, N. 22–4, 25, 26, 33–4
Kamien, M.I. 55, 66
Kennedy, P. 150
Keynesian economics
post-Keynesian 3, 22–4, 25, 33, 183
Kleinknecht, A. 57
Klepper, S. 56, 62, 63, 73, 131, 178
Klevorick, A.K. 124, 132
Kline, S.J. 6, 40, 75, 79, 93
knowledge
definition 3, 4–5, 9, 10, 19, 39
human capital and 21, 24, 26, 39
use of 23–4, 39
knowledge acquisition/distribution 42,
    43, 79, 175, 182–3, 184
learning by doing 10, 15, 19, 107
knowledge generation 8, 9, 14, 19–24,
    39, 40, 42–3, 70, 181, 184
see also innovative process; research
    and development; technological
    change
knowledge sector 43–4
knowledge spillovers *see* technology
    flows
knowledge-based economies 11, 20, 30,
    42–5, 69, 131
see also economic growth

labour
division of 13, 14, 25, 48, 61, 97
Marx on 48, 65
quality of 43, 44
specialized 49, 65
technological change and 12, 13, 14,
    18, 23, 26, 48
see also human capital
labour market 65
labour productivity 12, 18, 23, 76
influences on 77
innovation strategies and 111, 121,
    122–3, 124, 130, 148, 149, 162,
    166
labour saving technological change 26
learning 40, 46
see also knowledge
learning by doing 10, 15, 19, 107
see also knowledge
    acquisition/distribution
Levin, R.C. 36, 55, 56, 58, 66, 124, 175

licensing agreements 8, 42, 46, 70, 79, 96, 108
  see also innovative process; patents and copyrights
Lichtenberg, F. 35, 36, 46
Link, A.N. 31
Lissoni, F. 32, 46
low technology firms *see* medium/low technology firms
Lucas, R.E. 21
Lundvall, B. 42
Lyons, B. 52, 65

Maddison, A. 29, 73
Mairesse, J. 31
Malerba, F. 40, 58, 72, 124, 132
Mangano, S. 179
Mansfield, E. 31, 32, 33, 58, 60, 61
manufacturing sector 78, 164–80
  innovation costs 94–101
  innovation sources 93–101
  innovation strategies 111–31
  innovative process 83–110
  technology diffusion 84–91, 169, 172
  technology use 174, 179
  see also process innovation; product innovation
market structure 13, 49, 52, 55, 65
  determinants of 53
  imperfect competition 49, 55, 56–7
  innovative process and 79
  new markets 16
  non-competitive 49
  perfect competition 54, 55, 56
  technological change and 47–67, 70–72, 76, 182–3
marketing costs 94, 97–8, 118, 159
Marshall, A. 49, 79
Marx, K. 10, 11, 12, 13–15, 25, 48, 79
massed resources economies 50
mechanization 5, 6, 10, 12, 61
  investment in 13
  labour and 12, 13, 14, 18, 23, 26, 48
medium/low technology firms 95, 169, 171–2
Meliciani, V. 30, 73
Mensh, G.O. 25
Metcalfe, J.S. 32, 40, 46, 184
Miles, I. 93, 99

minimum efficient scale (MES) concept 52, 53, 65
Mirrlees, J.A. 26
Mohnen, P. 34, 36, 46
monopolies 16, 54, 56
Morroni, M. 51, 65, 79

National Research Council (CNR) (Italy) 35, 74–8, 83–110, 112–85
Nelson, R. 26, 39, 58–9, 61, 65, 66, 67, 72, 175
neo-classical economics 3, 17–22, 49
neo-Schumpeterian economics 11, 38–9, 47, 54–7, 58, 59, 64, 71–2, 76, 124, 125, 182
Netherlands 46
neutral technological change 26
new growth economics 24, 72–3, 183
  see also economic growth
new industrial organization 65, 66
new products 101–3, 120, 160, 184
  see also product innovation

OECD 28, 42, 43, 44, 46, 73, 79, 184
  Oslo Manual 70, 79
OECD countries 29, 30, 34, 43–4, 46, 184
  innovating firms 86, 87
  innovation surveys 74, 79, 87, 97, 99, 104, 109–10
  see also Italy
oligopolies 49, 56
operating systems 4, 5
organizational structure *see* industrial structure
Ornstein, S.I. 66
Orsenigo, L. 58, 72, 124, 132, 175

Papaconstantinou, G. 34–5, 46, 73
Pashigian, B.P. 66
Patel, P. 30
patents and copyrights 7, 8, 36, 44–5, 46, 57, 70, 108
  acquisition of 42, 79, 97
  data collection on 28, 29, 30
  see also innovative process
Pavitt, K. 30, 37–8, 41, 46, 61, 66, 73, 79, 93, 132, 176–7, 181
perfect competition 54, 55, 56
Phillips, A. 58

Pianta, M. 30, 73, 95
policy *see* technology policy
post-industrial societies *see* knowledge-
    based economies
post-Keynesian economics 3, 22–4, 25,
    33, 183
Pratten, C. 50, 52, 53, 55, 65
process industries 50
process innovation 62–3, 70, 73, 74, 76,
    91–3, 101, 108, 109, 111, 152–9,
    166–8, 172, 174, 181, 184
product cycles 61–3, 176–7, 178
product innovation 51, 53, 74, 76, 91–3,
    109, 111, 152–9, 163, 165–8,
    172–4, 181
    new products 101–3, 120, 160, 184
production capacity 41, 65–6
production function 29, 131
    capital intensity and 52, 53, 62–3, 66,
        121
    definition 26
    economies of scale and 49–53, 65, 66,
        72, 79, 175–6, 177
    disembodied technological change and
        164–80
    embodied technological change and
        164–80
    innovation patterns/strategies and
        76–8, 111–31, 132–50
    innovative process and 53–4
    investment in 31, 33
    literature survey 28–32
    Marx on 48, 65
    in neo-classical economics 17–19, 26
    research and development and 21
    technological change and 4, 5, 6, 10,
        12, 13, 16, 17–19, 26, 48–51,
        164–80, 184
    trial production 79, 97–8
production indicators 112, 113
production intensity 61
production sector 37–8
productivity
    in knowledge-based economies 42
    labour 12, 18, 23, 76, 77, 111, 121,
        122–3, 124, 130, 148, 149, 162,
        166
    research and development and 31–2,
        35, 36

raw materials 16

Reijnen, J.O.N. 57
Reiss, P. 36
research and development (R&D) 7–8,
    21, 22, 31, 37–8, 44–5, 181–5
    data collection on 28, 29, 30, 31
    economies of scale 55–6, 77
    economies of scope 56
    entrepreneurial 54
    entry barriers 55–7, 66, 175–6, 182
    by industrial firms 87, 90, 96–8, 108,
        123–5, 136–7, 150, 152–9,
        165–79
    measurement of 57, 70
    production function and 21
    productivity and 31–2, 35, 36
    Schumpeter on 17, 54–5
    by small firms 136–7, 150
    see also innovative process;
        knowledge generation; techno-
        logical change
research and development expenditure
    36, 42, 46, 55–7, 79, 94–100, 109,
    114–22, 139–44, 152–63, 169,
    172–4
    GDP and 44
    in science-based sector 98, 99
    see also innovation expenditure
research and development intensity
    56–7, 66, 173–4, 178
research institutes 106, 107, 108
    industrial laboratories 17
research spillovers *see* technology flows
resources
    massed 50
    raw materials 16
Ricardo, D. 11, 12, 13
Robinson, E.A.G. 49, 50, 79
Romer, P. 20, 21, 72
Rosenberg, N. 6, 25, 26, 39, 40, 75, 79, 93
Rosenbluth, G. 66
Ross, D. 50, 51, 52, 65, 66
Rothwell, R. 45

Sakurai, N. 34–5
Salter, W.E.G. 19, 33
Saviotti, P.P. 40
scale
    economies of 49–53, 55–6, 63, 65, 66,
        72, 76, 79, 175–6, 177, 180, 182
    of research and development 55–6, 77
scale-intensive sectors 99, 153, 166

Index

Scazzieri, R. 26, 79
Scherer, F.M. 35, 36, 50, 51, 52, 58, 65, 66
Schmookler, J. 22, 25
Schumpeter, J.A. 22, 56, 58–9, 61, 65, 77, 125
    on embodied technological change 69
    on innovative process 15–17, 26, 38, 39, 54–5, 66
    neo-Schumpeterian economics 11, 38–9, 47, 54–7, 58, 59, 64, 71–2, 76, 124, 125, 182
    on research and development 17, 54–5
    on technological change 15–17, 69
Schwartz, N.L. 55, 66
Science Policy Research Unit (SPRU) (UK) 66
science-based sector 37, 38, 97–8, 99
scope
    economies of 51, 56, 65–6
Scott, J.T. 55, 58, 66
Scott, M.F.G. 21–2, 72, 183
service sector 43
    innovation costs 94–101
    innovation sources 93–101
    innovative process 83–110
    product/process innovation 91–3, 109
    technology diffusion 84–91
Shaked, A. 65
Simons, K.L. 63, 73
Sirilli, G. 99
Small Business Administration (US) 66
small firms 135–7, 162, 175, 177, 178
    research and development by 136–7, 150
Smith, A. 11, 12–13, 14, 25, 48, 61, 79
Smith, K. 42, 184
Soete, L. 21, 30, 45
Solow, R. 18, 19, 29
specialized labour 49, 65
Sterlacchini, A. 110
Stiglitz, J. 58
Stoneman, P. 45, 61
Structure-Conduct-Performance (S-C-P) concept 49–50, 55, 65, 66, 76, 182
Suarez, F.F. 63
Suits, D.B. 150
Summers, L.H. 31, 73, 188
sunk costs 50, 53, 55, 56, 65
supply sector 37, 43, 98, 99, 181

supply-side economics 16, 49, 53, 99
Sutton, J. 56, 65, 118, 159–60, 163, 176, 180, 182
Suzuki, K. 36
Sveikauskas, L. 35
Sylos Labini, P. 49

technical assets 5
technical change 5, 22
    definition 10
technological accumulation 41, 46
technological capabilities 41
technological change
    biased 17–18, 26
    'black box' concept 26, 38–41, 45–6, 69–70, 72
    capital investment as form of 6, 72–3, 182–3, 184, 185
    capital saving 25, 26
    in classical economics 11–15, 25, 183
    cross-country differences 29, 30, 45
    definition 4, 5–6, 7–8, 9, 10, 24, 26, 68, 69
    disembodied 3–6, 7–8, 10, 17–22, 24–5, 26, 27–46, 47, 54–7, 59–60, 68–72, 73–7, 164–80, 181–5
    embodied 3–7, 9, 10, 11–15, 17–25, 27–46, 48–54, 59, 68, 69, 72–7, 164–80, 181–5
    endogenous 19–22
    firm size and 47–67, 182–3
    as generation process 5
    industrial firms and 47–67
    industrial sectors and 164–80
    industrial structure and 68–79, 164–80
    innovation output as 101–4
    intermediate inputs to 6–7, 10
    labour and 13, 14, 18, 23, 26, 48
    labour saving 12, 26
    literature survey 27–46
    market structure and 47–67, 70–72, 76, 182–3
    nature of 70, 101–3, 108, 183
    in neo-classical economics 17–22
    neutral 26
    in post-Keynesian economics 22–4, 25
    production function and 4, 5, 6, 10, 12, 13, 16, 17–19, 26, 48–51, 164–80, 184

research methodology 73–8
Schumpeter on 15–17
time scale of 39, 40
see also innovative process; research
and development
technological distance concept 178, 179
technological indicators 57, 71–3
definition 7–8, 9
in innovation surveys 112–14, 183
patents and copyrights 7, 8, 28, 29, 30,
36, 44–5, 46, 57, 70, 79, 97, 108
see also research and development
technological information
bibliographic data 7, 42
sources of 104, 106–7, 108, 110,
138–42
technological interdependencies 35
technological opportunity 39, 58–9, 66
technological regimes 39–40, 46, 176–7,
181
technology
definition 4–5, 8, 9, 10, 19, 39, 41, 68
disembodied 3, 4–5, 8, 28–32, 40–41,
68
dual nature of 39
embodied 3, 4–5, 9, 28–32, 68
industrial structure and 48, 58–9,
63–5, 66
innovative process and 72, 79
literature survey 28–32
'new perspective' on 45–6
upstream 34
technology diffusion 32–4, 45–6, 60–61,
72, 79, 182–3
capital goods as 95
importance of 184
manufacturing sector 84–91, 169, 172,
174

service sector 84–91
technology flows 4–5, 6, 7, 10, 34–6, 37,
46, 79, 182–3
definition 36
technology gap 29, 30
technology policy 183–5
technology spillovers *see* technology
flows
technology-push 21, 23
Terleckyj, N. 34, 35, 46
time scale
of technological change 39, 40, 79,
179
tooling-up *see* trial production
training *see* education and training
trial production 79, 97–8

United Kingdom 37
innovation process 66
United States 44, 45
innovation process 66
upstream technologies 34
Ure, A. 25, 48
Utterback, J.M. 61–3, 73, 178

value theory 13, 26
Vernon, R. 62, 178
Verspagen, B. 29, 30
von Hippel, E. 93

Wakelin, K. 31
Waterson, M. 66
Wilson, T.A. 66
Winter, S. 26, 39, 58–9, 61, 65, 67, 72,
175
Wolf, E.N. 31, 45, 73, 183

Yamawaki, H. 30, 32, 45